OVERCOMING FEARS OF INTIMACY AND COMMITMENT

OVERCOMING FEARS OF INTIMACY AND COMMITMENT

Relationship Insights for Men and the Women in Their Lives

Herb Goldberg

ROWMAN & LITTLEFIELD
Lanham • Boulder • New York • London

Published by Rowman & Littlefield
A wholly owned subsidiary of The Rowman & Littlefield Publishing Group, Inc.
4501 Forbes Boulevard, Suite 200, Lanham, Maryland 20706
www.rowman.com

Unit A, Whitacre Mews, 26-34 Stannary Street, London SE11 4AB

British Library Cataloguing in Publication Information Available

Library of Congress Cataloging-in-Publication Data

Names: Goldberg, Herb, 1937– author.
Title: Overcoming fears of intimacy and commitment : relationship insights for men and the women
    in their lives / Herb Goldberg.
Description: Lanham : Rowman & Littlefield, [2016] | Includes bibliographical references and index.
Identifiers: LCCN 2016010493 (print) | LCCN 2016017294 (ebook) | ISBN 9781442266841 (cloth :
    alk. paper) | ISBN 9781442266858 (electronic)
Subjects: LCSH: Men—Psychology. | Intimacy (Psychology) | Man-woman relationships.
Classification: LCC HQ1090 .G6425 2016 (print) | LCC HQ1090 (ebook) | DDC 155.3/32—dc23
LC record available at https://lccn.loc.gov/2016010493

Printed in the United States of America

For Frychettya Randall

CONTENTS

PREFACE

Getting to Know Him . . . More Deeply

It has frustrated me that so few men do the work needed to overcome their relationship dysfunctions. However, as a psychologist, I understand the reason why. Men's egos and denial mechanisms are their worst enemies and greatest obstacles to creating the change and growth they need.

It continually surprises me that most men have not truly taken in and absorbed the lessons, experiences, and treacherous relationship journeys of their grandfathers, fathers, and other men who, as they age, have become personally broken and have retreated into themselves, unable to break through enough to create the kind of personal, close, and loving connection that at some earlier point in their lives they believed they were capable of. This is one of those instances in which the supposedly most rational of men reveal their utter irrationality. They believe they will be different from other men and can have a quality relationship experience they have rarely seen in other men without having done the significant work required to create and maintain it.

As a therapist, I have been witness to countless men who *have* worked hard to develop healthy relationships. This book contains the stories of these men, struggling to recognize, grow, and transform themselves into insightful, empathetic people.

While acknowledging the many relationships that are not male/female connections, in this book I have kept the focus on the dynamic of the complex issues and difficulties that arise in the traditional coupling of men and women.

I created the case studies and scenarios contained in this book as illustrative of many men's experiences and thoughts based on my forty-five years of experience as a psychologist working in private practice with men in individual, group therapy, and counseling settings. Any resemblance to a specific man or woman, living or deceased, is coincidental.

ACKNOWLEDGMENTS

Because *Overcoming Fears of Intimacy and Commitment* was written over a period of ten years, many people made contributions to its final shape. The late Dr. George Bach, my mentor and friend, would conduct male/female communication and conflict-resolution seminars, and I worked with him as one of his trainers. This sparked and sharpened my interest in the psychodynamics of gender. His workshops were my first experience in observing, understanding, and exploring the complex and difficult aspects of the male/female relationship connection. Some of the conversations in which I participated and the insights I developed took place as I worked with him and are reflected in this book. Every couple begins to confront painful issues, usually beginning after the first six months of their relationship. Some deny them and then pay a painful price, while others acknowledge, confront, and grow through them to a healthy and grounded relationship. *Overcoming Fears of Intimacy and Commitment* is a compilation of what I have learned since my beginnings with Dr. Bach and his pioneering work with gender communication, and then later in my own work as a psychotherapist working with individuals and couples in their relationships.

My writing assistants, who were particularly helpful in the early stages of this book, include Dr. Marguery Lyvers and Max Rappaport, who were then inspired to become psychologists themselves. Mr. Zavier Cabarga, a fine writer and publisher himself, made a significant contribution to the titles I used for the insights in this book. As the book was being reshaped and expanded, Dr. Nazila Sayahzadeh brought her enthusiasm and skills to the project as well. I am grateful to them all.

When it was time to find the right publisher, Cissy Wechter brought her acumen and literary judgment to first identifying and then placing the book with my publisher, Rowman & Littlefield. A heartfelt thank you to her and to my editor, Suzanne Staszak-Silva, who believed in this book and gave it a publishing home.

Finally, I am grateful for the loving support and helpfulness of my partner in life, Frychettya Randall, who contributed so much to this book as well as to my life as I was struggling to put *Overcoming Fears of Intimacy and Commitment* together.

I

INITIATING THE RELATIONSHIP

Men initiate relationships by doing, not being, and by acting, not react ing. These ways of relating set the template that fuels and propels the relationship, while it lays a foundation for its dysfunctions and inevitable destruction. Men are raised to be do-ers, not be-ers, so it's no surprise that that is how they prove themselves attractive and desirable to the women they desire.

It would surprise most women to know how scared and threatened a man can feel when he's interested in initiating a conversation and relationship. He anticipates that she'll be annoyed and he'll be rejected. When he's strongly attracted, he sees her as all-powerful, because most of the time men initiate the first contact and assume the role of *actor*. The way a woman responds gives her the power of the *reactor* or reinforcing agent. She can make him feel like a star or a loser. Simply by being approachable and friendly, women can make themselves immediately attractive, if not irresistible, to men, because they have allayed their insecurities and fear.

When men are interested in a woman, they look for ways to perform for her. While this may not always *feel* good to a woman, it does reassure her that he cares and loves her. "He's so sweet. He's so thoughtful," she tells herself. The relationship initially comprises planning activities, like going to restaurants and movies, watching television, or taking trips, during which he needs to make choices that will appeal to her and bring her closer. When what he chooses doesn't please her, he feels responsible and guilty. Because of this dynamic, a woman establishes power with her response. When he makes a poor choice and she says, "Oh, sweetie, it's no big deal, we can still enjoy ourselves because we're together," he's reassured that he's chosen a partner who cares, who understands and loves him.

Exploring these experiences with my male clients, I might say, "It seems to me you're scared because you've turned her into an object who can validate you, rather than simply relating to her as a person you want to get to know, share, and have a conversation with." I suggest they ask themselves, "What do I really want to say to her?"

Once a woman decides she's open to a man's interest, a rhythm is set into place in which he takes on the role of *actor* and she becomes the *reactor*. They are putting in place an age-old dynamic that initially feels necessary and romantic, but it sets the stage for dysfunction and destruction and may leave her enraged and him guilt ridden.

Though it's been fifty years since the beginnings of feminism and the emergence of women as social equals to men, the deeper gender undercurrents remain mired in the traditional.

The prefeminist dynamic between men and women in romantic relationships, with most men assuming the role of initiators and many women remaining the gender-in-waiting, is still entrenched. Often women still hesitate to initiate the first conversations or ask for phone numbers. The first date is still frequently the man's responsibility, as planner, driver, payer, and sexual initiator. If he declines or resists taking the lead, he may be perceived as less than a man or even unattractive and unromantic.

What's wrong with this time-honored actor-reactor romantic model of a relationship's beginning? The problem lies in its process (the how), not its content (the what). The *actor-reactor* dynamic lays the foundation for the deterioration and negative endpoint by creating a progression that moves the relationship from romance to boredom to rage. *Actors* feel responsible for what happens. When they make the wrong choices, they feel guilty. *Reactors* can come to feel controlled, discounted, and diminished. Even if a man's choices are right, in this dynamic he is viewed as the controller and the responsible one. The woman who reacts may begin to feel controlled, with a sense of losing her identity. The classic complaints of these women are the basis for her anger building to rage, and a feeling she needs to leave, believing, "The only way I can be myself again is to get out of this relationship." The man is blamed for being controlling. The endpoint of this man-woman dance that began so sweetly is an inevitable one, though neither sees that when it begins. The blame game ensues—comprising a depressed and angry woman with low self-esteem whose partner becomes a guilt-ridden, self-hating, and bewildered man who feels like a failure, though he may hide his vulnerable feelings behind a veneer of coldness, withdrawal, and resentment.

To put an end to this cycle, so deeply embedded in the man-woman courtship ritual that it is rarely recognized or challenged, requires replacing it with an interaction in which each takes equal responsibility for *acting* and *reacting* right from the beginning.

The other dynamic in the beginning of the relationship that sets it on a path of toxicity and destruction is *objectification*. Romantic relationships do not begin person to person but *object to object*. A man's attractiveness comes from his image as a provider. The man as a person disappears behind the pressure to be a success object, while a woman's initial objectified appeal comes from her physical attractiveness. Who she is as a person is secondary and gets lost as well.

When one is objectified, one is dehumanized and found attractive for one's function or usefulness to the other and not one's personhood. It creates feelings in the objectified person of not really being known or seen as who one is or how one sees oneself. One comes to feel used, not loved, as well as feeling pressured to maintain the image that made one initially appear attractive out of fear that revealing one's true self will kill the attraction. He's under pressure to always be the successful provider, while she's under pressure to always be beautiful and sexy. Losses of either trigger anxiety, depression, and self-doubt. Feelings of being objectified also produce an accumulation of resentment that will eventually engulf the connection. In the end, there is a terrible sense that he or she has been living with a stranger.

INSIGHT 1: FIRST IMPRESSIONS

Women who emphasize their physical appearance and sexuality risk transforming themselves into sex objects, just as men who flaunt their symbols of material success and professional status may invite being used as a provider object.

The Conversation

Michael is an attractive, successful, single male professional who, at thirty-three, feels stuck in his dating relationships. Finding women to go out
with is no problem, but getting close and making a commitment is. The
problem has gotten worse as his level of success has increased. "I'm
becoming the male equivalent of the woman who doesn't know whether
men who express interest in her are relating to her for sex, or as a person
they want to get to know, love, and be close to."

Michael: "I don't trust women. They only consider a guy attractive
based on what he can provide or buy for them."

Dr. Goldberg: "Then why do you drive a high-end car and take wom-
en to expensive restaurants when you first date them? Why don't you
downplay all that?"

Michael: "I'd never get the good-looking, hot women that way."

Dr. Goldberg: "Then you are creating your own nightmare. Aren't
you just asking to be used?"

The Insight Explained

Many men use their money and job status to attract women the same way
women sometimes use their physical attractiveness and sex to attract
men. Both are objectifying themselves and inviting being used. It leads to
the cycle of distrust in relationships that will transform initial attraction
into resentment and even hatred. As a man may sense he is being used but
rarely sees how he helped set it up, he's doing the same things to the
woman he accuses her of doing to him. To change this, he can set aside
some of his material comforts in favor of experiences that might help him
get to know a woman, and she him, before they go any further. He can
still show up in his expensive car, but perhaps instead of a fancy restaurant, a hole-in-the-wall cozy date might set a better tone from the start.

What a Woman Can Do

It's scary to break an addiction to objectification when you feel being an object is what makes you attractive to the opposite sex. The man who resists turning himself into a success object through the flaunting of his symbols of success out of fear of being "invisible" otherwise embarks on a path of authenticity that can facilitate his growth and produce caring relationships. The price a woman pays if she chooses a man based on his material success symbols is the need to live with the personality that made him "a winner"—namely, his single-minded focus on achieving nonpersonal external goals.

After the initial "romantic high" of courtship with a man who objectifies himself as a success object by wining and dining, a woman will probably experience a man's progressive withdrawal and limited capacity for personal relating. Often when women look back on relationships of this kind, they primarily remember feeling controlled and diminished.

The short-term excitement and rewards of these romantic beginnings come with a large price tag—namely, the frustration and pain that could have been avoided had a woman's choice been based on the man's capacity and ability to care and relate and not on what he can provide for her.

What a Man Must Do

Some men don't seem to care, or they are so insecure about their ability to relate intimately that they unwittingly try to buy a woman's interest and love by showing off their symbols of success. That's much like a woman who captures a man's interest by dressing and acting sexy and like a trophy he can win in order to gain the envy and respect of his peers.

While this may give him a short-term victory, the price for objectifying himself is great. His already present tendency to hide his true feelings and self is exacerbated and leaves him with the all-too-common feeling men have that nobody really knows him or genuinely cares about him.

Showing off with material and success symbols is an attempt to avoid the hard work of finding an appropriate partner and building a loving relationship by opening himself up authentically to someone he really cares about and who cares about him, revealing his insecurity and fear of slowly developing a relationship of love and trust by *being* rather than by *buying*.

Initially, it's not as exciting and magical as when he pretends to be Prince Charming, but the work of being real at the start will be worth it in the end. Otherwise the relationship will begin to unravel and his partner will pull away because she never loved the real him. He never showed her the real him, so how could she?

It would be a great step forward in a man's relationship experience to resist creating a seductive image that is essentially a manipulation and will result in his ultimately being experienced as a stranger when his relationship begins to crack open because it lacks a foundation of authenticity.

INSIGHT 2: CHEMISTRY LESSON

Relationships that last are those that develop slowly and unevenly. "The higher the high, the lower the low" is the inevitable course of instantly passionate, romantic beginnings, as they launch the progression from romance to boredom to rage.

The Conversation

William described himself as a romance junkie and was beginning to think he had a problem because his relationships seemed to resemble and repeat themselves. The progression of excitement to deadness leading to mutual hostility seemed to be happening sooner with each new relationship.

> *William*: "When I meet a woman, it's that feeling of excitement I get that makes me want to pursue her. Without that initial high, it just isn't happening for me."

> *Dr. Goldberg*: "How many times have you followed that path of instant chemistry in choosing your relationships? And how did those relationships end?"

> *William*: "Well sure, after a while the excitement fades. That happens more and more quickly. I start getting bored, then it all collapses and we both end up angry and disappointed. Then I'm out there once again, searching for that initial high."

The Insight Explained

Those who crave a high level of excitement initially are using relationships as a drug to fill a void, or for some women, the childlike need for reassurance that she is attractive and lovable. The creation of such a process has nothing to do with developing an enduring relationship. Instead, it's more about repeatedly experiencing an initial addictive rush. Men and women for whom the awareness and recognition of this tendency to rush becomes apparent can benefit from slowing things down.

What a Woman Can Do

A woman who rates her new relationships based on their level of excitement and chemistry needs to ask herself if that measure had ever before succeeded in bringing her a lasting and satisfying relationship. A definition of relationship insanity is the belief that you can do something in the present that never worked in the past and experience a different outcome.

To break this pattern of failure, treat the craving for instant chemistry and excitement the way you would handle the craving for an addictive substance. Control the addiction by denying its demand for gratification one day at a time, as you work toward an authentic and meaningful relationship. Slow the relationship down, get to know the man as a person, and ask yourself whether you really like and trust what he is all about. Lasting relationships tend to build slowly and unevenly, but they have a way of getting better and better with time.

What a Man Must Do

The hunger to find a relationship that immediately clicks and in a flash ends a man's deep and denied loneliness and desperate need for closeness shines a light on his insecurity and inability to form a genuinely loving relationship. In relationships, if it's too good to be true and happens too easily and quickly, it suggests the relationship is based on fantasy and projection. The more that holds true, the more likely it is that the relationship will crash and burn just as quickly and intensely as it started.

Men's relationship dysfunction is highlighted by the fact that they willingly spend years building a career or a secure future in order to have something solid, and yet they somehow ignorantly believe the difficult struggle to form a well-fitting and loving relationship requires little effort or understanding and somehow love is "just there" and they'll know it when it happens.

As the world becomes more technological and less personal than ever, men need to make their choice for an intimate partner based on profound self-awareness and a clear perception and understanding of who their partner *really is* rather than who he imagines her to be. Putting the work in early through undergoing counseling or therapy, reading relationship literature, and finding other vehicles available to him to prepare himself will help him become healthy and make a healthy choice in a lifelong partner. It may seem like too much work, but it is the difference between a satisfying and challenging growth-filled personal life and a life of escape, loneliness, and pain.

Don't expect relationships to be easy and magical. Relationships are hard and complex. Prepare as you would for anything that will take the center stage of importance in your life.

INSIGHT 3: INSTANT ROMANCE

Women who are fearful of men and feel the most resistance to getting involved tend to look for intense romantic beginnings. By transforming a relationship into a magical fantasy, they can tell themselves that it will be "different this time."

The Conversation

Arthur wanted to know if there was something wrong with him because his matter-of-fact approach to his relationships frustrated and angered his girlfriend. She called him romance phobic and said he was afraid of love. "Are women who seem to crave being treated romantically really more capable of love than I am?"

> *Arthur:* "It seems like I keep meeting women who become super romantic quickly, and act as if I'm the soul mate they've been searching for. They tell me how different and refreshing I am to be with compared with other guys they've known, but as time passes they say I'm just the same as every other jerky male they've known before."

Dr. Goldberg: "Does that intense initial romantic attraction feel real to you when they express it?"

Arthur: "Well, I do wonder if they're seeing the real me. It puts pressure on me to try and be this perfect guy who won't hurt them or let them down, and who is different from all the other men."

Dr. Goldberg: "Then why do you keep buying into that initial romantic bubble?"

Arthur: "I guess it just feels so damn great to believe I'm that unique, special guy."

The Insight Explained

The more a woman fears and resists men, the more she will need to romanticize a man and see him as completely different than other men in order to let herself get involved. The romantic bubble she creates gives her a short holiday from deeper feelings of fear and anger. Inevitably, though, these deeper resistances and fears return and she will tell him she feels deceived and he's really "just like all the other men."

What a Woman Can Do

A woman needs to question her belief that her relationship problems and/or failures are primarily a matter of bad luck and poor choices. If she believes her past failures occurred because she never found the perfect man, she needs to ask herself whether that belief is disguising her fearfulness of men in general, causing her to search for an unreal man who doesn't behave like "all" the other men. Overcoming and working through her negative feelings and reflexes toward men will make it possible for her to perceive the men she meets more objectively.

I tell men to be wary of women who want to idealize them and fall instantly in love, and who tell them how unique and different they are. That kind of beginning is a set-up for an inevitable experience of disillusionment. For men, however, a woman's initial intense romantic enthusiasm feeds into their desire to believe that somehow they actually are the one-of-a-kind male who is different from all other men.

What a Man Must Do

Men who seek out extremely magical and romantic experiences with a partner and believe that a relationship is not the right one if those experiences don't exist are likely to be uncomfortable with or dislike the reality of women. Men who genuinely like women don't need to search for the perfect soul mate partner or someone who seems to be different from all the others.

Before a man begins to look for a lasting relationship, he needs to confront with great honesty how he really perceives and feels about women. That usually begins with asking himself how he felt about his own mother, his sisters, and the women who surrounded him when he was a young child. If his experiences have been good ones, he won't be inclined to seek intense romantic highs or need to fulfill the illusive fantasy of perfection. A man who does that must question himself as to what is motivating it.

If a man can recognize his tendency to fall for fantasy women rather than real ones, he should reach out for help to overcome his denied resistance, antipathy, and fear of being close to a real woman because of his negative experiences with the females in his life when he was young.

INSIGHT 4: ROMANCE IN THE DARK

The level of excitement a woman feels when she falls in love is related to the intensity of her needs and not the reality of the man she falls in love with.

The Conversation

"How do I know whether my girlfriend, who tells me how wonderful I am and how much she loves me, is for real?" This haunting skepticism kept Chris, an attractive teacher at age twenty-nine, from developing a long-term relationship. "Do I really have a problem letting someone love me? Is there something wrong with me because I don't instantly feel the way she feels?"

Chris: "When I first met her, she told me she was 'ready to fall in love.' I thought, 'Does she even know who I am?' But even though I realized she was idealizing me, I pushed aside my doubt."

Dr. Goldberg: "You sensed she wasn't seeing the real you, but you didn't care because it felt so good."

Chris: "I guess I don't believe the real me is very lovable."

Dr. Goldberg: "Does that initially wonderful, seemingly unconditional love of hers last?"

Chris: "I never tried to hide my true self, but eventually they come to see 'the real me' and then aren't as in love anymore."

Dr. Goldberg: "Still, it's hard to resist her initial fantasy-based response that somehow magically you're different than all the other men."

The Insight Explained

Women sometimes "fall in love" when they have needs to be met, causing them to temporarily deny and block what would usually cause them to avoid or push a man away. In those cases, the feeling lasts until they get what they want. Then real feelings begin to emerge and disillusionment can set in.

What a Woman Can Do

Just as a man often believes he is falling in love when he meets a woman who is welcoming and relieves his momentary loneliness and horniness, a woman may be vulnerable to falling in love when she has intense and frustrated personal intimacy needs that are pressing for fulfillment. Once these needs are fulfilled, her feelings toward her partner will tend to diminish and dissolve. Avoiding the letdown and feelings of disappointment and lessened interest that occur when we choose a partner because they fulfill our urgent and momentary personal needs is a major challenge. Intense personal needs can warp judgment, like when a woman chooses a man mainly because she wants a baby or needs to be rescued from economic hardship or the fear that she is getting older and less attractive and may never find a suitable partner.

What a Man Must Do

When I speak to and work with men who agonize over everything they say and do with a woman they are strongly attracted to, I tell them their focus is misplaced. A woman's attraction to a man has more to do with what she needs than who he is. The same holds true for men.

If a woman needs a man, for whatever her reasons, she will tend to overlook or deny the things about him that might interfere with, spoil, or end the relationship. A man who is obsessed with and afraid of saying or doing something that will cause a woman to abandon or reject him is experiencing a misplaced preoccupation and revealing a blind spot in himself that he needs to work on.

If he is the right man at the right time for a woman, she will tend to deny or rationalize whatever undermines her pursuit of a relationship with him. Psychologists call it *cognitive dissonance*, or the tendency to block out of awareness whatever contradicts a deeply felt need or belief. Similarly, if she doesn't have a deep need for him that he seems to fulfill, there is nothing he can do to win her over and change her mind.

Rather than point an accusing finger at his supposed shortcomings or obsess about what he believes he should have said or done to make the relationship happen, men need to learn that in these cases, even so-called perfection on his part won't be enough to win her over, so it is time to let go of that pursuit.

INSIGHT 5: WOMEN AND SEX 101

Men interpret personal interest from a woman as sexual. Women interpret sexual interest from a man as personal. These polarized perceptions create the basis for a serious breakdown in communication.

The Conversation

Ronald was shocked when he found himself accused of acting like a pig after he made a physical advance toward a woman he was sure had been coming on to him at a party. "When it comes to sex I'm as scared, confused, and cautious as women are. I know I've hurt and used women in the past, and now I'm feeling as defensive as they are when it comes to sex." Getting it right and diffusing the sex bomb was one of Ronald's preoccupations.

Ronald: "She came on strong to me—smiling, touching my hair, and holding my hands. So I'm getting excited and go to kiss her and touch her breasts, and she pulls away and gets angry. Women are crazy! They come on like gangbusters—then freeze when you respond in kind."

Dr. Goldberg: "Because she was warm and friendly, you thought it meant she wanted to be sexual with you."

Ronald: "The way she kept smiling and laughing and touching my hand, anybody would think that!"

Dr. Goldberg: "So, when you have sex with a woman you've just met, does it mean you're falling in love with her and want to be with her?"

Ronald: "Of course not. Why?"

Dr. Goldberg: "Because many women think it does."

The Insight Explained

Nowhere are the profound differences between men and women clearer than when it comes to matters of sex. When a man pursues a woman for sex, she tends to believe he's attracted to her as a whole person. She doesn't think sex is all he wants. When she discovers the latter is true, she tends to become bitter and cynical about men. Similarly, just because a woman is nice to a man doesn't mean she wants to go to bed with him. A major reason women hold back from being too friendly with men is the fear they'll be misinterpreted.

What a Woman Can Do

When a man has sex with a woman, he's not expecting it to unleash her feelings of attachment and longing. When he doesn't follow through personally, women may end the relationship abruptly, to the surprise of the clueless man, believing a woman will stay involved because of the "great sex."

Women sometimes do want sex simply for its own sake, but this interest in having sex without closeness rarely lasts. A sexual relationship usually has to be accompanied by a movement toward commitment. Often when a woman senses a sexual relationship is not progressing toward commitment, she may terminate the sex and not miss it at all. *Men fail to grasp the fact that sex means something entirely different to women and that being sexual triggers a desire for closeness and an ongoing personal relationship, which is ultimately the goal for everyone, but perhaps more important to women at this early stage of a relationship.*

Equally important, the connected and personal side of a woman's personality can make it hard for her to recognize when she's merely being used sexually, because that experience is foreign to her. Women need to learn not to expect anything personal from a man just because he desires sex with her. Out of feelings of guilt and responsibility after sex, often men may pretend to care and to love, but the pretense tends to diminish, dissolve, and finally disappear.

What a Man Must Do

The tendency for a man to misinterpret a woman's friendliness and seeming niceness and interest as meaning she desires him sexually is a psychological Achilles' heel, and a dangerous one for even the most intelligent of men. In recent years, we have witnessed the downfall or degradation and destruction of highly intelligent and successful men who misinterpreted a woman's warmth and openness as a green light to make a sexual advance, sometimes even persisting when she makes it clear that it is not what she wants.

To avoid the tendency to make a fool of oneself or self-destruct, it's a good idea in general for a man not to initiate sexual contact with a woman he doesn't know well, assuming she desires him just because she has opened herself up to a warm and friendly encounter. If a woman really wants physical intimacy, she will let him know, and he needs to wait for that to happen. It is better to err in the direction of not making an advance when she wants physical closeness than to assume she does want it because he is misreading her friendliness.

At the same time, men need to understand that when it comes to sex, most women are not casual about it; when a man shows strong interest in being sexual, a woman will often believe he has a strong interest in developing a close and committed relationship with her. If that doesn't happen, he shouldn't be surprised or think she's crazy if he gets a response of anger or complete withdrawal. "This weekend we had great sex, but when I called her a few days later she seemed distant and uninterested." The "craziness" is his, for his inability to correctly understand her experience and feelings about this very intimate experience.

INSIGHT 6: LOVE AND ANXIETY

Romance can amplify the feminine anxieties some women experience— their tendency to need reassurance, lose boundaries and sense of self, and see themselves as giving much more than they are getting.

The Conversation

In his ongoing confusion about his capacity to care and love, Gerald was bothered by his feelings of impatience, criticalness, and cynical distrust in response to his girlfriend's anxious preoccupations with their relationship. "Is she just manipulating and trying to rope me in by acting so vulnerable?"

> *Gerald*: "I like being in love as much as the next guy. It's what comes along with it that bothers me. It seems like women get crazy and childlike when they fall in love. They get clingy and needy, the opposite of the cool, independent women they appeared to be when we first met. When I'm honest with my girlfriend now, she acts wounded and tells me I'm being hurtful and selfish."

> *Dr. Goldberg*: "What do you do when that happens?"

Gerald: "At first I try not to spoil her romantic fantasy. Then I start backtracking and apologizing, closing up and pulling away. I feel like a jerk because she seems to be trying so hard. Usually, she senses my withdrawal and it goes downhill from there."

The Insight Explained

Falling in love tends to trigger intense intimacy needs in some women, making them feel vulnerable and fragile. When that happens, they often regress and lose the strength and independent spirit that initially attracted their partners.

What a Woman Can Do

The recognition on a woman's part that falling in love may go hand in hand with a growing need for reassurance, a difficulty maintaining boundaries, and feelings that she is giving much more than she's getting will go a long way toward making it possible for her to create, maintain, and build the relationship. She needs to recognize that a man's responses often are the polar opposite of hers, and that men respond best and with the greatest interest when a woman maintains strong boundaries and a separate identity. A woman's need for reassurance and her need to get closer to the point of losing herself in the relationship actually have a repellent and toxic effect. Even if a man remains in a relationship under these circumstances, his feelings of interest and attraction will diminish, sometimes turning into indifference and even disdain.

I warn my male clients that if they sense a woman is becoming too romantic too quickly and building them up as Prince Charming, they should proceed with caution and skepticism, because those feelings come along with the pressure to reassure her and repeatedly tell her how much she's cared for and with an overreaction to any withdrawal or conflicted feelings on his part.

What a Man Must Do

In a relationship that brings out a woman's romantic feelings, many men seem bewildered by the woman seeming to regularly or repeatedly seek reassurance of his love and interest. That tendency is a counterpart to a man's tendency to assume that once he's expressed his loving feelings to a woman once or twice, it should be a given. Her need for reassurance is no more an issue or dysfunction than his need to remain silent about his feelings once he's expressed them.

Rather than becoming irritated or annoyed, a man needs to see it not as insecurity but as a result of her bewilderment about his seeming distance or emotional withholding. Or it may simply be her way of building and maintaining an emotional connection with him. If he withholds a response, it invites or promotes her doubts about his love.

Being honest with himself as to whether expressions of love make him uncomfortable is a necessary first step. Withholding is a man's dysfunction that needs to be acknowledged and worked on in order to try to meet his partner's needs. The more he initiates expressions of love and caring, the less likely she is to ask for reassurance.

Men need to regularly "check in" with a woman to make sure she recognizes and feels his expressions of caring.

INSIGHT 7: HEROES WELCOMED!

Some women become more romantic when their lives are in trouble and they feel in need of being rescued. In these cases, their feelings may turn to coldness and hostility when the need dissipates and they no longer require a man's support.

The Conversation

Because Walter had a history of being a love addict, he was drawn to women when the beginnings of the relationship felt like being "stoned." What he found repeatedly was that the woman who seemed so magically in love with him turned out to be in some kind of personal crisis. Since he loved being the white knight, feeling needed and powerful, he'd ride to the rescue. Instead of appreciation and love when he got the job done, however, what he experienced was disappointment and confusion as women began to pull away.

Walter: "Why is it that when most women fall for me, it turns out their lives are in trouble? Either they are unhappy with a present boyfriend or worried about finances, or want to get away from their parents or to get pregnant."

Dr. Goldberg: "So, you think you're so attractive that a woman will just fall head over heels for no reason at all; no agenda and no neediness on her part."

Walter: "Well, I always thought falling head over heels was a normal thing in love, so why shouldn't a woman fall for me? After all, I usually fall for a woman if I like how she looks and acts."

Dr. Goldberg: "You mean that you have no agenda?"

The Insight Explained

When it comes to romance, we can learn a lot from fairy tales. From Sleeping Beauty to Cinderella, the stories are always about romantic feelings that blossom when a woman needs to be rescued and protected, and how a man becomes desirable, attractive, and a hero when he can fulfill that role. Once her need is fulfilled, she may no longer want to be with him. She may even become hostile because his presence is a reminder of her prior dependence and weakness.

What a Woman Can Do

After she satisfies it, frequently a woman's need to be rescued bears a resemblance to a man's feelings after his need for sex or ego validation from a woman is satisfied. Once a man "gets what he wants," he often discovers he doesn't want to be with the woman. From this perspective, a man should both understand and have empathy for a woman who falls "madly in love" with a man when she feels vulnerable and in need of being rescued.

In the midst of stress caused by anxiety over her troubles and vulnerability, there's a strong tendency for some women to objectify men and fall in love with the men who seem as if they can deliver her from her difficulties. Her need and fear bathe him in a glowing light that can fade as her anxieties recede.

Women need to recognize that their judgment in times when they are feeling personally endangered can be distorted, and if they make commitments based on them, they may be laying the foundation for a future relationship disaster.

What a Man Must Do

A woman's tendency to feel romantic toward a man who is there for her when she is in need is a counterpart to a man's excitement when he can play "hero" and do things for a woman she critically seems to need and for which she expresses her adoration.

When we're in life-threatening trouble, such as with a house on fire, in a dangerous crime situation, or when seriously ill, the fireman, policeman, or doctor who rescues us, doing his or her job well, will ignite feelings of warmth and loving. However, when the danger is past, the feelings we have toward them dissolve and disappear, and we may forget that person entirely.

Men who are most comfortable when they are "doing for" need to learn that by trying to win a woman over by "doing for her," they are setting themselves up for disappointment and heartache—not because they were coldly being used and discarded, but because "doing for" may be worthy of appreciation, but it isn't a basis for a continuing love relationship.

Men who refuse to recognize their relationship insufficiencies will become frustrated and embittered, and therefore need to understand and learn that it is *how* they relate to her that will create a meaningful and lasting connection of love, not the things they can do for her or provide materially.

INSIGHT 8: SMART MEN, CRAZY CHOICES

Though he hardly knows the woman, a man may pursue closeness and the intimacy of sex based solely on a woman's looks, breast size, or hair color. When he calls women irrational, he overlooks the insanity of this common male response.

The Conversation

Owen, a thrice-divorced engineer of forty, thought of himself as a logical person. His oft-repeated response to women was "That makes no sense." His marriages had ended, according to him, because "the women all turned out to be 'crazy.'" But his criteria for becoming interested in a woman were the size of her breasts and the color of her hair. Even highly "rational" men lack self-awareness when it comes to their ridiculous and crazy selection criteria.

Dr. Goldberg: "What attracts you to a woman?"

Owen: "Her hair, usually blonde, her body, particularly her breasts, and then her smile. I fall in love and I'm immediately ready to say, 'Marry me!' even though I hardly know her."

Dr. Goldberg: "So you're ready to commit solely based on her physical appearance?"

Owen: "Aren't most guys that way?"

The Insight Explained

Men are known to assert that women are crazy. What they don't see is how their own behavior, particularly when it comes to choosing a woman, borders on crazy. Married men, with wives who are willing and loving sex partners, may prefer to masturbate to pornography or have sex with women they barely know, risking an STD and creating a messy, destructive situation. Some men have sex with a woman they've just met without using a condom. If men could deal with women with the same clarity and caution they bring to their business affairs, they would avoid the insanity of the way they respond in relationships.

What a Woman Can Do

A man's vulnerability in attaching to and falling in love with a woman based on her physical attributes demonstrates the superficiality of his attraction and connection to her. The craziness is extreme; yet he seems unable to recognize the obvious irrationality.

If a woman finds herself referred to as crazy by a man because he can't understand her emotional response, she can take satisfaction in knowing that the man is unknowingly and actually describing and projecting his own irrational distortions. However, confronting him about *his* craziness rarely works because of his embedded and defensive conviction that he does everything rationally.

What a Man Can Do

A man can gauge the extent of his personal development as a related being rather than as a performing/doing machine by the degree to which he is drawn or attracted to a woman based primarily on the physical. Basing a relationship interest on external superficial characteristics is what I term *macho-psychotic*, or masculine craziness.

The same men who tend to do so are also those who are quick to decide that a woman is crazy or irrational because her response to him doesn't make sense. If a man is going to label his partner's behavior or response as crazy, deciding that in fact all women are crazy, he needs first to recognize and acknowledge the craziness of many of his own behaviors, such as watching porn while avoiding sexual contact with his partner, getting enraged or overly excited as he watches his favorite sports team in action ("Kill that fucking referee!"), or even his impulse to engage in an altercation with another driver who cuts him off or with a man who seems to look at him the "wrong way," thereby laying his well-being on the line in his crazy tendency to immediately engage in a fight.

INSIGHT 9: MAMA'S GIRL

The man who receives unexpectedly intense and romantic attention from a woman he's just met would be dismayed to discover he may just be a mother substitute.

The Conversation

Molly, a divorcée who at thirty-eight dated extensively, complained to her boyfriend, Brian, that while men would act romantically at the start of a relationship, they couldn't keep up the closeness she needed. Her parents had divorced when she was seven, and her angry, frustrated mother turned her into the adored child and a substitute love object. Without knowing it, she had sought to replicate with Brian the intensity of the love bond she had with her mother, and Brian was trying to provide the intensity of love she needed. Even if he could manage for a brief period, he was ultimately doomed to failure and hearing from his partner that she was frustrated by his lack of intimacy.

> *Brian*: "Whenever a woman gushes over how great I am after we've just met, I've learned that if we stay together long enough, her feelings will change to the opposite. I'll always end up disappointing her and hearing I don't give her what she needs."

> *Dr. Goldberg*: "Perhaps no one could."

> *Brian*: "That's not entirely true. They usually seem to talk about their mom, or sometimes even a dad, who just adored them. That intensity of love is what they're looking for and what they're measuring me against."

The Insight Explained

Acting from their own neediness, many mothers, and sometimes fathers as well, create an emotional fusion with their children. This resembles love but is expressed to meet the parent's unmet needs. In the children, this faux love produces an addictive craving that, when they are grown, they will seek to replicate with their partners. Finding that no one can fulfill their depth of desire and need, they may be doomed to disappointment and frustration, which they may think is caused by others.

What a Woman Can Do

Men are perceived as being shallow and unfeeling because of their supposed inability to maintain and grow their romantic feelings. However, this may be a failure only of the woman partner, who, as a child, became addicted to the "center of the universe" feeling she experienced as a young girl with her mother. That intensity of closeness becomes the internal and emotional standard by which she measures the love of the man.

Even with the best of intentions and great effort, men will fail in their attempt to satisfy this craving for closeness.

Acknowledging this can help a woman overcome her profound feelings of dissatisfaction with a man's supposed inability to be intimate. Those feelings of frustration she attributes to his limited capacity for closeness and warmth can be softened and balanced considerably once she recognizes that her longing may come from an inner template for a love no man could ever satisfy, having originated with a mother whose loving intensity was an outgrowth of her own frustrations. Grasping that reality would allow a woman to perceive a man's genuine efforts at closeness and love more positively, and let go of the fantasy that motivates her hopeless search for a man with an impossible motherlike capacity for closeness.

What a Man Must Do

Women who have had an intense and adoring relationship with their mother tend to be drawn to men who respond to them in a similarly intense way.

This can launch a loaded inflammable dynamic. While a man can provide the intensity that ignites and draws a woman's passionate response initially and for a short time, he won't be able to maintain that intensity, at which point his partner will believe his love and interest in her are fading, thereby triggering a relationship crisis in which he has to prove that his love continues and is real.

Insecure men tend to be excited by a woman's intense and immediate initial passion because it validates their grandiose beliefs about their irresistible attractiveness. Understanding that a woman's immediate and intense passion for him is probably a projection based on her early connection to her mother is something the aware man must learn in order to distinguish this unbelievable excitement on a woman's part from being a genuine, rooted enthusiasm for him as a person.

Men also must ask themselves why they need to believe that instant and extreme passion is real. An aware and emotionally healthy man will not be drawn to or find appealing an "over-the-top" response, and he will not be attracted to a relationship simply because the woman seems to be so intensely attracted to him.

2

HOW RELATIONSHIPS WORK

Man-woman relationships traditionally have been based on gender roles. The woman played out the *feminine role* and the man played out the *masculine role.* That generated and reinforced the compartmentalization and stunting of personality that brought about psychological dysfunctions and feelings of failure and inadequacy that not even the so-called perfect man or woman could escape. This brings light to questions and conundrums previously seen as mysterious and unanswerable: "Why do men and women who seemingly were raised in loving, 'normal' and even 'perfect' families develop serious psychological dysfunctions like depression, addiction, sexual confusion, and low self-esteem?"

Understanding this requires a brief excursion into the psychological underpinnings of feminine and masculine socialization and the massive price men and women pay for being raised to become the socially acceptable or admired feminine woman and masculine man. Recognizing this, answers to age-old gender-warfare questions and issues become possible—questions like "Why do men and women have difficulty hearing and understanding each other?" and "Why," as one pop psychology writer put it, "do men and women seem to inhabit different worlds?"

The human potential of each gender is significantly damaged in this process of gender socialization. A part of each man and woman's psyche is lost to repression as important response capacities disappear from consciousness.

What is blocked and lost in one gender is expressed in an exaggerated and defensive form in the other. For example, men whose response to physical and/or intellectual challenges is an aggressive one, and who deny or are ashamed to experience fear ("coward" or "sissy" are threatening and humiliating labels) find its counterpart in the women who are uncomfortable with and incapable of direct displays and expressions of conflict, anger, and aggression, and whose cherished sense of themselves is as peaceful, loving, and spiritual beings.

Assertion, autonomy, sexuality, emotions, and *intellect* are compartmentalized and polarized in many traditional men and women. Those men have exaggerated autonomy and denied dependency. They seek space, freedom, and separateness, particularly under stress, and avoid displays or expressions of help-seeking and dependent behavior. Childhood memories of Dad were Mom saying, "Leave Dad alone. He's tired. He needs peace and quiet! Don't bother him." Their polar opposite equivalents are the women who crave connection, intimacy, and closeness to the point where two can become as one.

Most men *assert* and *initiate*, while many women tend to *wait* and *react.* Men usually initiate relationships, while often women are reluctant to express clearly, directly, and immediately what they do or don't want. A typical, frustrating conversation would be:

He: "What would you like to eat?"

She: "It doesn't matter."

He: "What restaurant would you like to go to?"

She: "You choose. Any restaurant would be fine."

He: "What movie do you want to see?"

She: "What do you want to see?"

Emotions and rationality become polarized and compartmentalized as well. A man uses cold logic, accusing his female partner of being overly emotional and irrational. He says, "You don't make sense," or "That sounds crazy." She in turn accuses him of being cold, detached, and unfeeling.

Sexual behaviors used to be the classic battleground of polarized, compartmentalized motives. Men "always" wanted it, while women "never" did. While that has changed somewhat in recent years, it still seems many women can do without "it," while most men torture themselves when they can't get "it."

The result of the polarization and compartmentalization of the psyche of men's and women's personalities is the creation of a shocking, invisible, and often tragic reality—namely, that men and women filter and experience reality in opposite ways. That becomes the basis for insurmountable, frustrating, and even tragic misunderstandings due to major distortions. Many men have blocks and overreactions when it comes to their emotions and the acknowledgment of their dependency, fear, and sadness, and are insensitive to the impact of their analytic, cold, and aggressive way of being. Some women, on the other hand, because of their feminine filters, perceive intentional hurts, rejections, and dangers where there are none, and may see a lack of caring, love, and closeness despite a man's best efforts. They may feel controlled even if a man tries to share decisions and power equally. Because of their polarized gender conditioning, he overreacts in one direction, she in the other. Eventually, each comes to believe the other is "impossible" to talk to, and communication breaks down completely.

While gender conditioning makes both men and women defensive, each is only able to see the defensiveness of the other. Fingers are pointed until one or the other gives up with a sense of hopelessness. They are blaming their partner without realizing the enemy is not the other person, but the unseen power and result of generations of polarized gender conditioning and compartmentalization, accepting the unfortunate belief that "that's just the way men and women are."

It's not unfixable, and it's not unmodifiable. The obstacle is only the anxiety-driven, rigid defensiveness of each gender seeking to validate and support *their* version of truth while attacking and blaming the reality of the other. After generations of polarized defensiveness and the compartmentalization of men's and women's psyche, the end result begins to look as if it is genetic and biologically based, but it's actually based on generations of socially learned responses heavily reinforced by social pressure (what boys and men and girls and women are supposed to be like), until it takes on the appearance of biologically rooted behavior.

Men and women need to support each other's quest to acknowledge, work through, and transform the disabled parts of their personalities and capacities in order to become fully expressive and transcend blaming and guilt making.

This chapter introduces you to men making various discoveries and exploring things that previously made no sense to them. Every step toward lessening defensiveness has its own benefits and rewards, generating a gradual dissolving of the rigidities that keep relationships from blossoming and growing. Without doing the work, the outlook for achieving fulfilling relationships is bleak. With the work, the potential is unknown and perhaps limitless.

INSIGHT 10: TO DO, OR TO BE

Externalization is the major cause of man's relationship dysfunction. The pressure of his socialization separates the young boy from his inner and personal self and pushes him exclusively toward performance, achievement, and success in a process that values him for doing, *not for* being.

The Conversation

Bart had trouble talking about his feelings. His recounting of his relationship experiences, while always precise, lacked any glint of self-awareness. This meant that in his relationships he could "never see it coming," nor could he make sense of the mood swings, conflicts, fighting, and breakdowns that regularly characterized his dealings with women and other personal relationships. While he could achieve and succeed with impressive skills, he never felt he was good enough. Whenever he couldn't perform at a high level, he'd be consumed by self-loathing and depression.

Bart: "I'm sick of feeling that in order to be 'somebody,' I've got to turn myself into a performance and competition machine. When I feel exhausted or get sick, like a machine that breaks down or becomes obsolete, I'm afraid I'm going to be replaced and become invisible. I'm beginning to think the stress isn't worth it."

Dr. Goldberg: "Yes, most guys accept all that because the alternative means focusing on becoming a whole person and not just a high-performance achieving machine, which is scary because it's uncharted territory."

The Insight Explained

The world applauds men for their achievement and rewards them for being better performers than other men. This is so ingrained that when men are pushed aside for not performing well enough, they buy into society's judgment that they are becoming worthless. It's no wonder that so many men are cold, doggedly goal oriented, and obsessively driven, and that they become depressed and lose their self-esteem when they are between jobs or can't perform at a high-enough level.

What a Woman Can Do

The way a man relates intimately is the end product of a pervasive early conditioning process that focused him entirely on external achievement and provided no support or reinforcement for his learning to become a personal being. Recognizing and understanding this unfortunate consequence of men's socialization will free a woman from taking personally a man's struggle to be the intimate and connected being she would wish for. It will be liberating for a woman to realize her partner is not intentionally choosing to make her less of a priority. Her understanding of the pervasive conditioning that crippled his capacity for personal and close relating is a crucial step in creating a safe place for him to develop his dormant and diminished capacity.

Love and intimacy that is not fantasy based means women recognize and understand the psychological soil men grew up in and the relationship limitations that were created, so they don't take his dysfunction personally.

What a Man Must Do

Psychologists who specialize in gender studies have recognized the dysfunctional essence of both masculine and feminine socialization. Traditional gender conditioning tends to create rigid, driven, defensive ways of being. Many men pay the price of masculinity by becoming externalized and therefore more or less dysfunctional in their close relationships, while the feminine woman may suffer from a vulnerability and weakness in dealing with the impersonal world, causing her to resist and struggle with her pursuit of achievement, autonomy, and the building of a strong economic future.

Men must recognize that externalization in themselves, and rather than defend their right to be that way as a man, understand that the price for remaining that way is the damage it creates by destroying his ability to relate in a satisfying, close, and intimate way.

It is difficult to transform his externalization because of its deep roots and society's reinforcement and praise when he "acts like a man," even when it costs him his health, the endurance of his personal relationships, and even his survival. Resisting strong and defensive masculine tendencies, sometimes labeled as "macho," requires lifelong vigilance and willingness to reach out for help and feedback, since rigid masculine defensiveness is hard for a man to recognize in himself and tends to be denied. Failing to do so by refusing to enter counseling, joining a men's group, or at least continuously inviting feedback from his partner's experience of him is detrimental to the quality of his personal life.

Failure to make the personal a priority will eventually negate the significance and usefulness of all his efforts to be a success, a winner, or "a great man."

INSIGHT 11: THE PRICE HE PAYS FOR BEING A MAN

Paradoxically and tragically, the externalization process of masculinity that destroys a man's personal self and capacity to relate intimately is the same one that validates him as a man in the eyes of society. The externalization process is illusive and almost impossible for a man to see in himself, though he can see it operating in other men, and some women can clearly see it in him.

The Conversation

Growing up, Robert seemed like the perfect male—star student, athlete, and all-around popular person. Everyone predicted a great future for him; yet after a short marriage and two children, he was watching his life unravel. Instead of being appreciated and applauded, his wife was complaining about his "cluelessness." His relationship to his children seemed thin at best compared to the way they related to their mother. He felt isolated and like a loser. The chronic buzz of depression brought him to despair.

> *Robert*: "It's somewhat ironic that the higher I climb on the success ladder, and the more money I accumulate, the emptier and less fulfilled I feel."

> *Dr. Goldberg*: "The more a man achieves and succeeds, the more he finds himself in competition with other men, and the more energy he puts into protecting his turf and closing himself off. Even when a man strives and doesn't succeed, he will cut himself off more and more from other men along the way."

> *Robert*: "That's true. I really wanted to be friends with certain guys, but sensed a wall and a distance from them, and usually gave up trying. The more successful I got, though it afforded me more leisure, the harder it got for me to make friends and just relax and enjoy. My refuge became work and money, which made me feel I had meaning and value."

The Insight Explained

There is a "damned if you do, damned if you don't" aspect to being a man. The "perfect man" template is characterized by increasing alienation from one's personal self and from closeness with others. Therefore, when life should be getting better, he becomes more rigid and unable to let go and enjoy it. Men can see that happening to other men, but not to themselves.

What a Woman Can Do

Clearly men are in a bind. The same psychological process that may allow him to feel he is a man destroys his personal self. The same personality ingredients that make the acquisition of success and wealth possible destroy a man's capacity for close and personal connection. The more extreme the socialization that may make him a winner in the eyes of the world, the less he is able to develop enduring personal and close, caring relationships. The average man has few friends, and the manlier he is, the more likely it is that he has none at all. He may rationalize, saying that other men are not worth the effort or he doesn't need their friendship because his wife is the best and only friend he needs. He cannot see that the socialization he has never questioned or tried to change is creating an increasing isolation from all his personal relationships, including his children and family. If he looks at himself objectively, he'll see that the conditioning that drives him blocks his motivation to change. After a personal crisis disrupts his life, he may glimpse the need to transform himself, and he'll discover that is the hardest thing for him to do. In the meantime, women need to see beyond men's outer shell and embrace the importance and power they have in men's lives.

Women who understand that, and can relate to a man in a less judgmental and personal way, make it possible to actually become best friends with him. Fully seeing and accepting him for who he is will be the true and best foundation for bringing out his suppressed capacity for intimacy and caring that can grow to the point where he can satisfy her desire for closeness.

What a Man Must Do

For a man to transform the underlying, deeply rooted process that shaped him to become an acceptable or admired man can be excruciating, elusive, treacherous, and even frightening and near impossible for a man himself to accurately access. Yet it is a journey well worth taking, and accepting the alternative is to become just one more mechanical, hollowed-out man who is desperately isolated and lonely, and though he may deny it, one who is rigid and predictable in his responses, attitudes, and perceptions and will ultimately witness the failure and emptiness of his pursuits and defensive beliefs.

In the last few decades, many men have attempted the journey of transforming themselves by joining men's groups, going on wilderness retreats, getting personal counseling, and experimenting with spiritual pursuits and philosophies. I congratulate and admire those men, though I can readily see in myself and others how easy it is to become deluded in claiming major personal changes, liberation, or even a transformation.

A man can have all the trappings of the new, balanced, emotionally aware man, but the true test of whether his changes are authentic is the existence and quality of his personal enduring and close relationships, and how he communicates and responds in them. If, as his journey progresses, he becomes more isolated and a lone wolf, he needs to acknowledge the failure of his efforts to free himself of the strictures of masculinity and then create an alternate plan. The pursuit is noble and worthy, even if the actual experience is filled with dead ends, disappointments, delusions, and uncertainty. The alternative of not trying to grow is simply to age in a disconnected and bitter way, witnessed repeatedly in most of the older men in our society.

INSIGHT 12: THE BINDS THAT TIE

A man's psychological journey goes from externalization to disconnection to oblivion.

The Conversation

Tim, an architect, saw at age fifty-three what was happening to many of his male peers, particularly those who had lost a spouse through divorce or death. He himself had become isolated, depressed, and unable to create and maintain a satisfying personal relationship. He was self-observant enough to realize that what he saw happening to other men as they aged and became increasingly withdrawn and out of touch was also happening to him.

Tim: "I saw it with my father, but he couldn't see it. Do guys believe they're so different that they can follow the same path in being a 'real man' and not experience the same isolating and distressing results?"

Dr. Goldberg: "Most guys do believe they won't end up like other men."

Tim: "Yeah, most of us think that when we're young and adventurous and full of life, but by our thirties we've already begun shutting down personally. By the time my dad hit his forties and fifties, he was impossible to get close to or to have a satisfying and spontaneous personal conversation with. And he didn't seem to care!"

Dr. Goldberg: "As men move away from anything personal, they generally can't see or feel it happening. By the time they're fully closed off, they're self-satisfied, like nobody is worth the effort. Every other man to them is an asshole. But just below the surface you can sense the loneliness and hunger, which they only feel during painful moments of truth."

The Insight Explained

Gender socialization is a defensive process and, as with all defensive processes, if left alone, it grows deeper, more extreme, and rigid. Externalization is a process that destroys a man's capacity for personal connection and empathy. He alienates, frustrates, and enrages those within his personal world. He is unable to create close relationships and becomes desperately isolated. Men who are distrustful, withdrawn, disconnected, detached, and controlling become even more so as they age. Finally, it becomes futile to engage them personally because the wall around them has become too strong to penetrate.

What a Woman Can Do

Women involved with men who seem to be progressively more difficult to talk to, particularly when that is happening in tandem with an increase in their own desire for communication and closeness, find themselves in many painful and frustrating life situations. Men's detachment, noncommunicativeness, and coldness may trigger depression, anger, and feelings of hopelessness and helplessness in those who try to relate to them.

What can a woman do? The most important thing to learn is what *not* to do, which is to badger, complain, cry, plead, or blame. Once having identified and resolved their own contributing behaviors to the problem, such as weak boundary setting and low self-esteem, women can become a support and a coach for their partners.

When women realize the enormous power they have and can access because of men's intense, albeit denied, dependency, they have many options. Once a man knows a woman is serious about her own welfare and growth and will abandon him unless he changes, it may become the wake-up call he needs to begin the process of change and reconnection.

As a last resort, sometimes if a woman leaves, it brings out the man's powerful need for the relationship. The "shock therapy" of a woman leaving often gets the message through, at least temporarily. If that doesn't work and the man has become too defensive and disconnected, abandoning him may be the only option for a woman in order to preserve her well-being and set the man free to face the reality he has created, hopefully triggering his change process.

What a Man Must Do

To change one's experience and become a connected, personally functional man, a man must first recognize the inevitable stages his untransformed masculine socialization creates. Then he needs to emerge from his need to deny that he will become just like the other men he knows and sees.

It requires continual work on one's self to escape the pathetic last stage of the masculine journey, which is a state of personal oblivion. That means he has become incapable of creating and sustaining a personal, humanized relationship, which requires his ability to connect and relate in a sustained personal way while being able to be empathic, to recognize and share his own feelings and those of another person, to allow himself to be vulnerable, to acknowledge his need for help and his fears, to maintain a personal connection over a period of time, and to remain connected even when his critical voice is pushing him to withdraw.

There is no simple way or how-to. Rather, it is a matter of personal vigilance and a willingness to ask for and get feedback about himself from someone he trusts and who understands the importance of what he is working to become.

INSIGHT 13: BUYING LOVE

In the masculine end-state of personal oblivion, a man is beyond personal reach and connection and can only relate in an abstract and intellectualized way. At this point he gets "love" only by providing or doing for others.

The Conversation

After his father experienced a heart attack at sixty-eight, Scott resolved to make their relationship a priority: "I don't want to have regrets later on. I love my father, I think, but it sure is challenging trying to get him to open up in any personal way. My dad just sees himself as a provider or 'wallet' for others."

> *Scott*: "Although he kind of acts annoyed by it, my dad seems to take it for granted that his kids, grandkids, and even people in the community only call him or talk to him when they want something."

> *Dr. Goldberg*: "In a way, it's probably validating for him. He might even like the power his money has over them. It gives him control."

> *Scott*: "Everybody says, 'I love you, Dad,' or 'You're the greatest, Grandpa!' Outsiders will say, 'We sure appreciate your generosity, Mr. Fleming,' as he's writing them a check. He feels good doing it, but I can see it also pains him that it is the only time people reach out to him. He'll make cynical comments about it, but then claim he's only kidding."

> *Dr. Goldberg*: "He believes his identity is tied up in his net worth and it's hopeless to even attempt to change that reality."

> *Scott*: "Sometimes I see him make attempts to connect, but he can barely hold a personal conversation. When someone is friendly in return, it seems there's always a motive or agenda behind it. They want something from him. But I think he's resigned to it."

The Insight Explained

When they're young, men get the message that their job is to provide for others. That validates them as worthwhile men. Initially they may resist that role. As they get older, however, every conversation is abstract and becomes a debate, argument, or intellectual exercise in proving a point and determining who's right. Others learn to leave him alone unless they need something from him.

What a Woman Can Do

Observing what happens to men as they age can give women an understanding of the constricting and dehumanizing effect of masculine conditioning. The origins of men's relationship problems and deficits become magnified as men get older—the sad consequence of a conditioning that has progressively cut them off from their personal selves and destroyed their capacity to create close and personal relationships. Those they do manage to create and maintain are mainly by-products of their ability to provide and "pay for" the people who are in their lives. Consequently, as men age, those without means often are those with no relationships.

Relating to men almost as if they were psychologically fixated children with limited relationship and communication skills may be the most effective and realistic template for success. This can make a difference in allowing women to not take personally men's limited relationship behaviors.

Older men with money tend to buy "love." It's the easiest way to postpone, circumvent, and avoid change. They often end their lives ludicrously attempting a replay of their younger days by seeking out young women. They may fantasize themselves as desirable, but that turns to pain and resentment as the realization begins to sink in that the attraction is not to them as people but to the financial security they can provide. Older men without money may have to accept the painful fact that no one reaches out to them.

What a Man Must Do

"No fool like an old fool." That description aptly applies to men as they get older and equate having a personal self with pursuing a young, "sexy" female who supposedly makes him feel young again and validates his need to believe he is unique as a man because he has a young trophy girlfriend or wife, which everyone but he can see is delusional.

Men in that kind of relationship are buying love by reining in a young woman looking to be provided for or become the last one swimming in his inheritance pool.

It is hard for an older, emotionally isolated man to recognize and resist the delusional trap he is falling into. He may rationalize that he is entitled to a little hard-won happiness since he has had to face the shambles he has made of his personal life with his children, wife, and friends more or less alienated and no longer in loving contact.

The idea that he can buy the love he needs is the final nail in the coffin of his personal self. He is "finding love" in the presence and body of a woman who is probably with him because of a cynical and obvious practicality. Once he is sick, vulnerable, and even dying, if he has allowed himself to engage in this May-December romantic fantasy, he will find himself in the middle of ugly, mean, and self-centered opportunism. It is hard to warn men of this because by the time it starts to happen, they may be entrenched in the oblivion stage of masculinity and therefore able to see no alternative to the nightmare their unchallenged masculine socialization has generated.

INSIGHT 14: THE PRICE OF "NICE"

The feminine qualities of "niceness" and "sweetness" that seem so attractive initially are also a manifestation of the dysfunctions of some traditional women, which later may cause them to be seen as irrational and unreasonable by men. Their compulsion to be "nice" and "sweet" prevents them from stating their needs clearly and openly, often causing them to become overly sensitive and defensively reactive to expressions of anger and conflict.

The Conversation

"When I was in my early twenties," Randy said, "I'd be proud to be dating a person my friends and family thought was nice or sweet. While those women seemed to be the easiest to connect with initially, they were the hardest with whom to maintain a healthy relationship. The nicer they were to me, the more I felt everything that went wrong was my fault. Their words still ring in my ears—'that's not nice' or 'why can't you be nice?' Hearing that frustrated me and drove me crazy.

"The 'nicer' *they* were, the more I'd hear about how controlling or hostile I was. I'd never know what they really liked or didn't like because the important thing for them was to be seen as agreeable and easy to get along with. They acted as if everything I did pleased them, but I knew that couldn't be real, and it wasn't. Their denied negative feelings would leak through eventually.

"The 'nicer' they were, the more it became impossible to negotiate our conflicts or for me to talk about something that bothered me about them or our relationship. They'd get upset and tell me how hurtful and mean I was. So instead of being straight about what I was feeling, I'd pretend everything was okay, rather than trigger a scene that might go on for hours or days.

"We could never resolve problems. If we tried, I'd always feel like I was wounding them. I'd get bored and the relationship felt like it was stuck because it only had two gears: either everything was 'nice and sweet' and phony, or there was a painful drama because unknowingly I'd hurt their feelings. It got tiresome, so I'd leave because I was frustrated, or they would end it because they felt I didn't really care."

Randy: "How come most women act so lovely and giving when I first meet them, but there's always a huge, hidden price?"

Dr. Goldberg: "Do you mean they're manipulating you by acting so nice?"

Randy: "I doubt it's a premeditated manipulation. But they act like overly sensitive children. They want to be reassured. They're always checking to see if I'm angry about something. If I do try to have an honest discussion about how I feel, they react badly and even call me 'mean.'"

Dr. Goldberg: "Quite often when the relationship goes past the infatuation stage and starts to get serious, women start pressuring for reassurance. That's when men back away."

The Insight Explained

The gap between fantasy and reality is great when it comes to the attractiveness of a traditional woman. It seems so good initially, but the "niceness" turns out to be a by-product of an inability to express or handle anger or be clear about what she wants and accept that conflict occurs in all relationships and needs to be acknowledged and worked out. Men have to accept the fact that there's little they can say that's safe or real and isn't misconstrued.

What a Woman Can Do

The "price of nice" is about the consequences of feminine socialization. That defensive process conditions women to repress, deny, and avoid displays of any negative responses, such as anger, resistance, assertion, recognition of conflict, and the ability to say "no," and be clear about their choices. This sets the stage for breakdowns and a midlife crisis because it blocks a woman's growth toward a strong, separate identity and generates feelings of helplessness, hopelessness, and low self-esteem, often causing women to readily feel bruised and abused.

The process that conditions a woman to be nice is her most powerful relationship and intimacy obstacle. It limits her capacity to be a strong equal partner and see herself as a contributor to, not a victim of, everything that happens in her relationships, so closeness becomes impossible.

The very thing women are taught as young girls that will bring them recognition and love, which is to be "as nice as possible," actually turns men off and makes women seem "impossible" to communicate with. Men may initially take advantage of a woman's desire to be seen as "nice," but then it brings out their abusive, sarcastic, and insensitive side. While it appears that men are just being jerks, I like to think that, in a deeper way, it's a man's indirect and ineffectual way of trying to give a woman he cares about a wake-up call—namely, trying to prod her in the direction of her strength and wholeness.

The following consequences are a part of that reality:

1. The man will be seen as the bad guy for wanting to talk about anything "not nice."
2. Resolving conflict will become increasingly impossible because discussions trigger tears or cause her to feel wounded.
3. He will despair over the futility of getting her to be clear about what she wants when she complains about being controlled.
4. When he makes decisions and takes action to fill the void, most likely he'll be told he's being controlling and selfish, and he'll have no idea what his partner is referring to.

5. There will be a continual pressure in the relationship for the man to apologize and prove he's not angry and still loves her. Those demands will grind him down, causing him increasingly to withdraw and become incommunicative.

What a Man Must Do

What a man must do to avoid the consequences of attaching to a woman who is "so nice" to him is to recognize and grow beyond his resistance and fears of actively creating and building a relationship. Some of those resistances are an extension of his false ego belief that a relationship can just happen because of his specialness. The greater a man's inability to do the work of building a relationship in a mutual way, the more he will seek out the "nice" woman, whose inability to assert herself and draw boundaries and whose willingness to make the relationship happen primarily with her energy and then keep it going for both of them confirms to him that he's so lovable that merely *showing up* and being willing to continue is a sufficient contribution for him to bring to the relationship.

Relationships that seem to happen too easily, with little to no effort, and feel like they are happening magically because of finding a "soul mate" lack the reality foundation created when a man has to actively work at making it happen through the continual sharing of his feelings, his needs, and his conflicts, while also creating a relationship climate that makes it possible for his partner to do the same.

Equating love with a woman's seeming continual willingness to please him, love him unconditionally, and allow him to always have it "his way" reflects a man's fear of an authentic closeness with a woman as a real person, not just an extension of his need to validate his own irresistible wonderfulness and specialness.

Overcoming that grandiosity is a man's challenge in becoming an emotionally healthy partner.

INSIGHT 15: THE URGE TO MERGE

A feminine woman's personal journey is from internalization *to* fusion craving, *which is an intense and insatiable need for an ever-growing intimacy, leading to the* dissolution of her sense of self.

The Conversation

"It's surprising to me," said Levon, a divorced humanities instructor at age forty-one, "that when it comes down to the nitty-gritty of being in a relationship and making it work, men and women have not just a different experience, but opposite." He went on to admit, "I was really traumatized when I divorced my wife, who I was sure I loved more than anything else in the world before I realized she had misinterpreted almost everything I'd said and done in our relationship. I couldn't believe her picture of me in the relationship was so different from my experience of myself. Even the times when I thought I'd been playful or funny, I later learned she saw as having been patronizing, sarcastic, or just plain hostile."

> *Levon*: "When I think I've found a woman who is different from the rest—both of us on the same wavelength—am I just kidding myself? Is it just a matter of time before those awful arguments start showing up because we see things in opposite ways?"

> *Dr. Goldberg*: "It's not what a woman says or thinks, or even how she acts, that indicates how different she is from other women. How women relate is revealed once they're in a relationship and issues of commitment and sex come up. It becomes apparent that often women's concerns and complaints are different than men's. They talk about intimacy and 'getting closer.' It gets harder for them to maintain their separateness and boundaries. They react to what men say and do rather than being clear about what they really want."

The Insight Explained

The differences between men and women generated by masculine and feminine socialization are profound, including how they respond to conflict, the values they have around sex, and their ability to make decisions and be clear about what they want. Most women are socialized to be significantly more focused on the personal. Their priorities are to develop close relationships and intimacy. Once bonded with a man, they lose their sense of self and move toward selflessness. When their male partners don't join them in their urge to merge, they view them as uncaring.

What a Woman Can Do

Though it isn't as much of a problem today as it was in the past, especially with girls participating in more team sports and academic activities, there are still many women who are familiar with how their socialization has them more focused on the personal than the competitive, on physical appearance rather than worldly achievements, and on accommodating and pleasing others rather than pursuing their own dreams. The typical progression of women's experiences as a result of their socialization begins as young girls with a primary focus on the personal ("How do I look?" "How do I feel?") rather than on other achievements. As they grow up, they can develop an increasing preoccupation with relationships and closeness, which at the same time may cause them to lose their unique identity and sense of self as they enter committed relationships.

These socialization forces are hard for a woman herself to see (though others can see them), but where they still exist, their toxic nature needs to be recognized and contained because they will become the major cause for many of women's most painful relationship experiences.

What a Man Must Do

Men tend to collude with a woman's tendency to submerge and lose her sense of self in a relationship and fuse with *his* identity—namely, *his* lifestyle, *his* friends, *his* preferences, *his* hobbies and interests—by their own resistance to sharing and joining a woman in the lifestyle, friends, and interests she had when she first began the relationship. When he resists, becomes bored, and refuses to join his partner in her world as much as she participates in his, he makes it possible, even inevitable, that in her desire to be close to him she will have to do it "his way" and give up, hide, or diminish her identity in order to be with him.

In an emotionally healthy relationship, both partners need to embrace each other's world, such as career choices, family focus, activities, and beliefs. When a man lets a relationship happen only when it's in sync with his needs, choices, and timelines, he is setting the stage for her fusion with him by not giving her identity equal breathing space.

While it is not a man's responsibility to make sure a woman doesn't fuse with him and thereby lose her identity, it *is* his responsibility to recognize his tendency and need to only do things his way in a relationship.

The price for a woman losing herself in the process of becoming close to him is not readily apparent initially. It becomes severe when she reaches a point at which her anger and rage can no longer be contained and denied and therefore begins to bubble up because she has lost herself as a separate person, therefore needing to leave him, usually in anger and revulsion, in order to reclaim herself.

INSIGHT 16: CLOSENESS—THE FINAL FRONTIER

The compulsive pursuit of closeness, which I call "fusion craving," is the woman's counterpart addiction to a man's obsession with space and autonomy. While these needs are opposite sides of the same coin and equally bottomless, a woman's fusion craving is viewed positively by society, while a man's compulsion to disconnect and withdraw is viewed negatively.

The Conversation

Tom: "I get into these ridiculous spats with women where every sentence seems to have the word 'always' or 'never' in it as we accuse each other of deliberately frustrating each other's needs." (Tom had been with his partner, Anne, for two years.) "It has to do with her telling me I never *really* want to be with her, or me telling her that no matter how much time we spend together, it never seems to register or be enough to please or satisfy her. The women I get involved with say, 'Why won't you open up and be more intimate? We're not really close and it's so frustrating to be with you. I feel pushed away, like you don't want to be with me.'"

Dr. Goldberg: "And like most guys, you don't understand it. So with your masculine logic you engage her in a futile interchange. 'What do you mean, I push you away? Give me an example. You tell me I'm afraid of intimacy, but I don't think so. Be more specific; I haven't got a clue as to what you're talking about!'"

Tom: "I know I struggle with closeness issues, but the problem is many of the women I've met rarely acknowledge their own part, which is that no matter how much a man gives, it's never enough."

Dr. Goldberg: "To be fair, it must feel terrible to women that guys are acting like they're being suffocated and need more space, no matter how much space they actually do have."

The Insight Explained

Masculinity externalizes men, so they're constantly moving outside of their inner personal selves. Many women call that a fear of intimacy, and there's truth to that. But they are rarely told how their pursuit of closeness is an insatiable and bottomless pit that no man can fill. Often women feel superior and righteous when it comes to relationships because they crave this closeness, even though it pushes away the men who feel hopeless trying to satisfy it.

What a Woman Can Do

Women are correct in sensing and asserting that men have great difficulty being intimate and that a man's quest for space and autonomy has an unquenchable quality.

Neither society nor those who care about her may be able to identify a woman's desire and quest for closeness or intimacy as being a bottomless need no man can fill. It becomes a woman's challenge to realize that she is not being deliberately pushed away, but she and her partner have a relationship pull in their personalities that moves them in opposing directions. Because many women view themselves as being denied fulfillment of their needs by their men, and society tends to reinforce the notion that the man is the cause of a woman's frustrations, it takes a high level of awareness and effort on a woman's part to see beyond the common wisdom as to who is doing what and to whom.

Men's fear of intimacy is the counterpart to women's craving for closeness. They are reciprocal bottomless needs and dysfunctions.

Some women righteously confront men about how hard it is to get close to them, but at times men are ignored when they confront women about their struggle with a corresponding hunger for attention, reassurance, love, and closeness that alienates and pressures. There is a tendency for women to feel criticized and attacked, when in fact they are just being told about their impact and their partner's frustrations.

What a Man Must Do

Beyond a certain point needed for a man to remain himself, men's need for space and freedom has to be recognized by a man as being defensive and damaging to his development into and quest to become a connected person, able to continually grow rather than shrink as a related person as time goes by in his relationships.

A man may think he is just being "a man" when he goes silent, withdraws, refuses to communicate, and insists on being left alone when he is not pleased or things don't go his way, but that is defensive relationship behavior. His partner and others in his life will eventually "give up" trying to reach him and pull him out of "his space." They will in fact "leave him alone," as he eventually winds up in an emotional place where he is truly and painfully by himself and begins to lose the ability to create close relationships. He ends up, as many men do, either all alone or with a partner willing to tolerate his distance in return for being taken care of, a relationship that will inevitably lead to dissatisfaction, arguments, accusations, and distrust.

A man needs to learn that the quest to have a relationship with someone who allows him to retreat at will and communicate only on his terms is dysfunctional—an illusion of a relationship—and will lead to his own disappearance from a world of connection to others. His mantra of "if you don't leave me alone, I'll find someone who will" will be his wish fulfilled, and that will erode his being a person in a world of others.

INSIGHT 17: VICTIM "MEN"-TALITY

A woman's potential for change and growth is in inverse proportion to her sense of being a victim, whose unhappiness, frustration, and pain are caused by others.

The Conversation

"I don't think I've ever been in a relationship with a woman who pointed the finger of blame at herself instead of me when we were having problems." Timothy, at forty-nine, a thrice-divorced real estate salesman, was struggling to understand his relationship failures. "It's so frustrating to try so hard and still hear about how I'm the bad guy. Lots of women in a relationship talk a good game about being fair and supporting a man's growth, but I don't see that as possible unless they can acknowledge that what they do that contributes to the problems they have with a man."

Timothy: "I once read that people who see themselves as victims don't think they need to change. Whatever their problem is, it's always somebody else's fault. Well, the majority of the women I know, talking about their frustrations with men, make it sound like it's the guy's fault and they are the innocent victims of a callous jerk."

Dr. Goldberg: "I've found that relationships can't be worked on or improved unless both partners acknowledge their part in generating the problems, and work on identifying their own contribution, first and foremost. That's the hardest thing to do when you feel righteous about yourself. The only way a woman can change or grow when she's with a man is if she can see her part clearly and is motivated to work on that. However, because many women mainly react to men, it's hard for them to see the part they play. When someone sees themselves as a victim, change just isn't going to happen."

The Insight Explained

People don't change when they feel self-righteous and defensive about their part in creating a broken-down relationship. To create change, a person needs to feel there's a reason to do it. When partners blame and point their fingers at each other, their motivation to change is not there.

What a Woman Can Do

Relationships will thrive when women and men are able to clearly see how a relationship is a dynamic where each player has a part in everything that happens. All a woman has to do to generate the love, devotion, and intimacy she seeks is to demonstrate her ability to see the full picture, the reciprocal nature of each partner's experience.

A psychologically meaningful definition of a loving partner would be a man or woman who points the finger at himself or herself *first* when there's an issue or conflict in the relationship, to acknowledge their contribution to the problem. Women and men who act as blaming victims are stuck and create the feeling of hopelessness.

What a Man Must Do

Men have to avoid relationships with a partner who portrays and sees herself as a helpless, vulnerable victim in a relationship or life situation. If she enters a relationship with a man while blaming others for her pain, failures, unhappiness, and fears for her situations at work or in her life in general, a man must recognize that as a dysfunction and know inevitably, after the romantic glow fades, he will also be seen as her oppressor or victimizer.

A partner who experiences herself as a victim may initially ignite in a man a quest to make life better for her by being a different kind of partner, one who appreciates her and knows how to love her and make life good, but he will become dismayed and embittered when suddenly he finds himself needing to continually prove he isn't just a repeat of her past painful life experiences, relationships, and choices.

INSIGHT 18: THOUGHTS FOR FOOD

When women celebrate together they tend to use food to satisfy their need to be close, while men usually use alcohol to bond with each other. Women may also use food to medicate and sublimate their craving for fusion, which can result in a destructive addiction.

The Conversation

Men talking about their women partner's relationship to food notice that sometimes women mask and deny their eating habits, even denying that their weight gain had anything to do with their eating behaviors. What seemed to affect many men was the woman's obsession with dieting and agonizing over whether to eat a food she craved but thought might put weight on her. Sergio is an engineering graduate student.

Sergio: "My girlfriend is always lecturing me about my drinking, but did you ever notice a group of women when it comes to food? They sometimes eat the worst sugary, creamy desserts while saying they know they shouldn't. It's clear they can't always control their eating."

Dr. Goldberg: "When they talk among themselves, a lot of women will admit they'd rather be eating than making love. That's exactly how alcoholics or druggies feel. They'd rather get stoned than do anything else. Guys get drunk when they're depressed or anxious. Women often use food to comfort and console themselves and medicate their moods. When they're frustrated or angry, they might eat a quart of ice cream or a whole bag of cookies. Of course, in some cases the situation is reversed. There are certainly many women alcoholics and men who are addicted to food."

The Insight Explained

Mothers use food to show babies love, to reward, and to calm them. The internalization of femininity lends itself to using food as a substitute for the hunger and frustrated craving for fusion and love that no man can fill.

As girls become women, they may not see how their preoccupation with eating is connected to this hunger for closeness and love, along with their lack of separation from mother. Women who use food to calm, reward, or fulfill themselves resemble all other addicts using their addictions to fend off and control their pain and frustration.

What a Woman Can Do

Women with food issues tend to be as secretive about them as men are who have alcohol addictions. They feel shame and don't want others to see their out-of-control behaviors. The consequences of food addictions are as damaging as alcohol and drug addictions but not recognized as such because society believes stuffing oneself with food is less destructive than getting drunk.

It's easy in a society that seems obsessed with the pleasures of eating, dieting, dining out, and discovering new recipes and foods to hide one's food obsessions. The resistance to acknowledging food issues is as great for women as men's resistance to acknowledging their alcoholism and drug addictions. Both are relationship killers that erode and diminish the relationship experience, and they need to be acknowledged and defused in order to surmount their potential destructive power.

What a Man Must Do

A man's vulnerability to becoming an alcoholic is something he tends to deny while it's happening. Though he may be with a woman who doesn't want to be a nag or mother figure by pointing out and warning him about his drinking, men need to recognize alcoholism as a killer of their intimate relationships and the family atmosphere.

Similarly, men should educate themselves about the role of food addictions and the damage that obsessions with food and food cravings have on health and the creation of diseases, such as diabetes and heart problems, and the development of the children. While "eating for fun" is something one hates to play the role of spoiler about, for the sake of the family and relationships men need to learn to recognize the signs of excessive food, diet, and eating preoccupation without allowing the creation of a mutually enabling relationship in which men feel free to drink to excess while their partners show signs of an unhealthy relationship and preoccupation with food and eating.

INSIGHT 19: POWER AND SPIRIT

The success-driven man and the highly spiritual woman are polarized equivalents or counterparts. Both are attractive from a distance but increasingly offensive to each other as they become intimate. Each tends to be rigid and fearful of personal change and is equally clueless and defensive about why they are repeatedly abandoned in their tumultuous close relationships. Then they become self-righteous in their attempts to understand what happened.

The Conversation

When they first "got serious" with each other, Eli and Ruth seemed to be exactly what the other needed. As an investment counselor, Eli was pure Type A: driven, competitive, ready for action, and cynical when it came to spiritual and psychological matters. Ruth was seemingly other-worldly in her way of being: gentle, compassionate, quiet, optimistic, and positive in the way she related to the world. Friends thought they were perfect and would balance each other.

Three years into their marriage, however, their communication had broken down. Eli sought therapy after Ruth threatened to leave him because of his "workaholic and dehumanized" way of being. "I don't want to lose her, even though her righteous ways always leave me feeling I'm the bad guy."

Eli: "Guys who are obsessed with their careers are a drag to hang out with. They're not ever really present because they're always obsessing. I can see why their wives end up depressed and angry."

Dr. Goldberg: "They're an extreme version of the masculine ideal—goal focused, aggressive, in control, and detached. You can admire their success from a distance, but as they get closer you want to get away from them, unless you just want to ride their coattails."

Eli: "I get a similar feeling around 'spiritual' women. You'd think it would feel good to be with them, but it doesn't. They're obsessed with their moral purity, peacefulness, selflessness, tranquility, and their idea of loving. I find them really annoying. Their ultrafeminine outer image is attractive, but I always want to get away from them when they start getting closer. They've always got some holier-than-thou platitude to say."

Dr. Goldberg: "It's much the same with success-driven guys. You want to tell them that just because they've got money, they think they know everything and everyone should be awed by them. But their macho bravado is offensive to be around."

The Insight Explained

Nowhere is the gap between outer image and personal reality greater than in these two polarized extremes. Success-driven men are the ultimate of the masculine prototype. While the world applauds their success, the people around them experience a whole different reality. The same holds true for very spiritual women.

What a Woman Can Do

A very spiritual woman might feel "out of place" in the everyday world where money and power seem to be the measures of one's value. Being involved with a successful man could be a solution to easing her sense of vulnerability in the competitive marketplace. But a spiritual woman needs to recognize two things: The more successful a man is, the more likely it is that he will be controlling and resistant to change. As his partner, the spiritual woman will be tempted to be both judgmental of him and prone to seeing herself as burdened by his "hardness," insensitivity, and lack of self-awareness. In order to navigate the relationship through its rocky waters, it's important for a woman to realize she is now critical of the very same qualities that initially drew her to him. In order to nourish the relationship, a woman needs to recognize her own issues—namely, the tendency to attribute their problems to her partner's lack of spirituality. The relationship will improve by focusing on becoming a strong, separate person and not by using her spirituality as a tool to transform him. *Strengthening herself rather than trying to humanize him is the key to making the relationship grow.*

What a Man Must Do

It is tempting for the cynical, success-driven, coldly competitive man to view a woman in his life who professes spirituality, deep love, and caring for humanity as being more evolved as a person than he is. Men who embrace that fantasy, perhaps in hope they can be redeemed or made whole through a relationship with her, may in fact discover quite the opposite.

A man who is drawn to a spiritual, peace-loving, God-fearing, humanity-embracing woman needs to realize she is probably just an extreme

version of the traditionally feminine woman who is incapable of express
ing negative feelings such as anger, has difficulty setting boundaries,
allows herself to be exploited, and may require others to take care of her
financially.

A man attracted to or in a relationship with a spiritual woman needs to
focus not on what he thinks or believes about her as a person but rather
how it actually feels when he is with her. If her spirituality is just a
defensive extension of her traditional feminine socialization, he will have
to acknowledge that he feels bored as well as reluctant to be his real self
around her because he anticipates that she will be judging him critically,
feeling he is in need of enlightenment. If all he has succeeded in doing in
such a relationship is reinforcing his self-loathing and guilt rather than
being uplifted by her spirituality, he will come to feel even more convinced of his unworthiness and her moral superiority. Clearly, that is not
a good way to feel and to be, and he needs to learn to understand that.

INSIGHT 20: RICH MAN, POOR MAN, BEGGAR MAN, GRIEF

*Whether CEO, plumber, or homeless, men obsess on similar themes when
they speak of women and relationships. Likewise, female movie stars,
business professionals, secretaries, waitresses, and housewives all sound
the same when they discuss men.*

The Conversation

In my practice, whether speaking with an ex-priest or a maker of porn
movies, when it comes to women the struggle and experience of most
men is similar. Anthony, a self-described street kid from a lower-class
ghetto who became a Wharton MBA and had been through many relationships, described his experiences.

> *Anthony*: "Before I became successful in my career, I thought once I
> had money and status, things with women would get much easier. The
> only thing that got easier was getting them to pay attention to me.
> Once I got involved, the same issues kept coming up."

Dr. Goldberg: "Women think the same way. The same issues and complaints plague them once they're in a relationship. When they're 'in love,' high-powered career women will describe and experience the same things as waitresses and secretaries."

Anthony: "Right, and isn't that true of guys, too? No matter what we do for a living, when we're talking about women we're involved with, the same guilt, conflicts, and complaints come up."

The Insight Explained

Embedded in the gender process is a powerful, cultural, grinding force that is the shaper and equalizer of experience. Everyone is brought down to the same level. Nowhere is the *content/process* dynamic manifested more clearly than in the love relationships of men and women. One man may have better *content* than the next, meaning more money or a better job, and one woman might be more beautiful than the other; however, the *process*, or how she looks and what he does for a living, is what will determine what they experience.

What a Woman Can Do

In addition to Mother Nature and Father Time, add gender process to the list of the great equalizers of life. Rich men and poor men, gorgeous women and plain ones, have similar complaints when it comes to their committed relationships. *Not money, nor education, nor worldly power, nor physical attractiveness changes what men and women experience when involved with each other.*

When a woman chooses a partner who seems to be "a real man," whether he is a poet or plumber, a musician or attorney, the moment-to-moment, everyday reality tends to be similar. Masculine socialization will cause a woman to see her man as out of touch with his emotions, focused on *doing* rather than *being*, resistant to expressing feelings or acknowledging his love or his needs, with a tendency to be controlling.

Working to rebalance the relationship on both sides is the way to change one's relationship experience, rather than seeking a new or "better" partner or feeling stuck and resigned to the man's way of being, which is conditioned by his socialization and is not a matter of choice.

What a Man Must Do

Relationship equalizers expose our common human vulnerability. We must add intimate relationships between heterosexual men and women as another equalizer, yet for many reasons it rarely seems to get acknowledged.

When women and men talk about their relationship experiences with others of their gender, the feelings shared are often similar, whether the individuals are high up on the social and economic ladder or way down, whether they are celebrity and royalty or working person and homeless.

Considering that, it is foolish for a man to believe that in a traditional relationship, simply by luck or great wisdom, he will escape these commonly felt and heard experiences of male/female relationships.

Women bemoan men's cluelessness, lack of communication skills, self-centeredness, controlling behaviors, inability to listen, short attention span, and emotional insensitivity. By contrast, men talking about women complain about their irrational, mystifying, moody, so-called crazy and crazy-making, intrusive, and impossible-to-understand-and-predict behavior.

What men must do in order to avoid these gender socialization traps that ensnare both the brilliant and the not-so-smart is first recognize and acknowledge that their experience is not likely to be different from that of other men, and that without working at it consciously they will surely repeat the experiences of other men.

To avoid the common psychological endpoints seemingly created by gender socialization, men must rid themselves first of the grandiose belief that they will make their experience different if they can only find the special woman, unlike all the others.

That belief is what I refer to as a *content error* because the experience of relationships is the result of how two people interact, not who the person is.

What men must do is acknowledge their commonly shared socialization and how that has shaped their relationship behavior, choices, and interpretations.

Once that is acknowledged, men must begin the hard work of reshaping or resocializing themselves to free themselves of embedded, traditional, and automatic masculine responses. This takes time, awareness, and focus because gender socialization generates deeply rigid, rooted, and anxiety-driven ways of responding and fears of being seen as unmanly.

Because these roots are deep, men need to know and see that having a different relationship experience outcome will require patience, as a slow, probably ragged self-transformation occurs that is neither all or nothing nor black and white. Changes will occur in a slow, incremental way.

Men must become self-aware and nondefensive and will probably require outside help in the form of therapy or group support.

Often, the greater the amount of success, wealth, and education, the more likely that one will repeat traditional relationship errors, misman-agement, and endpoints.

Finally, men must applaud the women who understand a man's quest to break time-honored and toxic-gender patterns, and avoid the women who make them feel aberrant for trying.

INSIGHT 21: ACTOR/REACTOR

When men act *and women* react, *the process leaves men feeling respon-sible and guilty and women feeling controlled, discounted, and angry. Women's rage toward men and men's guilt in relationships are in direct proportion to the degree to which this* actor/reactor *dynamic exists.*

The Conversation

The more a man has a need to control, even when he denies it, the more he will be drawn to women with low self-esteem who need to be rescued by a man. She readily gives him control initially. This lethal gender rhythm was experienced repeatedly by the highly successful, power-and-control-driven Gregory, who by age fifty had numerous relationships with beautiful women that all began with sexual fire, then became filled with resentment and rage. As a result, no matter how different or unique the women seemed at the beginning, the relationships all came to feel the same.

> *Gregory:* "I'm optimistic when I start dating a new woman. I feel I've learned from past experience and I'm expecting a great new relation-

ship with someone who will be better or different than the ones before!"

Dr. Goldberg: "And then?"

Gregory: "After the first few dates, each woman starts to act like all the others. The arguments and accusations sound the same."

Dr. Goldberg: "Like what?"

Gregory: "Like telling me I'm a control freak or I treat her like a child. No matter what I do, I wind up feeling a combination of guilt and boredom."

The Insight Explained

Traditional courtship is about men being *actors* and women being *reactors*. This *actor/reactor* dynamic, which characterizes the beginning of the majority of romantic male-female interactions, is the process at the heart of the dysfunctional, painful experience of relationships. The *actor/reactor* dynamic is so powerful in its impact that the good stuff between a man and woman readily gets lost and drowned out. Many women get angrier because they feel they're losing their identity and being controlled by the men, and men start to freeze because they feel blamed and responsible. The emotions that build most strongly in men as a result of being actors are guilt, boredom, and self-hate, while the feelings that build in those women who are reactors are rage and a sense that they are being diminished and abused. The more extreme the polarization, the more toxic and painful the feelings will become.

What a Woman Can Do

Women who have grown tired of unsatisfying and irritating relationships with controlling men need to look at the dynamic of their relationships for the solution to breaking the frustrating pattern. Instead of looking for a different kind of man or feeling frustrated and angry at all men, women need to look at how their relationships begin and evolve and do the difficult work of breaking the *male as actor/female as reactor* pattern, in which men take the lead and responsibility and women react to their lead.

Once that dynamic is balanced, the relationship will start to take on freshness. Men will no longer be experienced as the irritating controllers, and deadened relationships will be revived.

It is folly to believe that by working hard at a relationship, one can transcend the feelings created by its *process* or dynamic. If a relationship starts to feel loaded down with anger, guilt, blaming, and irresolvable arguments, the solution is to change or alter its process rather than change its content. Unless both partners are able to engage fully in working on the balance of *actor* and *reactor*, the inevitable breakdown will repeat itself.

What a Man Must Do

To avoid the common relationship endpoints of traditional masculinity that include feelings of guilt, self-hatred, and failure and a woman's anger over having felt controlled, deprived of her identity, and diminished self-esteem, men must be wary of relationships with women who lack a clear and positive sense of themselves and don't take responsibility for whatever happens to them in their relationships.

From the very beginning, there must be a continual conversation about who decides and who initiates—who drives, who pays, and who initiates sex.

Responses by a partner such as "whatever you want to do is fine," "why don't you decide?" "I'm open," "It doesn't really matter," or "I don't know" must be rejected, deemed unacceptable, and confronted before these gender-based toxic interactions become entrenched.

Men must talk themselves through their feeling that "if I don't romance her by taking charge and acting like a man, she won't want to be with me or she will see me as weak, unmanly, and therefore undesirable," because taking the role of *actor* to her *reactor* will become a bottomless and thankless pit of taking responsibility and generate a pattern that once set in motion may become almost impossible to alter.

INSIGHT 22: A WOMAN'S POWER

Asking a woman to take power and control in a relationship can be like asking a man to relinquish it. Once a woman takes direct responsibility for initiating and participating in the dynamic of the relationship and its decisions, she may lose the form of indirect power that was traditionally hers.

The Conversation

At twenty-eight, Marvin, an aspiring Los Angeles writer, describing his experiences with a woman he thought might be the one, became cautious when he realized he'd taken on the role of decision maker, entertainer, and social director. It left him feeling bored and negative about himself when he made choices like a disappointing restaurant or getting tickets for a sporting event his partner didn't enjoy.

She didn't say so directly, but he could sense her disapproval. It made him feel anxious and reminded him of previous experiences with women in which a similar pattern had occurred.

Marvin: "Women always tell me I am controlling. Even with women who seem independent and strong, they almost never want to take charge or make decisions. Some complain about having no say but resist and almost panic when I ask them to take charge."

Dr. Goldberg: "Maybe some women control men that way. If they get a man to take responsibility for what happens, instead of making the decisions, when things go wrong, it's never their fault."

The Insight Explained

It is not uncommon for some women to freeze, go passive, and get silent when a man asks, "What do you want to do?" or "Where do you want to go?" because making decisions about activities is giving up the power they get indirectly by simply responding positively or negatively to a man's choices. They may not acknowledge it, but it's also a lot less stressful.

What a Woman Can Do

While it may seem that most men like to take charge in the early stages of a relationship by initiating dates, choosing restaurants, and making the plans, this is actually the beginning of a pattern that leaves men feeling bored, frustrated, and discontent. While hesitant to press a woman to make the decisions, most men would respond positively to clear and strong responses to such questions as "What are the things you don't want to do and that turn you off?" or "Is there anything about how I relate to you that bothers you?"

By taking responsibility for decisions and choices, some women may lose the power of passive resistance, causing a need for them to learn to be comfortable expressing their choices directly, which, while sounding appealing initially, can make them uncomfortable. They may be tempted to assume the reactive role again, but for true and enduring change they must resist that temptation.

What a Man Must Do

When men behave passively or reactively in the beginning of a relationship and their partners become the active initiators, it may create feelings of discomfort and the sense that something is not right. That is usually the consequence of changing long-standing, entrenched patterns of man-woman interaction.

Men must realize that the reason men and women resist changing the socially entrenched ways of responding is because it *is* initially uncomfortable, scary, and accompanied by a sense that one is entering unknown and risky relationship territory.

Men must respond positively to the woman's choices and decisions while appreciating and loving her for taking the responsibility, and stating clearly, when appropriate, that he does not want to take all the responsibility for choices and decisions with the confidence that that does not make him less of an adequate partner. This is a necessary step toward breaking deeply entrenched, time-honored, and toxic gender patterns that, if left to continue, will have distressing, negative emotional endpoints.

It may be uncomfortable for a man's partner to deal with this in the initial stages of a relationship in regard to matters of money, sexuality, and the like because it tends to threaten both parties, particularly the man, who is giving up the importance he gets from behaving in a manly way. For women, it may be a threat to their sense of femininity to be asked to take active, visible control and power with a man early in the relationship.

Finally, the ideal endpoint is for both men and women to become equally comfortable taking or giving up power and control, thus making it possible for both to do so in a natural, easy, and comfortable way.

INSIGHT 23: WOMEN AS THEIR OWN OPPRESSORS

Women who react to men are not expressing their real selves. Rather, they are accommodating men and adapting to them. Reaction generates in women a sense of being controlled and having their identities denied, regardless of men's intentions.

The Conversation

Craig was thirty-five and tired of the single life when he began his counseling sessions because he feared he could not really trust his judgment or read his partners well enough to allow him to make a permanent commitment.

Craig: "At some point in my relationships I get this weird feeling that I don't know who this woman I'm with really is or what she really thinks or needs."

Dr. Goldberg: "You're saying that most of the time she's just playing off your energy and responding to your lead? She's so busy accommodating you that whoever she is and what she really thinks and feels gets lost. And up until a certain point, your ego hides awareness of the fact that everything that goes on happens at your initiation, not hers. It's your choices that are shaping the relationship."

Craig: "It makes me nervous because by waiting for me to make the moves, everything she's doing is to please me, while everything I'm doing seems to be all about my ego."

Dr. Goldberg: "Do you think maybe you like that arrangement, or you wouldn't be going along with it? You want to believe that she likes you being the strong, in-control man, and she just happens to like whatever you like."

The Insight Explained

From the time they're little girls, most females learn that being lovable is about being nice and being pretty. Their real selves—specifically, their independent feelings, thoughts, needs, and preferences—may get lost, and they may disappear completely as a separate person. Then they may become paralyzed when asked to choose or make a decision. After getting into a committed relationship, a woman begins to feel the full impact of having "no self," but she blames it on her partner. It started when she was a little girl. He didn't cause it.

What a Woman Can Do

Women who *react* and accommodate a man in his *actor* role may tend to see themselves as being nice, loving victims of his selfish ego and need to control. "I try to please you, but you don't really care about what I think" can become a woman's reality, while the man is left wondering what he did wrong.

Women need to know it doesn't *please* a man to be with someone who just goes along with his choices and decisions—it *bores* him. A woman's initial willingness to take on the accommodating role often is replaced by feelings that she is being controlled, taken for granted, and diminished by the relationship. These feelings may create a sense that she is the man's "victim," feeling unsupported or respected by him.

Once the sense of being controlled, diminished, or even abused becomes embedded in a woman, it may be too late to change its course because she may have lost the awareness and perspective of how she participated in setting up the situation.

This *reactor* role is so embedded and intractable and invisible that it becomes impossible for a woman to acknowledge its existence. This needs to be changed before marriage, before a woman's good feelings about the relationship have been replaced by the feeling that she's being oppressed by her partner. Once the latter sets in, it is often too late to alter the relationship.

What a Man Must Do

The toxicity of gender socialization is that it blocks the emotional development of both men and women in becoming fully expressive people capable of a full range of responses.

Women who have only learned to react to men often rationalize that men don't like women who initiate and take charge and are clear about what they want and don't want, whether about seemingly trivial matters such as choosing a restaurant or more difficult ones, such as having sex, scheduling, experiences, deciding on marriage, and having children, or simply clearly stating activities she wants to participate in, such as going to sporting events or watching porn.

Men collude with women's defensive accommodation by wanting to have things their way. In that sense, men must see beyond the moment, that it is unhealthy for women to accommodate men.

Men must applaud the woman who maintains a clear sense of self, seeing it as a loving act that will create trust and diminish the possibility that she will one day decide that she has been controlled by her partner and cannot be herself as long as she remains with him.

Men must make it clear early in a relationship that they appreciate when their partners initiate, take responsibility, and are clear about their choices, and they must support women who do this.

3

HIS RELATIONSHIP EXPERIENCE

It takes a man most of his lifetime to acknowledge the truth of his relationship limitations, dysfunctions, and disabilities. There are multiple ways to escape the hard look at what he has done to keep personal connection at arm's length, frustrating partners, family members, friends, and children to the point where they stop trying to have a satisfying experience of closeness, communication, and understanding. For men who never realize what their socialization has done to them, and who find endless ways to justify, rationalize, and deny their enclosure, the end stages of their lives find them transformed into beings who, while seemingly friendly, jovial, or playful, cannot open up or recognize what their emotional and psychological impact and effect has been on those close to them, who even when they seem to be loved, feel that love is limited by a sense that what he is feeling and thinking remains unknown.

From someone who has worked intensively with men and their relationships with women, and who has been a focused observer of men in general and men written about by the media as a result of their relationship crises and tragedies, one reality consistently comes through. Women have enormous power and control in a healthy, positive, nonexploitative way over the man they're involved with because the abandoned man falls apart, and unless there is another woman, his despair and desperation are often extreme to the point of triggering crazy rage and destructiveness. When women are disappointed, mistreated, cheated on, or abused, it is because underlying needs have caused their power to leak away. This can be due to personal issues of low self-esteem or childhood socialization emphasizing "niceness" and the fantasy of having a romantic relationship that is conflict free and close in a way that causes women to lose their boundaries and limits. The men then close up and become distant and cold in response.

Simply stated, in intimate relationships women are their own worst enemies, because men need women far more than women need men. Once men commit, even when they have a roving eye (which is rare if they are with a woman who has strong boundaries and keeps a separate distance), they become deeply attached even as they deny their dependency. In fact, one could speculate that a man's roving eye may only be his attempt to deny his infantlike bond with his wife. It may also be his way of igniting a flagging libido that is a by-product of his intense dependency on his wife or partner, whom he transforms into a mother figure. He is tied to her and can't objectify her enough to turn her into a lusted-after sex object, something he may need in order to become sexually aroused. It's a cruel paradox and the result of his masculine socialization that the more "intimate" and personal he is with a woman, the less of an object she becomes and the more he will tend to relate to her in a nonsexual, protective, and dependent way.

Women's boundaries need be clear and strong, unwilling to overlook or forgive transgressions of disrespect and insensitive behavior. While men may balk, like children they are at their best when limits are set, the consequences of their behavior consistently enacted, and clear conditions set forth, such as "I'll only stay with you if you commit to couples counseling," or "I expect you to get therapeutic help for yourself," or "You can't stay away evenings or weekends without letting me know where you are and what you're doing." He may chafe and balk, but he won't leave. Rather, it will deepen his appreciation of his partner, particularly if the message behind the boundary is "I won't let you manipulate, lie, or hide yourself from me." When that message emerges from her need to have a respectful, authentic relationship, its effects will be positive.

Why do men need women more than vice versa? Because most men's relationships with other men are emotionally thin, activity focused, and not really close. Who else is there for him to be close to? Who will nurture and care for him? Men's connection to family members, parents, siblings, and others is usually limited and lacking in authenticity.

Older men with grown children tend to have relationships with them that are limited, consisting of infrequent and superficial conversations that usually involve discussing material needs.

With friendships that are limited in substance, family connections that are even thinner, and mainly goal-focused connections to their children, who is left? That is why men describe their wives as their best friends. They're really describing a profound dependency so great that when they are left, they are in crisis, with great pain and desperation.

Further evidence of men's dependency on women is the fact that few men ever leave a relationship they are in without having another woman waiting. Divorced or widowed men tend to remarry much sooner than divorced or widowed women. Men have great difficulty tolerating the aloneness they themselves create. They almost always need a constant companion. Indeed, many married women perceive their men as "big babies," always wanting to know where his wife or partner is.

Generations of increasing externalization during which men have been conditioned and validated to be performers, competitors, and achievers, making external goals happen, has crippled their capacity for non-goal-motivated or task-focused relating. Men arrive at a personal endpoint that I term "oblivion," where the ability to create any kind of personal and intimate relationships that are genuine and based on caring and love becomes impossible. They progressively retreat into a shell where the only human connections they make are based on materialistic concerns.

INSIGHT 24: A WOMAN IS NOT A CAR

A man tends to find a woman incomprehensible because he tries to understand her based on the observable information, the way he would analyze a mechanical problem. Her reality, not his logic, needs to be the starting point for truly understanding her. Men who use their logic to make sense of their relationships are left confused, frustrated, and eventually embittered.

The Conversation

Men whose strength lies in handling the mechanics of everyday life, such as engineers, accountants, and construction workers, bring that same logical way of making sense of things to their personal and intimate relationships. Thus they tend to get lost and feel helpless when a relationship they have become dependent on begins to unravel.

Leslie was suddenly and "inexplicably" abandoned by his wife of twelve years, and he went on a period of binge dating in his attempt to escape intense feelings of loneliness. In his counseling sessions, he began to see the mechanical way he had interpreted and attempted to understand, manage, and fix his relationships, which led to experiencing a string of failures.

Leslie: "Freud was right. You can never figure out what a woman really wants. I've given up trying."

Dr. Goldberg: "Men think they can fix relationships like they fix their cars. Then get frustrated trying to talk women out of what they feel and trying to use their logic to make them see things their way. Not only are men wasting their time, but they're also alienating women to the point that women feel hopeless about being able to communicate with them."

Leslie: "You're the expert. What's the right way to do it?"

Dr. Goldberg: "Get over the notion that she can be talked into seeing things your way and listen to how she experiences things, without interrupting or interfering. Just listen. You may not like what you hear, but at least you'll have a choice based on her reality, not yours. You can learn to adapt and accept that, or you can end the relationship."

The Insight Explained

Masculine socialization externalizes men so they learn to process their experiences with logic and "objectivity," except that men's ideas primarily seem logical to themselves. Relationships are founded on each person's total inner experience, not the so-called objective facts. In relationships, it doesn't matter what a man may intend. What matters is how his partner experiences him. Using reason to resolve issues with an upset woman makes her feels like a man feels when he's trying to have a conversation with a woman in tears. The more he uses specifics, facts, and reason to connect with her, the worse it gets.

What a Woman Can Do

Men's obsession with "the truth" and solving personal problems with their logic alienates their wives and families, who come to feel they can't make their husbands/fathers really listen, hear, understand, and empathize with their experiences.

Foremost, women need to recognize that these are not intentionally alienating behaviors. A man's "cluelessness" in his personal relationships is *not* deliberate. The missing piece of his understanding and awareness in his personal relationships needs to be strongly and patiently built up. A woman's important message to him should be as follows: "I know you love me and are doing the best you can, but you need to learn to understand my experience and recognize how the mechanical way you use everywhere else is pushing me away."

Growth for most men begins when they realize their so-called truth is only *their* truth. If ever a man's relationships are going to work, the starting point will have to be paying attention to and acknowledging the other person's experience and reality. Men who can't do that will be alone and frustrated by "all those crazy women" who can never understand a man's "superior logic."

What a Man Must Do

A man who wants to avoid a breakdown in communication with his partner must recognize and acknowledge the impact of his lifelong orientation to solving problems. Typically, men want to "understand things" and make sense of them rather than simply empathizing with their partner's experience.

Men who want to create an enduring, loving relationship must see how their tendencies to communicate and solve problems with a detached, cold, and mechanical logic may allow them to win the battle but causes them to lose the war. In return for believing he is always right and all-knowing because of his logic, he will alienate his woman partner, who experiences him as mechanical, arrogant, and uninterested in her perspective.

While a man may prove his so-called brilliance using his traditionally masculine way of solving problems, he will generate the sense in his partner that he doesn't really listen to, care about, or appreciate what she says or thinks.

A man's mechanical, "logical" way of dealing with personal issues creates a distance and a wall between himself and his partner. He may think he is appreciated, convincing, and helpful when he focuses on "the facts," without recognizing how his partner gradually "gives up" trying to communicate with him, begins to "tune him out," and distances herself from him.

A healthy starting point for men is to not immediately try fixing matters with his logic. To understand and develop a growing bond, men need to focus on and hear the experience and feelings of their partners without interruption, judgment, and argument, while also inviting feedback that he listens to seriously and acts on. Relationships are based on the other person's reality, not on one's own. Contrary to what men believe, women do not want a display of a man's "brilliance," but will connect and love him for his ability to hear and accept her feelings, thoughts, and reality and not force his own onto her.

When women share their concerns, they don't want to be "fixed" with a man's cut-and-dried matter-of-fact solutions. They want a show of empathy, appreciation, a sharing of feelings and recognition of being a person who is respected for the way she sees and processes matters of concern.

INSIGHT 25: "I'M NOT LIKE THE OTHERS!"

A man's willingness to believe a woman when she says he is different from other men indicates that, in fact, he's just like them.

The Conversation

Alexander, at forty-five, after a long string of failed relationships, still spent his adult years convinced he was not like other men and could understand, communicate, and give to women what other men supposedly couldn't.

> *Alexander*: "I feel great when a woman I meet tells me how refreshing and nice it is to be with me because I'm not like all other guys."

Dr. Goldberg: "And you believe her? Do you really think you are different?"

Alexander: "I'd like to believe it's true."

Dr. Goldberg: "But don't you think about work, sex, and sports most of the time? Doesn't that make you just like other men?"

Alexander: "I think what she means is I'm more sensitive and a better listener."

Dr. Goldberg: "I'll bet later on, these same women tell you the opposite."

Alexander: "Actually—now that you mention it—that is usually the case,"

The Insight Explained

When a woman tells a man how different he is from other men, she's probably responding to something he's doing at the moment. For example, if a man likes poetry, seems to be a patient listener, and doesn't come on sexually, a woman may conclude he is different. However, what ultimately creates a man's impact is *how* he relates. A man's belief that he's different from other men reveals his competitive ego need, which makes him just like other men (who also see themselves as better).

What a Woman Can Do

While some men may seem to be cut from a different cloth, that supposed difference is usually there only in the initial or early presentation of himself. A man's belief that he actually is different is misleading and reveals his competitive nature and desire to be better than other men, while a woman's quest to find the different man, and her periodic belief that somehow she miraculously has, suggests that in her history she's had painful or traumatic experiences with men and needs to believe a man she falls in love with is different. Rather than pursuing the fantasy of finding the one-in-a-million man, a woman needs to resolve the issues of her past relationship traumas to avoid continuing her cycle of relationship disappointments.

There's no way a woman can make an intelligent assessment of a man as "different" when she first meets him because his personality can only be revealed over time and by how he relates on an ongoing basis. When a woman declares that a man is different soon after she meets him, she's manifesting her need to believe that in order to justify getting involved.

What a Man Must Do

Men are vulnerable because of their competitive orientation of believing the unbelievable—namely, that on a personal level, they are unique and different from other men and somehow magically cut from a different cloth.

While a woman who is infatuated, or who wants to please him, may tell him she has never met a man like him before, men who believe this are displaying quite the opposite: that in fact they are just like other men.

Men must become aware of how their ego makes them vulnerable to flattery and believing that on personal matters they are different and better than other men.

To not recognize that grandiose vulnerability is for a man to open himself up to manipulation and be pulled into a relationship simply because he likes being put on a pedestal and adored. At the same time, the man who wants to become fully aware needs to ask himself why he needs to believe he is better or different than other men and what he should be looking at is the depth, transparency, and authenticity of his personal experience.

INSIGHT 26: CHASING THE "DIFFERENT" WOMAN

Men who think women differ from one another significantly, and that past relationship disasters were the result of choosing the wrong ones, are destined to repeat their histories and the patterns they deny, rationalize, and want to change.

The Conversation

After dating more than a hundred different women in search of the "right one," Richard was forced to consider that he was pursuing a mirage. The idea that the problem was really more about him than the woman was difficult to accept.

> *Richard*: "I've kind of given up trying to find the right woman. I've had so many bad experiences where I thought initially, 'This is the one,' only to find out, once I got to know her, that she was just like all the others."

> *Dr. Goldberg*: "Apparently, you believe love is about finding just the right person, rather than looking at the way in which you and she relate."

> *Richard*: "That sounds like 'shrink-talk.' The right woman is out there! And once I find her, I'll make it work. But for some reason, I just keep finding the wrong women!"

The Insight Explained

A man who honestly examines his past relationship failures will notice a repetitive pattern in the problems that occurred. That pattern should tell him that his relationship experiences were about himself rather than the past women in his life.

What a Woman Can Do

Women who get involved with men who talk of all their past failures in relationships being the result of having made poor choices and having been deceived need to prepare for the fact that they will inevitably be added to his list of relationship "disappointments." The man who has had countless relationship failures is definitely waving a "red flag" that women need to recognize so they can avoid the temptation of believing they can provide him with a different experience.

What a Man Must Do

What a man must do to transform his relationship experiences is reject the false idea that his disappointments and failures in past relationships occurred because he hadn't found the right partner. While we all need to find a relationship that is a good fit, very few of us are that unique or evolved that we have to search worldwide to find the person with whom we can create a meaningful relationship. Men who believe that to be the solution, and take on that kind of self-deluding search, are inviting a nightmare, and in all likelihood they will wind up with a woman who can read his desperation to find his fantasy and allow him to play that out with her.

A man with a healthy sense of himself as a related person can in fact form a relationship with a wide variety of women. Personally damaged and relationship-wounded men who actually fear committed relationships are the ones most likely to believe that the answer to their problems is to find the magically right partner.

Men must learn that repeated relationship failures and bottomless dating with an unending string of women speaks more to their crippled relationship capacity and is not the result of having been unlucky in love.

Continual attempts and failures and disappointments are more about who a man is and not about finding the perfect partner.

Men who engage in numerous short-term dating and relationship experiences need to turn the focus on their own issues and seek help in finding out how and why they're alone and can't maintain a relationship in order to discover what they need to do to repair themselves.

INSIGHT 27: STONE, NOT CRYSTAL

When men see fragility in women, it is a projection of the vulnerability they disown in themselves. Men are naïvely oblivious to the anger and negative feelings building behind the feminine mask of accommodation.

The Conversation

Marcus had a relationship pattern of being extremely protective of the women with whom he had relationships because he saw them as fragile, weak, and vulnerable. But he acknowledged after being badly hurt by these women that it took him months, if not years, to recover from the pain of these experiences, but they seemed to do fine without him. He still continued to believe he was strong and women had to be protected and shielded from conflict and confrontations.

Marcus: "When I'm in a relationship, I'm always afraid if I'm real and honest about my feelings, I'll hurt my partner."

Dr. Goldberg: "You think men are the tough gender and women need to be protected."

Marcus: "Well, they cry at the drop of a hat and always seem to want everything to be positive and conflict free and harmonious."

Dr. Goldberg: "If that was the real her, she'd be capable of being 'not nice' and showing you her anger at times when she's been wronged in some way. If she can't do that, her 'niceness' isn't authentic. It is automatic. And if women are so fragile, how come they bounce back so fast when a relationship ends, seeming to bend and not break, and moving on easily?"

The Insight Explained

Women learn growing up that being feminine and lovable is about pleasing others and avoiding aggressive displays. Men's superficial interpretation is that women's lack of assertiveness is a sign of weakness and timidity. The reality is more about men's vulnerability and women's resilience. Women have extensive support systems of friends and can ask for help more readily than men, allowing them to cope more easily with painful events. That, to me, is real strength.

What a Woman Can Do

This is one area where women's reality and men's perceptions of them differ widely. Women know they aren't the fragile, weak, or vulnerable beings some men believe they are. While being with a protective man may have its upside and charm early on in the relationship, and while it may give women a way to control and manipulate him, when men treat women as if they need protection, they also come to see them as children who can't handle tough realities. Women begin to resent these patronizing behaviors. Because of the initial benefits, however, women may not show what they know themselves to be: resilient, competent, and able to handle stress better than men, but fearing that a man could be scared away if they show him their true strong selves. Men get bored with, cheat on, and eventually leave dependent, "helpless," or "childlike" women, but they rarely leave the autonomous, strong, competent, and fearless ones.

When they view women as too fragile to handle tough issues or face a man's real feelings, men monitor and censor themselves. They begin to hide what they *really feel*, becoming withdrawn and silent. They interpret women's "niceness" and "sweetness" as fragility rather than a muting of anger and overt displays of power and aggression as a consequence of their feminine socialization. The fragile gender turns out to be men, whose dependency, desperation, and even collapse are evident when women leave and the relationship ends.

What a Man Must Do

Most men continue to hold on to the deluded and dangerous belief, in spite of all evidence to the contrary, that women are the weaker sex, whom men must protect and provide for.

Men need to educate themselves about the realities of gender. Men have significantly shorter lives than women, and suicide rates several times as high; they contract major diseases at significantly higher rates, are more prone to alcoholism and drug addiction, and are more vulnerable emotionally because they lack the support system of close and loving relationships that women tend to have. Even men's bond with their children is typically weaker than the children's bond with their mother.

Men need to realize the serious, self-destructive tendencies they need to change even if it threatens their masculinity. Instead of feeling responsible for the welfare of their partners and guilt ridden when they can't adequately provide for or "take care of them," they should instead learn from the habits of women that make it possible for them to be the healthier and longer-surviving gender. Men must learn to identify and avoid feelings of guilt and responsibility for a woman's well-being that comes at their expense and make sure they don't self-destruct in the process of playing hero, rescuer, or guardian angel.

INSIGHT 28: THE OBJECTIFICATION OF MEN

A man can recognize he is being used when most of the conversation and activity revolves around spending money, discussing commitment, and making marriage plans.

The Conversation

Because of his insecurities, Emanuel displayed his success symbols by wearing expensive clothes and driving a luxury car to pick up his latest flame for dinner at an upscale restaurant. He became dismayed, defensive, and withdrawn, however, when inevitably the conversations would turn to commitment, marriage, babies, and buying a house together. It made him skeptical of their feelings toward him being genuine. "They hardly know me, and they're talking about being together forever." At the same time, he wondered why they repeatedly said he was afraid to be close, feared commitment, and couldn't accept being loved.

> *Emanuel*: "My girlfriend showers me with affection when I take her to an expensive restaurant or tell her how much I love her, and when we talk about engagement and marriage. But whenever I pull back a little and say, 'Hey, let's not go too fast,' she withdraws and gets cold."

> *Dr. Goldberg*: "It sounds like you're being groomed like a circus animal or SeaWorld dolphin. When you perform as expected, you're rewarded. Otherwise, you're ignored or rejected."

> *Emanuel*: "You mean women actually exist who will love you without your spending money on them and buying them stuff, or talking to them about commitment and marriage?"

The Insight Explained

The traditional relationship was based on men doing for women and providing for their security. But those same traditional marriages are also the ones that inevitably bring out women's anger or rage toward "male chauvinists" who control everything.

What a Woman Can Do

While most women can sense when they are being objectified by a man because the man's conversation and focus is fixated on sex, few women acknowledge the ways *they* objectify men as "security and success objects" whose job it is to make them feel safe, secure, and prosperous.

To overcome the sense of being used by a man as a sex object or relationship trophy and to free relationships up to become their best and most vital, women need to become aware of how they choose men based on success symbols and an ability to provide materially, rather than choosing a man for what he's all about as a person.

When men get a woman's love by spending money on her and fulfilling her desire for marriage and security in order to please and hold onto her, they are diving into a bottomless pool of endless needs. This sets the stage for the melting down of the relationship because what he provides will never be enough. The love is conditional and superficial, and it will dissolve when he balks or is no longer able to make her fantasies, dreams, and needs come true.

What a Man Must Do

Dysfunctional relationships between men and women occur when they relate to each other object to object—specifically, when the woman is seen as a sex object while the man is viewed as a success and provider object, loved and found attractive primarily for his status and image in life.

Men as success objects who are attractive because of their "power," position, and finances, and who choose women as sex objects and trophies to boost their egos, are embarking on a seemingly irresistible and compelling dynamic (e.g., the extremely wealthy businessman with his sexy model wife or the athlete with his adoring cheerleader girlfriend). While these relationships are initially compelling, they are also brittle, readily break down, and turn ugly because they lack a genuinely rooted, person-to-person foundation.

Objectified relationships are ones of fantasy to fantasy.

Men must develop a personal self to the point where they are no longer drawn to a woman based primarily on her physical attributes. Men must learn to see women in terms of the people they are—their ability to communicate, deal constructively with conflicts and issues, show love and caring, and have the ability to take equal responsibility in recognizing their part in creating relationship problems rather than blaming their partners.

They must grow to the point where they no longer indulge in shallow, image-to-image relationships with women. Such relationships are doomed to fail, and when they do, mutual antipathy, rage, and the desire to punish and hurt the other for not being the person they initially fantasized about are all that remain.

INSIGHT 29: RECOGNIZING FALSE LOVE

A man can discern whether a past relationship of his was genuinely loving and caring by asking himself whether the woman's interest and affection continued after she'd determined he had no desire to marry her. If the break-up was abrupt and final when he resisted commitment, then he was not a person to her, but rather an object discarded because he was found to be useless.

The Conversation

As Marty, divorced and in his forties, spoke of the "great loves" of his life, he was struck by the realization that once his love relationships ended, they never saw or spoke to each other again.

> *Marty*: "I really thought the last one was meant to be. I thought our love would last forever, at least as a friendship, even if we couldn't hang together as a couple. Then she dumped me; now she won't even answer my calls. I'm in shock, and it hurts."

> *Dr. Goldberg*: "So you discovered that all that love was conditional and based on her wanting a commitment from you."

The Insight Explained

Authentic love, as in a good friendship or a family bond, continues even as external circumstances change or the focus waxes and wanes. When a relationship is based on each partner's personal objectives and not on a loving attachment, it exists for the function the other person serves and the agenda the other person can fulfill. If that's the case, when either party decides they're not going to get what they want, the end of the relationship is near.

What a Woman Can Do

The haunting preoccupation many lovers have is whether the relationship is authentic and will survive when the going gets tough. Women, as well as men, can learn about themselves, their choices, and the true nature of past relationships by recalling what happened when these relationships ended.

Relationships founded on friendship, genuine caring, and love will continue even if they are no longer as romantic or passionate. Relationships based on objectification and mutual using to assuage momentary needs and fantasies have little to do with the reality of their partners and will fade and end once one partner can no longer fulfill their expected function.

By reviewing their past love relationships, men and women could see that if the relationships were based on objectification, fantasy, projection, and momentary needs, nothing remained once the other person was no longer willing or able to fulfill their expected role. If their partner "disappeared" once the relationships ended, those relationships were not based on friendship but on self-centered need. Relationships founded on authentic friendship and love remain in some form, even as they change and evolve.

What a Man Must Do

Just as women are repulsed and enraged at being viewed as an object where the man's primary interest in them is sexual, men need to recognize the poisonous nature of being viewed as a "good catch" based on their vocation, success, and commitment potential for a woman who feels pressure to be married and have children, and a desire to be provided for.

When relationships end suddenly for a man, with a woman he believed was "the love of his life" but wasn't ready to marry, he must think about how his partner related to him once they were no longer a couple.

If a man's partner has no interest in his welfare and no longer wants a connection with him when she believes she won't get the commitment she wants, then the relationship was one of exploitation, not love.

Having a way to identify the real essence of the relationship when he has been rejected and abandoned will help free a man from self-condemning ruminations, feelings of failure and unworthiness, while allowing him to see his good fortune in losing a relationship that existed primarily to fill his partner's needs, allowing him to let go of the self-loathing notion that his relationship failed because of his own inadequacy.

INSIGHT 30: HIS DESPERATE FEELINGS

When a man feels desperate about a relationship, he is misreading the signals, being manipulated, or in the process of being rejected. Relationships based on genuine caring and love will not generate out-of-control or desperate emotions.

The Conversation

Most men don't reach out for help until they become desperate. These moments of truth temporarily open men up to reveal their vulnerability, fragility, confusion, sense of isolation, and "cluelessness."

Harry spoke of the latest of many events that led to his feeling of desperation. He recognized that the obsessive love that lay underneath his feelings wasn't based on genuine caring. "How could I really be in love if I feel continuously insecure, always worrying that she will leave me?" It had begun with him being feverishly pursued by her, but once he was attracted in return and began to really need her, the "power balance" shifted. He became the insecure one who needed reassurance.

> *Harry*: "I was 'madly in love' and I could see I was losing my emotional balance. I obsessed about everything she said and did, and overreacted to any sign of rejection."

> *Dr. Goldberg*: "You must have been sensing something was seriously wrong."

Harry: "Yes, I thought, 'I've given away my power again. She's probably just toying with me and now I'm hooked.' She senses my insecurity, and it's just a matter of time before I get that dreaded phone message."

The Insight Explained

In a mutual, authentic love there isn't fear, desperation, and obsession. Those feelings are almost always the signs and indicators that you aren't experiencing genuine love, regardless of what your partner says. Also, it suggests they may be hiding something important, such as another relationship they're continuing to carry on.

What a Woman Can Do

Obsessive preoccupation or jealousy occurs most with severely dysfunctional men who have a mixture of ambivalence, hostility, and a childlike dependency that they deny. While it may seem romantic to be with a man who is obsessive and jealous about you, the downside is they become controlling in their possessiveness, readily triggered into displays of anger and aggression, and present a severe problem if and when you decide you want to end the relationship. While initially attractive because of the passion, such relationships become dangerous and suffocating, with cycles of raging outbursts followed by cringing and sentimental apologies.

Desperation, clinging, fear, dramatic emotional extremes, and exaggerated responses indicate that something is seriously wrong. When love is based on reality and not maintained by fantasy and projection—when love is healthy and mutual—continual reassurance, suspicions, doubts, and pressure to "explain" one's actions are not part of it.

What a Man Must Do

Men who feel desperate in a relationship, continually ruminating and anxious about whether they are really loved and becoming desperate to the point of depression, high anxiety, and frustrated rage, must understand that relationships characterized by this continual drama of highs and lows are due not to his inadequacy but to the fact that his partner didn't really love him in the first place.

Authentic love occurs when there is good communication and a sense of personal calm and completion. A relationship characterized by emotional extremes such as "she loves me; no, she hates me" suggests that the relationship is dysfunctional and not one of love.

Excruciatingly painful relationships are readily misunderstood and misinterpreted and lead to self-destructive behaviors and responses such as outbursts of rage, violence, and self-injury.

Because these relationships are difficult to perceive clearly and understand, men need to reach out for help in order to free themselves from their unhealthy fixations and make the inner changes needed for them to see their experience accurately.

Men who feel desperate in a relationship must understand that they have not been loved and there was no genuine caring on the part of their partners.

4

HER RELATIONSHIP EXPERIENCE

How do I, as a man, presume to make sense of a woman's experience in relationships? When it comes to the actual experience itself I don't, although I've often caught more than a glimpse of the frustration and feelings of hopelessness women commonly experience when they try to get a man to open up and be forthcoming about his personal feelings and thoughts. In fact, when I'm not working as a therapist but simply trying to have a deeper, more personal conversation with another man and getting almost nothing back from him besides intellectualizations, superficial comments, or silence, I wonder what, if anything, is actually going on inside of him. Perhaps he's just thinking about his work or having negative or critical thoughts. Or maybe I'm making him uncomfortable and he doesn't like me. I'll have to figure it out myself, though, because he won't disclose it. He'll probably withdraw completely if I ask him. Sometimes I feel fear and anxiety that if he did tell me how he *really* felt around me, the feelings would be negative and critical. I know I don't *really* want to hear them, although I tell myself I do.

The times I bring all this into focus and see the dilemma clearly, I get a sense of what women go through when they want and need personal connection and conversation and can't find a way to make that happen. The woman in a relationship with a man largely for practical reasons such as marriage, children, and support probably makes peace with it as a necessary trade-off, or she may even be okay with it because what she really wants is her partner's *function* and not his *being*, and she doesn't want to hear anything that might threaten her.

In prefeminist days, when the earlier model of traditional relationships prevailed and was unquestioned, apart from a man's functional role as provider and doer, what could actually feel good between a man and a woman? He most likely valued drinking, sports, and declaiming about the state of the world, the economy, and his philosophies about life, with no suggestion of any interest in the ideas and opinions of the other. These "clueless" men never talked in connected and personal ways in their conversations. Other than taking care of practical matters or solving problems, they remained largely silent, like the old-time ideal man in movies who said little or nothing at all beyond whatever was absolutely necessary.

Those times when I'm with a guy and wondering how to create an easy, meaningful, or personal conversation and am unable to do so, I "get" how months and years of such frustration can produce in a woman feelings of depression and the desperation that comes from feeling trapped in a lifeless connection. In that way, I believe I know how women in traditional relationships feel and why when feminism opened the windows and doors of inner and private experience what emerged was intense rage, scorn, and hatred. Years of feeling like just another household appliance, as Betty Freidan portrayed her experience being a traditional housewife, has to create a build-up of terrible feelings. While much of this kind of relationship interaction is changing, the struggle of trying to emotionally connect with the goal-driven, workaholic, sports-obsessed, alcoholic, sex-obsessed, and otherwise reticent man continues.

The conversations, academic or otherwise, about men's and women's relationships tend to focus on who treats whom better or worse and who is more dysfunctional, but my understanding and interpretation of men's and women's socialization is that the power of sex-role conditioning has made men and women polar opposites and counterpart equivalents in an excruciatingly painful dance by causing them to be drawn together in intense initial romantic attraction in which they seek completion through closeness with someone of the opposite sex. The initial romantic attraction transforms into frustration, anger, and revulsion as each realizes what they have seen in the other doesn't really exist. Repeatedly bumping up against this illusion or mirage creates frustration, burnout, and the need to escape completely from these relationships.

Masculine socialization externalizes men, exaggerating in them defensive tendencies in the areas of aggression, assertion, autonomy, sexuality,

and intellectualization, while closing them off from developing their inner and vulnerable self.

Feminine socialization defensively reinforces and enlarges tendencies
in the other direction, creating personal issues for women that are opposite to men's. Women become obsessed with needs and cravings for
closeness that can never be satisfied by most men, causing depression,
despair, and feelings of failure and low self-esteem.

Many women struggle as well with establishing and maintaining
boundaries. They have problems with matters of aggression, such as acknowledging anger, dealing with conflicts, and undue fears. Similarly,
while men's socialization causes them to be obsessed with long-range
abstract goals that have no limit, feminine defensive socialization may
cause women to become mired *in the moment*, resulting in shortsighted
misjudgments and overreactions.

Some men clearly have relationship problems. Women's relationship
problems are elusive and more difficult to bring into focus because the
exaggerated responses created by feminine conditioning create tendencies
to err in the direction of an overemphasis on the personal, giving women
the appearance of profound caring or loving. How can a man challenge
that without seeming to be critical or hostile?

I believe men and women care and love and bring problems and dysfunctions to their relationships equal in weight for each, but opposite in
their surface appearance. The resolution and transformation of this difficult dilemma lies in each gender being able to acknowledge and transform their own defensiveness, distortions, and the resulting dysfunctions.

INSIGHT 31: THE MR. GOOD-AS-GOLD FANTASY

*Men who are bewildered and in pain because of unexpected abandon-
ment by a woman to whom they've been as "good as gold" are confusing
their reality and intentions with her experience of the relationship and
are out of touch with their own dysfunctional relationship behavior.*

The Conversation

Seymour had the reputation among his peers of being the "nicest" and
most generous guy. But while many women were happy to go out with

him, few continued to see him after a few dates. Some would say they just wanted to be friends. Others would simply abandon him. Sensing there was something wrong in the way he was coming across, but stymied in identifying what it was, led him to seek therapy.

> *Seymour*: "I've heard men whine about how wonderfully they treated their women and all it got them was rejection. They don't understand it and it embitters them."

> *Dr. Goldberg*: "Phony and inauthentic behavior is one of the last frontiers of psychological relationship cluelessness. Maybe because of political correctness issues or simply the desire to not be confronted with the falseness of one's own niceness, most people seem to welcome and praise phony, nice behavior, viewing it as behavior that's positive and real."

The Insight Explained

The components of good-as-gold behavior are usually denial and manipulation designed to benefit Mr. Good-as-Gold himself under the pretense of selfless, goodhearted behavior, but they are hiding an underbelly of resentments and negatives that builds behind their "nice façade." Or maybe they are only being as good as gold to get something in return.

What a Woman Can Do

A healthy relationship has a whole continuum of responses, from selflessness to selfishness, love to anger, desire for closeness to needs for separateness. But repetitive, rigid behaviors of any kind, even when the individual appears to be acting out of love, hide and disguise underlying defensiveness.

It's common for women (and men) to feel embittered when their heavily socialized "nice" behaviors bring them insensitive, self-centered, and abusive responses from their partners. These are dysfunctional patterns that are difficult to acknowledge and understand because there is so much social support for the "nice person" by well-meaning others, who reinforce the notion that the "nice person" is simply "too good" for the "hurtful" or "abusive," unappreciative partner. This reinforces the self-defeating and dysfunctionality of the so called nice or good-as-gold person.

The missing ingredient in understanding your relationship experiences is not what you intend, but what the "not nice" partner's reality and experience of the relationship is. The chronically "nice" person is unable to freely express any "not nice" feelings. This creates a sense of being with someone who is unreal or inauthentic, causing pressure to live up to the unspoken demand that others have to be "nice" in return or risk being seen as hurtful. The oppressive atmosphere this creates, and the sense of being stuck in a relationship where conflict, anger, or negative feelings or thoughts cannot be expressed, is what poisons these interactions.

What a Man Must Do

A man who plays the part of being Mr. Nice Guy in order to gain love by compulsively accommodating and pleasing a woman will be disappointed when he is treated badly in return.

"Nice guy" behavior is usually inauthentic and manipulative, and men who are "overly nice" must get in touch with the real feelings they are blocking and denying. Compulsive "nice guy" behavior communicates anxiety, falseness, low self-esteem, and manipulation.

Friends may console the "nice guy" who is treated badly or rejected by telling him that his partner didn't deserve him, and women don't know how to appreciate and love a man who treats them well. What the "nice guy" who is being distanced needs to do is learn to view himself truthfully, to see how he is creating the response he gets, and hopefully get in touch with his deeper motives for being "nice"—specifically, the hidden dark side he resists expressing.

The "not nice" guy often seems to be treated better, not because women are masochistic, but because these men provide a sense of greater authenticity, self-esteem, and confidence in just being themselves. As a result, they are more likely to be trusted emotionally because their boundaries and preferences are clear and feel genuine.

INSIGHT 32: MR. NICE GUY PLOY

Men who try to "nice" their way into a relationship or maintain and try to win love through "being nice" may win the sympathy of friends when the relationship abruptly ends. However, the woman's rejection may be a functional, authentic reaction to the man's inauthentic and fear-driven behavior, toward which her healthy and life-preserving response is either avoidance or contempt.

The Conversation

It took Max two years of therapy to grow past his belief that he had been unappreciated and badly treated by his girlfriends, whom his friends reassured him had been "selfish, opportunistic bitches." This brought him to some powerful realizations.

> *Max*: "It seems to me that women rarely leave guys who act like callous jerks, but they're merciless in the way they treat and desert the 'nice guys.'"

> *Dr. Goldberg*: "Men do the same thing. They cheat on and leave the women who are devoted and selfless and put the so-called 'bitches,' or self-centered, narcissistic women, on a pedestal."

> *Max*: "People may give the nice guys sympathy, but underneath they sense there's something wrong with this picture."

> *Dr. Goldberg*: "The one thing that emotionally feels worse to women than being abused is the inauthenticity and phoniness of constant niceness."

The Insight Explained

What passes for or is described as "niceness" may be composed of dishonest, out-of-touch behavior combined with an unhealthy lack of boundaries and manipulation. It tends to be anxiety driven and designed to get reassurance that one is "nice" and loved and won't be abandoned. Because such behavior is dysfunctional and phony, its impact is toxic. The contempt, hostility, and rejection it engenders is functional and life-preserving for the partner.

What a Woman Can Do

Nowhere are the terms *being out of touch* and *confusing one's intention with the other person's experience* more apt than in the response to "nice" behavior that is put on for show. Constant niceness is inauthentic, and it covers up denied hostility, manipulation, and self-serving motives that are disguised as caring and altruism.

The insensitive, critical, hurtful, selfish, and even abusive response the "nice" person receives in return typically is perceived critically by well-meaning friends and acquaintances. The supposedly hurtful partners in these relationships may be experiencing boredom, a sense of inauthenticity, and of being manipulated by the rigid and oppressive "niceness" of their partners, which triggers negative responses. This is one area of relationship experiences in which the commiseration and support of friends not only is unhelpful but also prevents the needed growth and responsibility that the wounded "nice" person needs in order to break the pattern of disappointment in their relationships.

What a Man Must Do

The "nice guy ploy" is essentially self-serving, which is why it is often responded to negatively. While it may generate a surface appreciation, "nice guy" behavior usually is composed of a lack of boundaries and automatic behaviors that communicate his fear over not being liked if he is real. He gets the response similar to the "nice" accommodating woman who is vulnerable to being abused and cheated on because her "niceness" communicates low self-esteem, neediness, and the fear of being abandoned.

The negative response a "nice guy" often gets should be seen as a "wake-up call" pushing him to become real and have the confidence to express his real feelings. His niceness communicates a weakness that makes him emotionally untrustworthy, because when one is nice to everyone across the board, much like a politician or salesman, it is primarily designed to serve the "nice" person's needs and motives and is not an expression of a genuine love and care for a partner who is special. "Nice guy" behavior disguises true emotion and thoughts that are hidden, which creates a sense of unreality and emotional untrustworthiness.

INSIGHT 33: NO AGGRESSION, NO LOVE

A woman's dream and longing for a world that is nice and sweet and free of conflict is a key factor undermining the closeness and intimacy she believes she wants.

The Conversation

Men's self-loathing and remorse is triggered and reinforced when they believe they have hurt or lost the love of their ever sweet, unselfish, and giving partner. They experience a chronic sense of guilt for being at fault. By twenty-three, Randolph had already virtually given up on the idea of being in a committed relationship because he couldn't tolerate the chronic feeling of being the flawed and hurtful relationship spoiler.

> *Randolph*: "Lots of women I meet don't get angry or tell you when they don't like something. They think everybody is supposed to be 'nice' all the time because that's how they see themselves and how they want to see the world."

> *Dr. Goldberg*: "Those women often have expectations that a truly loving situation means men will avoid conflict or expressions of anger. If I ask how a man and woman can get close to each other without conflict, I hear, 'You men are just so cynical.'"

> *Randolph*: "Many women perceive anger or hostility in a man even when he doesn't feel it. He gets defensive trying to prove it isn't so, which convinces her even more that she's right."

> *Dr. Goldberg*: "Since the guy is sometimes the one who shows anger or brings up conflicts, he becomes the 'dream spoiler' or the one who's 'diminishing the relationship.'"

The Insight Explained

Just as many men deny their vulnerability, dependency, and expressions of fear, many women will block acknowledgment of anger and conflict. Some women who are obviously being mistreated can't express anger or clearly draw a boundary that says, "You can't do that!" They believe that if the love is "true," you only have loving feelings. As a result, the intimacy women want becomes a romantic illusion they'll never realize. They blame that on men because they assume that avoiding conflict and anger and acting nice will pave the way for that intimacy and love.

What a Woman Can Do

The niceness and sweetness women are praised and rewarded for as little girls, and which later produces a hypersensitive and wounded response in the face of anger or any conflict or negative feelings, is a chief factor in the frustration and helplessness women experience in trying to make their relationships with men feel like the loving ones they believe are possible.

It is a giant step forward in self-awareness when women can see how their socialized inability to acknowledge the negatives of conflict, anger, and assertion of boundaries is a major factor in causing unhappiness and dissatisfaction in their relationships with men. Looking for the perfect guy or confronting men they're with about their insensitivity or lack of niceness guarantees that genuine intimacy, which requires the full spectrum of responses, positive and negative, will not happen.

The blocking of anger and the denial of conflict gives women a sense of moral superiority. The man is seen as the "bad guy" when he inevitably expresses these negatives. When a woman cries or acts wounded, the message is clear: he is the hurtful and insensitive one. A man involved with such a woman finds himself continuously apologizing or feeling guilty for being hurtful. It leads to his withdrawal and/or sense of futility. Once he's aware that he is seen as the bad guy, he must accept hopelessness and even depression as a fact of the relationship (or else leave).

What a Man Must Do

While being with a woman who shuns and disdains arguments and negativity and needs to have a conflict-free, peaceful relationship may initially seem refreshing and appealing, particularly to a man who has had rancorous experiences in recent relationships, a woman who is conflict adverse and will not "fight it out" means her partner will inevitably be cast as the "bad guy" and love spoiler.

If a woman's "peacefulness" is so rigid that she cannot engage in an argument or disagreement without crying or acting wounded, the man is doomed to be seen as the relationship spoiler when conflict arises. Conflicts in an authentic relationship are inevitable, particularly in a male-female relationship, because men and women are so different in their consciousness. With a conflict-phobic partner, the man who brings up painful issues will be viewed as the heavy and be seen as a negative person.

Denial and avoidance of conflict prevents a relationship from growing, and men shouldn't feel guilty because they carry the responsibility for bringing up the difficult issues in the relationship. Healthy relationships can tolerate conflict and threatening discussions.

Men must see what they're getting into when they begin a relationship with a woman who can't seem to acknowledge and negotiate conflict, and who cries, acts wounded, and seeks to make a man feel guilty for wanting to discuss "uncomfortable feelings."

Men must recognize the unhealthy nature of relating to a woman who expects a continually loving and peaceful interaction. Men who bond with such women must acknowledge and confront this issue early on and know that if they remain with a woman who can't tolerate dealing with the "negatives" in a relationship, the relationship will stagnate, and when it finally deteriorates and falls apart, the man will be blamed for having destroyed it.

INSIGHT 34: HER AGENDA

Most women need commitment as a goal to motivate them in relating to men, just as most men need sexual interest to motivate them in relating to women. That is, women usually need to feel there is movement toward commitment, just as men more often need to feel there is movement toward sexual involvement.

The Conversation

At age thirty-three, Carlos, a strikingly handsome and charismatic man who'd led the life of a vagabond, with careers ranging from managing a restaurant to crewing on a yacht, arrived in Hollywood to pursue a career as an action-hero actor. In his twenties he developed a relationship pattern he boastfully described as "managing my stable," meaning he had numerous girlfriends at the same time, most of whom were readily available for sex. A number of years later, his "luck had run out," as he put it, finding himself being dumped regularly and not understanding why. He attributed it to losing his touch, and it depressed him. At the advice of his physician, concerned about Carlos's depression and anxiety, he reluctantly sought counseling.

> *Carlos*: "When I meet a woman, I can tell if she's sizing me up as potential husband material. I understand marriage and commitment are important, but I can't stand the constant pressure and ongoing questioning about 'where this relationship is going.'"

> *Dr. Goldberg*: "What about you? What do you think about?"

> *Carlos*: "What she'll be like in bed."

> *Dr. Goldberg*: "Do you think she feels that pressure? Do you think it bothers her if she senses that's what is keeping you there?"

The Insight Explained

A man likes to believe a woman's interest and love for him will be without any kind of agenda, and that just being with him should be rewarding enough for her. That's a delusion created by his defensive ego. If a woman can't see a relationship going where she needs it to go, she'll end the relationship no matter how "perfect" the man is, just like the man who leaves because sex is not happening.

What a Woman Can Do

In relationships, a man will often feel pressure for commitment, even if it's unspoken. Until a man evolves to a point where he chooses a woman just because he likes being around her and not because he's excited by the prospect of getting her into bed, he shouldn't be surprised that a woman will have an equivalent motive.

Contemporary relationship books geared toward single, dating women try to teach them the rules of the game insofar as getting a man to commit. While this may result in a short-term benefit, the positive results of such manipulation won't last very long and will produce long-range negative consequences.

Women have enormous untapped relationship power because many heterosexual men without a partner are lost at sea and hungry for a partner, even when they deny it. Knowing that, a woman's focus initially should be on developing the relationship rather than using tactics to "catch him." At any time after a positive relationship has been established, she can openly state her desire for committed permanence (marriage) and make clear that if not provided within a specific period of time, she will terminate the relationship. She needs to mean it for it to be effective, not just use it as a ploy. This will trigger in her partner his dependency and fear of being alone. If his feelings for her are genuine and loving, he will agree to a commitment.

What a Man Must Do

Many men complain that once they have sex with a woman, or indicate a desire to have sex, it is accompanied by pressure to commit themselves.

Men's egos and inability to empathize lead them to believe that while they may have a motive such as sex for relating to a woman, women don't need to have an agenda or motive to want to be with him. Men's egos tend to prevent them from understanding that anyone who embarks on a relationship has to have a reason, and his belief that just having his company is sufficient reflects a man's delusional grandiosity.

Both men and women want their needs met and will only remain in a relationship as long as they believe that will occur. While sex may be a man's dominant motive, commitment tends to be the dominant female motive, and once a woman with that motive determines commitment will not happen, she will end the relationship regardless of the so-called quality of the sexual experience.

Men must recognize the ego vulnerability that leads them to believe it is enough for a woman to just be with him because of his supposed attractiveness. Often men resent the pressure to commit, and their egos prevent them from seeing that in a world of innumerable choices, if a woman enters a relationship with him, she must have her unspoken reasons that are keeping her in it. There is no such thing as a person in a relationship without a motive, and recognizing and acknowledging that motive and seeing it as a response to a man's agenda will make it possible for men to have realistic and not ego-delusional experiences.

Men must see that their resistance to commitment denies the woman's agenda and reality, which is as valid as his. To protest, deny, and view her need for commitment as a negative is self-centered, and men must understand that if they only want to be with a woman for the momentary pleasure, the relationship will be fragile, and it is only a matter of time before she will end it.

A man must learn that relationships are not toys, there for his pleasure, and that he should probably avoid getting involved with a woman if he sees no potential to commit to her.

INSIGHT 35: COMMITMENT FLIP-FLOP

In building a relationship, women and men unconsciously treat each other the way good business people treat their clients. Both tend to put on their best faces in the beginning of a relationship, projecting alluring images, giving the other what he or she wants, and acting interested, warm, and caring.

The Conversation

Howard, divorced and remarried shortly after, saw how his distrust and self-protectiveness was sweeping him into an isolated corner. His fears revolved around concerns that women who wanted marriage couldn't be trusted to tell the truth about their feelings. "They'll do what it takes to get married, and a man won't know how they really feel until they've achieved their goal," he said.

> *Howard*: "What I hear from my pals is once they got married or had a baby, their wives changed. They didn't seem to care as much, and

were always 'out of energy.' It's like 'now that I got what I wanted, I don't have to be at my best anymore or show love or caring.'"

Dr. Goldberg: "It sounds like what businessmen do with their customers or clients. Before they close the deal they'll do and promise anything. Once the deal is closed and the money is in the bank, they're not as eager to return phone calls or follow through with customer service."

Howard: "I get that, but I wish women would acknowledge what they do. Instead, after marriage or a baby, the decline in affection and caring is often blamed on the man. He's told that 'he's being too needy, immature, or competitively jealous and resentful of the baby.'"

Dr. Goldberg: "A man doesn't acknowledge the role he might have in expecting too much from his wife after children are born. Why expect the woman to acknowledge that her needs have changed as well?"

The Insight Explained

In traditionally based relationships, partners are at their best when trying to get what they want and need. Nobody likes to think of themselves as opportunistic in this way, so when things start to turn sour, *they tend to blame it on the other person and deny that their own feelings changed after they've achieved their goal.*

What a Woman Can Do

A source of resistance to commitment in men is the fear that after marriage or commitment of exclusivity there will be a loss of control and power, and the loving and devoted feelings of women will change into something else. It's the "car salesman" phenomenon, where the attentive and accommodating attitude ends soon after the deal is closed.

Women are damaged as well by the "flip-flop" of feelings when a man's delight in the relationship is replaced by emotional distance and a closing off after marriage. To avoid this, women need to get comfortable expressing the full spectrum of their feelings early on, *before* commitment, with the knowledge that if the bond with a man is healthy, it will sustain and grow in the face of some negatives. This will avoid the "shock" later, with men feeling betrayed and fooled and women feeling disappointed and distrustful as men pull away after commitment because they are confronted with the negative feelings that were previously hidden in their partners.

What a Man Must Do

In the process of learning to relate to women as people rather than magical beings who enter a man's life in order to make him happy, to complete him and provide an emotional foundation, men have to understand and see women as complex people struggling to create the best life.

What men must do to have healthy, stable relationship experiences is avoid romanticizing those relationships and viewing their partners as above and beyond the everyday realities and motives they see in themselves and others.

Women are exactly like men when pursuing a goal. Their negative feelings only emerge after they have achieved it. Therefore, men must have a rooted and realistic sense of who a woman is before entering into a relationship with her.

INSIGHT 36: VICTIM RAGE

There is a correlation between the extent to which a woman is a reactor to a man and gives away her power to initiate, make decisions, and set boundaries and her build-up of feelings of being controlled, diminished, abused, and victimized.

The Conversation

"Not only is it boring and deadening when a woman seems to take on my identity, likes and dislikes, interests and passions, and seems overly agreeable and pleasing, it makes me distrust her," is how Rudy, age forty-four and single for six years after a traumatic and sudden ending to his seeming idyllic marriage, expressed it.

As we talked about his "relationship barriers," he acknowledged his deep fear of facing the accusations he was confronted with at the end of his marriage—that he'd damaged his wife's self-esteem and she couldn't be herself around him and therefore had to leave. After a number of years of dating, he explained why he had made no commitments since then.

Rudy: "I get really confused when a woman tells me I'm controlling her or I'm abusive, and she feels like my victim. Frankly, I never know what she's talking about. If any of that is true, it's certainly not intentional on my part. All she'd need to do to is point it out when she thinks it's happening."

Dr. Goldberg: "At what point does she usually tell you this? Early on, or once the relationship is committed and going strong?"

Rudy: "Not until she's ready to break up with me. I'm left dumbfounded because the last thing I wanted to do was to control or be abusive. Why would I want that? I'm not a monster."

The Insight Explained

A woman's feeling of being controlled comes from *how* she relates. Feeling controlled and abused comes from giving away her power and being fearful of asserting herself and drawing boundaries. No matter how thoughtful a man tries to be, it will eventually feel like abuse and control if she always follows his lead, accommodates him, and loses her identity.

What a Woman Can Do

What is often omitted when women feel they must end a relationship for their survival's sake is their own contribution to creating a relationship that leaves them feeling controlled, diminished, and abused. Assuming the reactor role in a woman's desire to please, avoiding conflict and negative feelings, and not setting and maintaining clear boundaries are all factors. When women change partners without changing their reactor behaviors, they will repeat their experiences with someone else. The inability to see and change their part in their painful relationship experiences will result in an increasing sense of hopelessness, anger, and bitterness.

Unless a woman asserts her power equally to a man's, she will come to feel controlled regardless of how "nice" he is or how much he tries.

What a Man Must Do

Most men are pleased initially to be with a woman who seems to let them be in charge, follow their lead, allow them to make the decisions, and control much of what goes on.

Men pay a price for buying into and colluding with a woman's seemingly selfless, adoring, and accommodating behaviors and believing she is happy to defer to him.

Men must understand that consistently selfless, all accepting, and accommodating behavior without boundaries in a woman is dysfunctional. Many men see themselves as fortunate to have found such a woman and others tell him how lucky he is. While he hears that and wants to believe it, his feelings of boredom, criticalness, and even hostility may begin to leak through, telling him something different about how this relationship really feels.

The price of being with such a "selfless, giving woman" are the feelings he will have of always feeling responsible and blamed when things go wrong and disappointments and problems occur. Once that dynamic is set, there may be little to nothing he can do to change it or the feelings he develops that whatever problems and pain his partner has he has caused.

5

THEIR RELATIONSHIP
EXPERIENCE TOGETHER

Who would have thought the journey from tradition to liberation, a transition that was supposed to level the playing field of love while creating vast new potentials for deeper intimacy, friendship, and equal sharing and division of the difficult responsibilities of life, would produce the psychological chaos, resistance, and trepidation that characterize today's man-woman relationships? When I wrote *The New Male-Female Relationship*, I envisioned a transition period away from traditional relationships based on the three "r's" of *role*, *ritual*, and *religion* that would be disorienting, and I called it "Driving Each Other Crazy on the Way to Liberation." In that book I proposed that following the transition there would emerge a new relationship, which I characterized as *playmates*, *companions*, *lovers*, and *friends*.

The transition period of liberation from traditional relationships to sex-role liberation has lasted longer than I anticipated and has made it very difficult, if not *too dangerous*, to fully commit to someone of the opposite sex. The happiest couples today seem to be gay couples, who have avidly fought for *the right* to marry, while for heterosexual men and women the ties of permanent commitment are growing more fragile. Relationships between men and women today often play out their unhappy progression from *romance* to *boredom* to *rage* in shorter periods of time. Is the love bond between a man and a woman becoming a shining artifact of the past?

Men, who can no longer simply play the provider role to secure their relationships, are retreating from commitment out of a fear of the dramatic shift of power to the woman once marriage and fatherhood occur. Yet the man's need for a woman partner is greater than ever, in tandem with his growing isolation. The fears of commitment are most clearly expressed by men with the men's rights movement, who believe the courts and the legal system are in a conspiracy to deprive them of their role as father after a divorce.

While men take on the traditional provider role after they marry and become fathers, the power balance shifts dramatically if the woman decides she is unhappy and wants to end the union. A man's nightmare is having her gain custody, continue to live in the house when he leaves, expect child support (money for which she will not be accountable), assert that he is an abuser, alienate the child from him, promote the child's bond with her new lover, punish him severely for any delays in child support payments, and poison the relationship sufficiently that he even gives up his efforts to remain close to his progeny.

This worst-case scenario occurs too often. However, men are complicit in creating and maintaining this nightmarish scenario by continuing to live in their ego-driven relationship fantasy land and refusing to understand and accept the necessity of doing the profoundly needed work of growing themselves psychologically in order to avoid impulsive, inappropriate, need-driven, superficial sexual and emotional relationships based on a woman's physical appearance and availability. The defensive male ego prevents them from working on understanding themselves, their relationships, and the realities of maintaining a relationship founded on healthy communication and love. Most men are certain they know all the answers to relationships and are masters of them. Smart women don't challenge that male delusion because it signals that he can be easily controlled and tamed.

Women see the reality of their relationships more clearly than men. Even when they seek a romantic experience, they remain rooted in the practical, real-life aspects of commitment and love. What partially poisons their relationship experiences, however, are mothers, grandmothers, aunts, and female friends who have been abused, cheated on, or unduly weighed down by oppressive responsibility because of a relationship with an irresponsible mate, passing along sour and painful memories of men.

Feminism didn't create women's anger and distrust of men. It simply triggered and released an outpouring of rage and even hatred that had been building for centuries as a result of women having been sexually objectified and psychologically and materially controlled in a society where economic autonomy eluded most women. The consequence is that many women became increasingly defensive and cynical postfeminism in their use of their relationships to get their needs met, with a guiltless ability to leave those relationships at any time. Some became zealously committed to a sense of "never again will I allow a man to control or abuse me." What was surprising when feminism unleashed women's long-suppressed feelings was the depth of the rage and defensiveness and the length of time it would take for the wounds to heal, the defensiveness to dissolve, and good will toward building a new and healthy model of relationships to return.

For those fortunate couples who have found their way to higher ground by developing the new, balanced relationship where each is equally and deeply committed, there exists great new opportunities. For those who still believe in the instant magic of romance, and who cling to the traditional role models, the path of love will continue to be painful and traumatic.

There is no quick or easy way around today's obstacles to a man-woman relationship. Without an awareness that to free oneself from old, toxic models of connection requires more than loving intentions and ideals, the relationship will hit distressing impasses as the ghosts and demons of past generational patterns leak through and engulf the relationship.

Today's relationship opportunities are greater than they've ever been, but so are the hazards and obstacles. Clear-eyed lovers can acknowledge and see that difficulty and avoid compromising or shortcutting the effort required to build a rooted love relationship.

INSIGHT 37: EGO—HIS AND HERS

Men tend to fall in love when they get their egos stroked and inflated. Women tend to fall in love when they can dissolve their egos and lose themselves in a fused relationship.

The Conversation

The phenomenon that seems to release the chemicals that produce seemingly delightful and addicting highs of early romance were embodied by Samuel, age twenty-three, in his experience with Shoshanna, his fiancée. While he was delighting in the ego bath of regularly hearing he was the sexiest and most perfect male, he also acknowledged concern when Shoshanna expressed the opposite feelings about herself, feelings of insecurity and a sense of unworthiness she projected onto him by accusing him of not really wanting her and secretly desiring to be with other women.

Samuel: "When a woman falls in love with me, why does it seem like she loses her identity and strength?"

Dr. Goldberg: "What happens when you fall in love with a woman?"

Samuel: "She makes me feel like I'm totally wonderful and brilliant and the world's greatest lover. That's the greatest aphrodisiac."

The Insight Explained

Feminine socialization produces a tendency in women to want to get closer and closer to a man, to the point where their selves get lost. When men are attracted and feeling "full of themselves," they bond. Women who understand that can flatter a man and give him everything he wants to make him fall in love. A man can hardly resist a woman who makes him feel like a king or a god.

What a Woman Can Do

What women often identify as intimacy, and the frustrating, elusive, and seemingly impossible quest to achieve it, is the loss or dissolution of their separate self, which feels like love but is also a core element in eventually creating an identity crisis. As women tend to lose themselves in love, men polarize in the opposite direction, feeling inflated and completely full of themselves. Both tendencies are dysfunctional and pathological.

Falling in love may have more to do with how the other person makes you feel about yourself than about how you feel about them. For men, that means feeling like Superman. For women, it seems to mean their sense of self has disappeared, wanting to "selflessly" give to the man. Both states, inflated ego and dissolved ego, are unhealthy and have negative psychological consequences. Men with inflated egos alienate others and become disliked, while women who lose their selves also lose their self-esteem and become depressed.

What a Man Must Do

Men must recognize the extent to which their feelings of attraction and love for a woman come from her ability to make him feel wonderful about himself, giving him an inflated sense of his attractiveness, intelligence, and manliness, because most men's egos need regular feeding.

All is well and good unless the fulfillment of his ego needs blinds him to an objective perception of the woman as a person who makes him feel that way. When a man gets into a relationship based primarily on how good a woman makes him feel about himself, he must see that as possible manipulation and salesmanship on a woman's part, clearly a risky foundation for a relationship.

Likewise, many women fall in love when they can lose themselves in a relationship with a man, sometimes including giving up goals and worldly pursuits as well as denying and losing the ability to identify, express, and fight for the right to express their preferences and choices. Early in a relationship, this may be seen as an expression of her "being in love," but when the "love fog" lifts, she will experience a combination of panic and rage over having lost herself to her partner and then feel she needs to leave him in order to regain her sense of self.

When men see their formerly strong woman partner begin to lose herself and her identity to their relationship, they must: (a) recognize that as unhealthy and dangerous for the future of their relationship, (b) make it clear that such a transformation is not something he desires from her, nor is it something she is doing for him, if she believes that she is, and (c) remain in the relationship on the condition that she expresses and maintains her own strong, separate, and passionate self.

While it may be initially flattering to a man that a woman is willing to give up her preferences and goals in order to fit into his life, men must recognize this as dysfunctional behavior that puts the future of their relationship at risk and is not an act of love.

INSIGHT 38: THE WORK OF LOVE

When women are serious about their relationships, they are as grim, humorless, ego involved, and intensely focused as the men who are serious about their work or competitive pursuits. The best and worst of women in relationships mirror the best and worst of men in the external realm of business.

The Conversation

Dan, a recent MBA from a prestigious eastern university and an admitted workaholic, was troubled that his relationship life gave him so little pleasure. At age thirty-four he was feeling the pressure to find an "appropriate" mate. Believing his time with a woman partner, their sex, and the companionship itself should be enjoyable and a holiday from the competitive, cold, everyday world of business, he questioned why he didn't enjoy his personal life more despite dating many beautiful, smart women.

> *Dan*: "I look at being with a woman as something that should be fun. But with women it's got to mean something serious. They say, 'Is this relationship going anywhere?'"

> *Dr. Goldberg*: "It's important for men and women to put a lot into relationships, though they must be careful not to get so intense about it that love comes to feel more like work than an evolving exploration of possibilities."

The Insight Explained

Men's self-worth is tied to their success at work, not their success in love. For most women, having fulfilling relationships defines and generates self-esteem and feelings of being successful, so they react as strongly to the ups and downs in their relationships as men do about their ups and downs at work and earning money.

What a Woman Can Do

Most women in relationships have experienced the frustrations of being with a man who is obsessed with his work. Men experience similar feelings when they enter into a commitment and experience the pressure that comes with feeling monitored, observed, and confronted with the minutiae of their relationship behavior. When even the smallest comments or behaviors are scrutinized and they are never sure how they've been "hurtful" to their woman partner, men tend to close up and shut down. Just as men have to learn how to lessen their workaholic behavior if their relationships are to thrive, women need to work at understanding the stress men experience in relationships when everything they do or say becomes a potential reason for criticism or hurt.

It's obvious to women when men are workaholics, with the distraction from the relationship that it brings. Many women could be termed "relationship-aholics," except society doesn't see it that way. Nevertheless, women who obsess about love and get enmeshed in their relationships are the psychological equivalent of male "workaholics."

What a Man Must Do

To understand women in relationships, men must learn to see them as counterparts to men, who then can be more easily understood rather than seen as a mysterious species that is impossible to fathom.

While times are definitely changing, traditionally, for many women, relationships have been and continue to be their primary focus and obsession. In their relationships, therefore, women behave much like men do in their primary pursuit of success, a career, and money.

It may seem like men's and women's priorities have changed greatly, but I believe that is largely a politically correct illusion. The reality is that women still get euphoric over receiving an engagement ring or becoming pregnant, just as men continue to become euphoric over their career achievements, job promotions, and financial rewards.

To understand the seemingly confusing ways of women, men must understand that women's moods and responses are largely tied to their experiences and the changes in their close relationships, much like men's moods are more vulnerable to the victories, threats, and losses in their work lives.

INSIGHT 39: EMOTIONAL FLIP-FLOPS

Just as men's true feelings sometimes come out after sex, at which time they may lose interest in the person of the woman and withdraw and become critical and hostile, some women's true feelings come out after they get what they want—namely, marriage or motherhood.

The Conversation

"Twice married, twice burned," and now very wary of committed relationships, Tod, forty-five, the proprietor of a small business, was feeling he was closing up dangerously and becoming increasingly isolated. He joined a men's therapy support group, sharing his experience.

> *Tod*: "It's a letdown and a painful moment of truth for me when I really like a woman, have sex with her, and then wish she'd leave. I ask myself, 'What was I thinking?'"

> *Dr. Goldberg*: "Were you being controlled by your penis?"

> *Tod*: "Maybe. Women don't seem to be like that—or are they?"

> *Dr. Goldberg*: "Well, yes and no. Guys tell me that soon after they marry or have a baby with a woman who pushed for it, her feelings shift. She can become critical of her partner and begin finding fault with little things he does."

The Insight Explained

When gender needs partially driven by biological drives dominate, the opposite sex often serves as just an outlet for one's satisfaction. Most people don't want to accept the idea that pursuing a strong attraction may just be seduction to get what they want at that moment, but after they get it, the way their feelings change reveals the truth.

What a Woman Can Do

Women have long known the terrible feeling of becoming sexually intimate and emotionally vulnerable only to have the man withdraw and fumble for reasons and justifications to distance her. While that kind of hurtful withdrawal is easy to recognize, it is useful for women to see the impact of equivalent distancing after they get what they want. Then men are left bewildered, confused, and withdrawn, which women tend to interpret as men's resistance to closeness and intimacy, when, in fact, it is an honest response to feeling distanced.

What a Man Must Do

When most men are first attracted to a woman, their thoughts usually turn to sex. After they succeed in their pursuit of sex, their real feelings begin to emerge. If she was primarily an object for his sexual gratification, a man will begin to lose interest in spending time with her. If his interest in her was much more than sex, he will continue to want to be with her. Thus, having sex becomes a test of how a man really feels toward a woman.

Men shouldn't feel guilty for losing interest in being with a woman after having sex with her. Rather, he should recognize that even if it is an unfortunate reality, his experience is telling him what he really feels.

When a woman gets involved with a man, if she is attracted to him, her thoughts will usually turn to a possible future commitment. He may be an object to be used rather than a person she really cares about and wants to love, but unfortunately for the unknowing male, this reality may not emerge until after she achieves her goals of marriage or becoming pregnant.

Men must therefore do their relationship due diligence on their own and not expect a woman in pursuit of her goal to show her true feelings. Indeed, she may not even know how she really feels until *after* her goals have been achieved. This is equivalent to a man not knowing what he really feels about a woman until after he has had sex with her.

Men must learn to recognize the true essence of a relationship before they commit to marriage and fatherhood, when it has become "too late" to discover the true feelings of their partner. To accomplish that important goal, he may be advised to reach out for professional help.

INSIGHT 40: OPPOSING REALITIES

In relationships, women don't just experience things differently; they also experience things in opposite ways from men.

The Conversation

Manfred, a twice-divorced German businessman, age fifty-three, was concerned he'd become too distrustful for relationships. Once a wild, passionate romantic, over the years he had become paralyzed by caution and the fear that he didn't really understand women at all. The final blow occurred when he fell deeply in love with Ingrid, a fashion model who was thirty-three. Intent on doing everything right, he found that his best-intentioned love notes, gestures, and even gifts backfired. What he intended to communicate wound up far from how it was received. He felt he had no alternative but to stop seeing Ingrid altogether. Communication seemed hopeless, and this generalized to women as a whole.

> *Manfred*: "Sometimes when I joke with a woman she'll say I'm being hostile. Or we go to a party and I think the people are boring, but she tells me how interesting everyone is. It's scary when I suddenly realize I haven't a clue how she really sees things and we're miles apart in our experience."
>
> *Dr. Goldberg*: "What do you do?"
>
> *Manfred*: "First I'll try to convince her about the validity of my feelings and explain to her my interpretation of what's going on."
>
> *Dr. Goldberg*: "Does that work?"
>
> *Manfred*: "Rarely. Even when she says she can see it my way, I wonder whether she's only humoring me."

The Insight Explained

Women filter relationship reality opposite to the way men do because their defenses are the polar opposites of men's. Women often block anger and aggression, while men often block fear and vulnerability. As a result, they experience the same things in opposite ways. What each blocks in themselves they overreact to in their partner. If a woman blocks her own anger, she'll experience a man's irritated or angry response as a major assault. Likewise, when men block dependency, they will react negatively when they see women seeking more closeness.

What a Woman Can Do

Many women come to feel that men deliberately speak and behave in ways that are insensitive and abusive. The truth is much the opposite. Most men want to be seen as excellent and caring communicators, companions, and lovers. To get close to a man, the best starting place for a woman is to focus on his experience and intentions—what he says and does—not her own interpretation of him, while assuming the best rather than the worst as a path to a deeper intimacy. When men and women feel continually misunderstood and misinterpreted, they give up, and intimacy becomes impossible. Polarized defenses are what cause men and women to experience relationships so differently. The quest for closeness requires an awareness of the polarized undertow that causes women and men to readily misunderstand, misinterpret, and ultimately fear and even hate each other's responses.

One of the basic aspects of man/woman communication is that each one's reality is true for that person and can't be denied. The starting point in the quest for intimacy is to recognize and accept their partner's reality and intentions, and not criticize, judge, or attack each other for them.

What a Man Must Do

A man must overcome the self-destructive fantasy and projection that causes him to believe the women he loves can and should feel, think, and see the world the way he does.

Men with the delusion of having found their clone in a female are vulnerable to entering a relationship believing they have found their soul mate, only to discover that what they thought was magical compatibility was something else. Then they may add insult to injury by coming to believe they had been manipulated, when in fact, they were just victims of their own lack of psychological awareness.

To make sense of the frustrating communication struggles and battles a man has with his partner, a man must recognize that on the deepest level, most women's emotional experience in life is not just different from that of men but also largely opposite to it.

That is not good or bad, nor right or wrong. It just is.

For men to deny the deeper polarization of the genders is to embark on a relationship nightmare. While that may sound like an overgeneralization, I believe on a deeper level, in many crucial areas, men and women have opposing experiences of the same things. To deny the deeper reality that may not emerge clearly until well into the relationship is to set oneself up for painful and enraging conversations in which partners accuse each other of not wanting to understand them and wishing to destroy the relationship.

Because of women's tendency to initially accommodate men, the deeper polarization may remain softened and reduced, and will emerge only after time and under stress. Until that time, it may seem as if they see things in similar ways.

Gender polarization can be seen clearly during the stress of a difficult argument. Typically, a man will withdraw, refuse to communicate, and ask to be left alone, while his partner will want to pursue communication and accuse him of being cold and uncaring because he has closed up. Similarly, their tastes in entertainment, social preferences regarding whom to spend time with, political views, the way they view life as loving or harsh and cynical, attitudes toward relationships with extended family, and even small matters like sleeping with windows open or closed and the desire for affectionate foreplay all expose the polarization and their deeper differences in how they experience reality.

Relationships between men and women are complicated enough as it is, but men must learn that without understanding the non-negotiable differences in how men and women experience reality, in frustration they will be prone to fantasizing about being with another partner who they believe will understand them better and see things their way. This unfortunate, self-centered delusion often leads men to replay their relationship frustrations and disappointments with a new woman, and with each new woman it will probably get worse after the initial euphoria of believing he has found somebody who sees things his way fades away.

INSIGHT 41: THE SCARIEST FACTS OF LOVE

A painful paradox in male/female relationships is that what a man believes is an act of love on his part, a woman may interpret as distancing and even hostile. Conversely, what a woman believes is a show of affection and love may be experienced by a man as engulfment, suffocation, and manipulation.

The Conversation

Hans was highly cultured, educated, and well read in the philosophical German literature on love and relationships, which turned out to be an impediment in his relationship experiences and efforts to find lasting love and caring. When things went wrong, he would pull out books and read to his partner in an attempt to "educate her" on managing relationships. He was shocked to see his attempt to bring rationality and harmony to a "crazy argument" only enraged and alienated women. "Women are just too thick to understand" was the conclusion he drew from his failures and frustrations in communicating. His male colleagues readily agreed.

Hans: "It's frustrating when I do something for a woman that I think is caring and designed to bring us closer, and she sees it as an attempt to push her away."

Dr. Goldberg: "Such as?"

Hans: "Trying to be helpful by giving her advice on living is definitely one example. After all, I study the philosophy masters. She'll say, 'I didn't ask for advice; I just wanted you to listen,' or 'I feel like you're patronizing me and putting me down.'"

Dr. Goldberg: "Women have a similar experience of feeling misinterpreted by men."

Hans: "Like what?"

Dr. Goldberg: "Like when they show affection with a man and he acts irritated, or when they tell him how much they care about him and he acts like he's being maneuvered and manipulated, or when they cry and he withdraws."

The Insight Explained

When men "do" for a woman to show love, it's often because they don't know how to just be fully present with her as a way of showing love. "Doing" is a man's way of running away from just being there with a woman. Similarly, women show affection or say "I love you" often because they're looking for reciprocity and closeness. Men, sensing that and feeling the pressure to reciprocate, close up and stiffen with discomfort.

What a Woman Can Do

Many women resent the notion that they have to make special efforts to understand men in order to have a relationship with them. Once women can acknowledge that men's "upside-down way of experiencing relationships" explains his supposedly hurtful behaviors, the relationship can get on track and become surprisingly easy.

When a man recoils from a woman's "loving" gestures and repeated statements of affection, he's told he has a problem and doesn't know how to accept love and is afraid of intimacy. In fact, he may be reacting to his idea that she's really doing it out of her neediness or to fulfill her agenda. Similarly, men will "do" for a woman—like mowing her lawn or giving advice on her finances—because that's the way they know to show caring. While a woman may be pleased initially, when that's all he can do to show love, it frustrates her deeper need to be emotionally close. In fact, he is giving her the best he has. Reacting negatively may cause him to close up permanently, feel unappreciated and misunderstood, and give up trying.

What a Man Must Do

Intense relationship frustrations and feelings of hopelessness over communicating successfully and effectively will occur when loving motives by a man and a woman are met with hostility, irritation, and negative interpretation.

Men must learn how the polarized realities of men and women cause each to negatively respond to behaviors that their partners believe are motivated by love. That is, a man will be dismayed when his light-hearted attempts at humor and playfulness are experienced by his partner as being expressions of hostility. Similarly, women become disillusioned and frustrated when their expressions of loving affection with a man are met with coldness or even irritation ("Can't you ever leave me alone?"). Even if he doesn't say anything, his partner senses his negative response.

A man must understand that in a relationship, what creates the reality is not what a man *intends* but what his partner *experiences*. Many men in such instances will try to talk a woman out of her experience by calling her "crazy" because he is unable to see the different nature of her experience. This will have a damaging effect that can destroy their feelings toward each other.

Likewise, a man's negative reaction and interpretation of a woman's needs and efforts to be close to him will systematically cause her to withdraw and become cold toward him.

Men must learn to interpret their partner's relationship responses with an empathy that emerges from the recognition of her reality and intentions in their interactions, without insisting that she see and interpret responses as he does.

INSIGHT 42: THE TOUCHING EXPERIENCE

Little or no affectionate touching from a man is as difficult to accept and deal with for a woman as the continual need to hold hands, hug, and kiss is for a man.

The Conversation

Jeff, a West Los Angeles hospital intern, typified many young, single men in his reaction to the physical contact needs of his girlfriend. "When I dated the ice-queen type I complained about the lack of affection. Now, engaged to Donna, who is warm and caring, I find I get irritated and impatient at her expectation of and request for hugs, hand holding, and snuggling. Maybe I'm the cold one. All these years I've been criticizing my girlfriends for being cold and unaffectionate, I should have been pointing the finger at myself."

> *Jeff*: "Whenever we go out, my fiancée wants to hold my hand or tries to make some other kind of physical contact. At home she's always asking for a hug or a massage. I end up trying to give her what she wants even when I don't want to, and it irritates me."

> *Dr. Goldberg*: "What else does that make you feel?"

> *Jeff*: "It makes me uncomfortable. I feel like running away or begging her to please stop."

The Insight Explained

Most men are made uncomfortable by too much spontaneous touching. It's almost like it takes them off track and renders them soft or powerless. Most men don't know how to express this discomfort because they feel too much guilt. Yet men don't see how their difficulty with affectionate, nonsexual touching feels like rejection to a woman. It's like how a woman's refusal to have sex feels to a man.

What a Woman Can Do

Many men are made uncomfortable by nonsexual physical displays of affection. Unfortunately, that is an outcome of their masculine socialization, and it can be distressing to women. With a physically withholding man, complaints, requests, and insistent demands for reassurance of his love is not an effective approach for women to use.

The need for physical contact is there in most men. They are hungry for affectionate contact, but they usually express that need only when they are the ones to initiate it.

While a man may complain about the cold woman, she excites and triggers the profound but denied need within him to be held and touched.

Clearly, men need to understand their partners' needs for touching, and the need to respond to and satisfy it or risk the deterioration of their connection and desire to remain in the relationship. The more they withdraw and reject a woman's desire for closeness, the more it will bring on a kind of desperation in her. It feels as bad to her to be touch starved as being smothered feels to him.

What a Man Must Do

Many men are secretly irritated by the continual attempts of their partners to make physical contact, but out of guilt or desire to please, they may pretend otherwise while thinking, "I wish she'd just let me be."

Once men can acknowledge their own negative responses to a woman's spontaneous attempts at affectionate touching and communication, and understand the polarized relationship experience of men and women, they can more easily empathize with the pain and frustration of women who rarely, if ever, get kissed, hugged, or affectionately touched by their partners.

Controlling men will tend to deny the importance to the welfare and maintenance of their relationship's survival of regular affectionate touching and verbal expressions of love. Doing without that is as frustrating for a woman as doing without sex is to a man. Men who want their relationships to survive must overcome their self-centered belief that they can relate to their partner in any way that is comfortable for them without any relationship consequence.

In the evolving world of male-female relationships, men who do not understand and educate themselves about women's experience, and continue to believe that it is not of importance for them to do so, will experience a rude awakening when they are suddenly and unexpectedly abandoned.

Men must develop a deep understanding of a woman's experience and how it differs from a man's, or else they can expect to live with the traumatic consequence of failing to do so.

INSIGHT 43: PRETENDING TO BE RATIONAL

In relationships, women seem irrational when they actually know exactly what they're doing and what's going on. Conversely, men may try to act rational and as if they are in control when they are confused, overwhelmed, and clueless.

The Conversation

Ivan, a married engineer in his late thirties, had a habit of trying to teach "reason" to his young bride. Like many men in committed relationships, he saw himself as the sensible partner, not driven by hormones, until he faced the painful fact that his wife was having an affair and planning to leave him. His response was what I term *macho-psychotic*, meaning the insane defensive response of the ego-threatened male. "I'll kill that ass-hole, and if you leave me, it'll be the last relationship you'll ever have" was his threatening and psychotic-like response. Typically, the men I have worked with and spoken to over the years were "rational" only so long as they felt in control of their relationships. Once threatened by abandonment or rejection, their response tended to be more in the nature of berserk.

We talked about his arrogant and chauvinistic view that men were the logical ones in relationships.

> *Ivan*: "I thought my wife had no idea of what was happening in our relationship, until I discovered it was me who was clueless."

> *Dr. Goldberg*: "I see that all the time. A woman announces she's leaving, and the man goes into a state of disbelief and shock. He had no idea how she really felt. When the guy falls apart, it's like he's discovering for the first time how needy, vulnerable, and dependent he is."

> *Ivan*: "And women, who seem irrational, helpless, fragile, naïve, and dependent, are just the opposite."

The Insight Explained

Men believe they can control and reason their way out of relationship problems. Relationships don't operate the same way as learning to drive a car or solving a mechanical problem. Sensing, intuiting, and empathizing are weak areas for men who are in denial of their emotional blocks.

What a Woman Can Do

Clearly inappropriate responses, such as violent outbursts, self-destructive and inappropriate lashing out, and attacking, are the ways men demonstrate their relationship craziness.

Because men tend to be "out of touch" with vulnerable emotions and needs, when a crisis situation cracks them open, their responses demonstrate extreme irrationality. When men get crazy and even dangerous, the most effective response for a woman is to listen and soothe and not counterattack, respond in fear, or try to explain what she's feeling, or he might use his "logic" to twist her responses.

What a Man Must Do

When relationships unravel and spin out of control, many men like to console themselves and support each other with the self-serving notion that relationships are impossible because women are crazy. Few men are aware that women see men the same way: as clueless, childlike, and crazy.

Male-female polarization generates these negative perceptions men and women have of each other. Still men must recognize, acknowledge, and overcome the "insanity" that exists on their side of the fence.

Why are men pulled into relationships based on the size of a woman's breasts, the color of her hair, and her willingness to perform oral sex? Why do men work so hard to provide for a family they claim to love and then rarely, if ever, interact and converse with them because they are "always busy"? Or why are men obsessed with sports such as football, boxing, and hockey where the game inflicts pain and often serious bodily injury?

When men argue and fight with their female partners, why do they repeatedly try to impose their logic to convince a woman about something when they have seen that approach fail time and again, only to despair about the so-called hopeless communication?

Contrariwise, women may become tearful and emotional in conversation with their partners, yet when they are ready to abandon the relationship, they seem fully in command of the situation while their partners are falling apart.

Most of all, men must see how their defensive egos prevent them from recognizing themselves as the clueless, immature idiots that women recognize them to be.

Men must acknowledge the truth in women's perceptions of them and then work to understand themselves and the nature of their relationships.

Indeed, if the degree of relationship irrationality were actually measured, I believe men in relationships would rate significantly "crazier" and more ignorant than women.

INSIGHT 44: INSATIABLE NEEDS

Men fear that giving into women's requests for intimacy will pull them into a bottomless pit of closeness. Women fear that men's requests for space will put them into a distant place with no limits. Initially they attempt to fill each other's needs but soon realize their best efforts are "never enough." They see that in their partners but not in themselves.

The Conversation

Nothing highlights the experiential and communication gap between men and women more clearly than the conversations and arguments regarding a woman's frustrated intimacy needs or a man's need for distance.

Dennis, a corporate workaholic, personified the hapless male who had given up in his efforts to satisfy his wife's desire to spend quality time together. "Less than a year after we married I realized I'd never succeed in satisfying her. I'd rather she be angry at me for not trying than to actually try and fail and face her contempt and negative feelings about my inadequacy."

Dennis: "I used to get upset when my girlfriend said I never wanted to just spend time with her or share my feelings."

Dr. Goldberg: "How did you respond?"

Dennis: "I'd get angry and say, 'Can't you stop asking me if I love you?' or 'No matter how close we are, it's never enough for you!'"

Dr. Goldberg: "Well, aren't there certain things you do or say that trigger her frustration and anger?"

Dennis: "Sure, when I'm telling her I need to be alone, or she's crowding me and I need breathing room."

Dr. Goldberg: "At first, most people try to listen to their partner's complaints, but eventually they give up trying, realizing that the more they try, the more hopeless it feels, and their partner's needs are impossible to satisfy."

The Insight Explained

Because the essence of being masculine or feminine is defensive—meaning that it requires a lot of blocking out of certain feelings and responses—the drives and hungers that build can never be fulfilled. The insatiable needs gender defenses create cause men and women to resent each other. Eventually each partner will give up on trying to fill what initially seemed to be understandable and acceptable needs.

What a Woman Can Do

The solution to this historic battle of the sexes is fairly simple. When men express their needs for space, a woman's healthiest response is to question why she wants to spend time with him when he's telling her he wants to be by himself. Surprisingly, when a woman stops resisting a man's insistent and pressuring request to be left alone, the result is a new interest and desire on his part to be together. Nothing gets the attention of a man more strongly than a self-contained, withdrawn woman, and nothing brings out his need and desire to spend time together more quickly.

There is a reality to a man's tendency to withdraw and a woman's hunger to be close and intimate. Men and women need to acknowledge the truth of what their partner says about them, even if they can't do much in the way of immediately fulfilling those needs.

What a Man Must Do

It is a distressing illusion, and one that generates painful feelings of failure and inadequacy in both genders, that somehow, simply with love, good will, and the best of intentions, men and women can satisfy each other's needs. *Until the existence and reality of the polarized and defensive experiences of men and women are both acknowledged and, with good will, effort, and intervention, worked through and depolarized, such that the experiences of both genders become in sync with each other, even the best efforts at communication are doomed to fail.*

The polarized needs of men and women, which typically mean men need "space" while women need closeness and communication, are at the core of the breakdown of male-female relationships.

Once the defensive and therefore "insatiable" nature of men's and women's needs are fully recognized, the challenging yet potentially very rewarding work to rebalance realities can begin.

Men must realize the bottomless aspect of their need for enclosure and withdrawal and the way it pushes away and alienates not only women but also family and others. It also leads men to end states of painful isolation and bitterness.

Only bonding with a woman who can also see the bottomless and defensive nature of her needs can give the needed support for a man and woman to create a mutual middle road.

INSIGHT 45: BLAMING THE OTHER AT THE END

Men can see women's defensiveness, and vice versa, but rarely can either gender see their own overreactions, rigidities, and distortions. When relationships end, both sexes tend to see what has been done to them but rarely what they have contributed to creating their failures and pain.

The Conversation

The effectiveness of couples therapy tends to be in proportion to how much both partners are able to focus on and take responsibility for their own dysfunctions and their part in triggering conflicts and making resolution impossible.

While men often acknowledge guilty feelings regarding the relationship problems they're having, they are unable to see how what they do and how they are to be with seem to the other person.

Lloyd: "Why is it that my relationships with women usually begin with little conflict and lots of good will, but end with blaming, finger-pointing, and defensiveness?"

Dr. Goldberg: "It is hard to believe that these are the same two people who were initially so in love and sure they had found their soul mates. The defensiveness on both sides is often so extreme they never even want to see each other again."

The Insight Explained

Men and women have been socialized to behave in certain ways that they were told would make them attractive, lovable, and normal. So when they then act out those behaviors in a close relationship and it alienates their partner, they assume it's the other person's problem. Women can see men's defensiveness when they are afraid to get close, out of touch with feelings, controlling, never truly present, emotionally cold, and objectifying women as sex objects. Men encounter women's defensiveness when they are engulfing, blaming, guilt making, unquenchable in their need for reassurance, irrational in their complaints and emotional responses, and manipulative with their sexuality.

What a Woman Can Do

The personal training that makes boys and girls "normal" and "well behaved" growing up can cause problems in a committed relationship. Because each is behaving according to their original script, they can't understand that the ways in which they've always acted need changing. To improve a broken relationship, each partner must (1) assume that his or her behavior is the cause of one-half of the problem, and (2) listen for the truth in what the other person is saying.

Because the role of *reactor* is so deeply embedded in most women, they tend to have a major blind spot when it comes to recognizing the ways they are an equal contributor to the relationship problems they experience. Women who feel controlled tend to not see the ways they resisted or even refused to take control by making important decisions. Women who feel invisible and insignificant tend to not see how they fail to directly assert their preferences, needs, and choices.

Contributions to the demise of a relationship can be manifested actively or passively, but the deterioration is always the product of the interaction between two people. Trying to isolate the true culprit is a hopeless and impossible task.

What a Man Must Do

The common tendency in relationships is to focus on one's partner's flaws when conflict and frustrations arise. To cast one's partner in the role of relationship spoiler seems irresistible, but doing so, though it may allow one to temporarily take the relationship high road, also means the potential for growth and change will be stymied.

Men, particularly those who have had many partners and relationship failures, must begin the journey toward taking responsibility, gaining self-awareness, and identifying dysfunctional communication patterns, behaviors, and blind spots that are part of a cycle that is damaging and destroying these relationships.

A healthy, growing relationship is one in which both partners focus with unflinching honesty on what *they* themselves repeatedly do to undermine the communication and what choices they make to cause their relationships to fail.

While courting prospective partners, men must choose women who are able to shine the harsh light of responsibility on themselves and know what their relationship issues and patterns are and have a history of working on themselves and not blaming their partners. At the beginning of the relationship, noting how a woman describes her past failures and the men she has been involved with will provide an immediate preview of how she will respond and handle conflicts in the future. If she was a blamer who portrays herself as the loving and innocent victim of her past experiences, she will do that again in her new relationships after the initial romantic fog has settled and the light of reality has begun to shine.

INSIGHT 46: ROMANCE, DESIRE, AND THE POWER IMBALANCE

Romantic relationships begin with both partners as equals but become power struggles. The person who dominates becomes bored and distant, while the one with less power and control remains excited and becomes needy. When this dynamic reaches its peak, the person with the power becomes hostile and ponders exit strategies, while the one who has given power away becomes obsessed with the relationship and desperate for contact and reassurance.

The Conversation

Can it be that intense feelings of love and sexual excitement are more a by-product of the balance of power than anything else? Relationship experts, when they advise about love, tend to focus on its content or "how-to" aspects: "Doing *this* is loving and doing *that* is not." Yet we've all had the experience of having tried and failed to be our most loving selves in the vain attempt to win over another. Similarly, we have seen others fall in love while being rejected or mistreated.

The power balance equation suggests that in a relationship, the person who controls comes to feel bored and falls out of love, while the person who is being distanced and rejected will obsess, remain excited, and think he or she is "so in love."

Manny, age forty-two, shows an example of how men respond, even when they don't understand why.

> *Manny*: "When I'm not sure where I stand with a woman, when she is strong, hard to read, and keeps me guessing, I get excited and fall in love."

> *Dr. Goldberg*: "Is it the challenge that turns you on?"

> *Manny*: "I'm not sure, but what I do know is when I'm in control and the woman acts insecure and needy, it's me who loses interest. And when I get bored, I start to look down on her and get hostile. I hate that."

Dr. Goldberg: "But when she's totally in control and you are kept off balance?"

Manny: "It's embarrassing to say, but it turns me on. I become desperate for reassurance."

The Insight Explained

It's a sad, difficult, and painful truth that excitement in a relationship often comes from the power imbalance and not from the content. A man who is bored with his wife, for example, may suddenly get interested and excited again when she becomes indifferent, takes a lover, or announces she's planning to leave.

What a Woman Can Do

When a man says a woman doesn't excite him, it has little to do with what the woman does but much to do with how she relates. If she's dependent and insecure, the man becomes bored and withdrawn or cold. If she remains solidly her own person, she will get and keep his attention. If she's indifferent to him, or even abusive, he may well become more interested.

Similarly, when women become obsessed and needy in their relationships, men tend to become indifferent and even abusive. This seems to be a predictable and consistent consequence of the power imbalance.

A woman will discover how quickly she becomes attractive to a man when she pulls away emotionally and physically, not as a strategy, but as a self-caring response to a partner who seems to be losing energy and interest. Nothing renews or creates excitement in a man more quickly than a woman's announcement that she is leaving the relationship and her ability to follow through.

What a Man Must Do

Power in a relationship can be recognized in its rhythm. The person who is less invested in a relationship working out is the one with the power. The less one cares about the outcome of a relationship, the more one gains control. The insecure, needy partner, who will accommodate and deny negative feelings because of the urgency to make the relationship work, has less and sometimes even no power at all.

The person with more power and less investment will act insensitively and may unknowingly even become hostile.

This power dynamic is the hidden reason many relationships become so painful and feel so desperate. When a man has less power, he will tend to pressure for reassurance of his partner's love. That will only make the problem worse.

Being a person with greater power is dangerous for men because they will be seen as and blamed for being abusive and uncaring. Rather than protesting that perception, men need to acknowledge its truth. Instead of feeling guilty for being hurtful, they need to seriously consider ending such a relationship or ultimately confront blaming, rage, and accusations of their so-called abusiveness.

When a man is the one with less or no power, he must first become aware of the reasons he has allowed this to happen, and then become aware of what generated his insecurity and fears of abandonment, causing him to give up power, and work to correct the imbalance. To achieve this, he will need outside help.

One step a man must take immediately if he is the less powerful or the powerless partner is to recognize how his urgency for reassurance will tip the balance even more to his detriment. He must refrain from asking for reassurance and find ways to pull back and distance himself until he can perceive his partner as a person like himself rather than a prize he feels he is unworthy of.

INSIGHT 47: HER POWER

Men's guilt is women's power.

The Conversation

When men assume the role of *actor*, initiator, or decision maker, they also assume responsibility and experience guilt when their choices, actions, and decisions turn out to be poor. As a *reactor* or the passive and reactive partner, a woman's power comes indirectly and passively from the way she reacts to what the man initiates and does. While it leaves a woman feeling controlled, invisible, and angry when she is a reactor to a man's choices, what is overlooked is the power she derives from reacting, whether with approval, praise, indifference, boredom, or displeasure.

Here's how Harvey, a "chronic bachelor" after five years of a painful marriage that ended with him filled with self-hate, expressed it.

Harvey: "I'm afraid of commitment because once I'm committed I'm always blamed for failing to be loving, thoughtful, and fully present."

Dr. Goldberg: "You mean that once you're in the relationship fully, you always need to be proving something or apologizing for something you did wrong. That seems like a pathetic way to relate."

The Insight Explained

For men who typically take responsibility for most relationship decisions, when things go wrong they feel it is their fault. Then they feel the need to apologize or make it up to their partners.

What a Woman Can Do

Men's guilt gives women an indirect handle for control in a relationship and gives them their strongest tool of control.

However, a guilt-ridden man becomes a powerless and uninteresting man and consequently one who will be unattractive and unappealing. A woman's indirect power gives her a level of control, but, at the same time, it diminishes and toxifies the relationship. To remedy this requires women to begin to maintain the relationship on an equal footing by taking responsibility for whatever happens in it. Once the relationship is free of guilt and blame, the possibility of a growing and healthy one can be put in place.

What a Man Must Do

Feelings of guilt in a relationship are insidious. They block a person's ability to get in touch with what they really feel, and they are damaging to the health of the relationship. In a relationship between two healthy adults, guilt is an unnecessary, unhelpful reality distortion and tends to become a tool for manipulation by the "guilt-free" partner.

Men must see how they are the ones in the relationship prone to guilt because they traditionally assume the role of actor.

While women may seem to not have the overt control, their male partner's feelings of responsibility or guilt give women the power to blame, withhold approval, and criticize.

Men need to discuss all relationship decisions, learn to listen, refrain from automatically taking over, and avoid relationships with women whose continual responses are "it doesn't matter" or "whatever you choose will be fine."

Men must know that by taking responsibility, they are handing their partner a powerful tool for manipulation that is difficult to recognize, but once established it is hard to change and transform.

INSIGHT 48: MEN AS THE NEEDY SEX

While men are often viewed as more powerful than women, in personal relationships women often have greater power because men need women more than women need men. Because of his enclosure and isolation, a woman is a man's personal lifeline. The reverse is not true, since women usually have caring and bonded relationships to buffer them. Most women can readily get along without a man in their lives, while a man without a woman tends to become lonely and desperate.

The Conversation

Reggie, a military career officer at thirty-three, had recurrent bouts of depression that sapped his energy and threatened his career as a recruitment specialist. One of his complaints was a lack of close friends. The conversations he had over drinks or dinner with other bachelor colleagues consisted of impersonal subjects such as sports, business, or teasing in the form of caustic barbs and jokes. The conversation would spark if an attractive woman approached their table. They would become energized and focused. It discouraged him to realize how dependent he was on female companionship in order to feel "human" and connected.

Reggie: "I used to say, 'I don't need a woman,' but that was usually when I was in a relationship. I don't think women are nearly as desperate. They seem to have close friends and close family ties. A man without a woman is alone and lonely, even if he pretends he isn't."

Dr. Goldberg: "Women would be surprised how powerful that makes them in men's lives. It's amazing that women think men have the power, when they do so much better on their own than men, and men need women's validation more."

The Insight Explained

By the time they reach adulthood, most men are so focused on external goals that their personal lives have dissolved. Without a central woman, they're locked in an isolation chamber. Because women don't define themselves solely based on achievement, placing at least an equal emphasis on relationships with family, friends, and children, they are less emotionally vulnerable without a man.

What a Woman Can Do

Because men need women more than women need men, women have an enormous form of power. While men may not admit it or realize it until a woman leaves, suddenly they're overwhelmed with loneliness, anxiety, and desperation. So building and maintaining a support system for himself outside of the relationship is his best protection, but few men are able to do so.

The greatest problem for a woman may become how to diminish the burden she feels being wholly responsible for a man's personal life.

What a Man Must Do

It's been a long and painful journey for men to see themselves as the vulnerable and needy, not the privileged, gender on many levels, from health, longevity, and social relations (or the lack thereof) to developing a loving bond with their children.

As men and women age, painful gender truths become clear. When a man loses his wife, he finds himself pathetically alone. When he divorces, he usually finds his children are bonded with their mother and have little interest in seeing or being with him. When he can no longer do his work, he may have the dreadful feeling that he has become invisible and useless.

The athlete he may have been doesn't translate into middle age and older, when he is beset by physical ailments and diseases and he begins to experience self-loathing.

The earlier in life a man can see the painful realities that will emerge as he gets older, the better. While it is never easy for a man to change, since men are notoriously resistant to asking for help or changing entrenched habits, men must recognize that what he sees happening to other men around him will also happen to him. Denying his isolation and a lack of a caring support system is a major roadblock to his growth.

Deluding himself into believing he will escape the all-too-common personal endpoints of his gender is perhaps a man's greatest vulnerability.

INSIGHT 49: AN UNCOMFORTABLE TRUTH

Men manipulate the world; women manipulate men.

The Conversation

When I first listened to what Ricardo, a professional gambler in his early fifties, experienced in relationships and love, I thought I was hearing the rationalizations of a psychopath. After a while, however, I found myself intrigued by the seeming directness and honesty of his perceptions. Many of his observations caused me to challenge some of my own preconceptions about closeness and love.

Ricardo: "It seems men who 'make it' in the competitive world understand that being a winner means knowing how to 'play the game.' Guys shake hands, smile, make eye contact, play golf, but all of that is really on the surface. Underneath, they don't really care about each other, though the successful game players know how to make it appear as though they do, and maybe even believe it themselves. But money, power, goals, and success is the bottom line, and they readily abandon even close friendships."

Dr. Goldberg: "But suggest to a man that he's manipulative, shallow, or opportunistic, and he'll get defensive and angry."

The Insight Explained

As boys, men learn the need to be competitive. It's all about performing and measuring their abilities. He's a hero if he succeeds and a "loser" and a "nobody" if he doesn't. Girls learn early on the need to win over a great guy in order to validate themselves. Women teach each other the "rules" of the game when it comes to getting the man they want. The manipulations may be blatant, yet denied. When they find the "right one," they act as if the love is a magical event or a fated meeting with their soul mate. It's when they're ready to leave that relationship that true motives and feelings emerge.

What a Woman Can Do

While the idea that *men manipulate the world and women manipulate men* sounds cynical, recognizing the deeper reality of what's transpiring in their relationships would allow men and women to grow and avoid depression over failed experiences. If they stayed aware of their deeper motives and feelings and were able to see themselves for who they really are, they could then start to change their experiences.

Because men are brought up to be competitive and to succeed, win, and triumph at the expense of close friendships or acquaintances, they lose their capacity for nonopportunistic, genuinely caring friendships. Fully realizing this would help women in relationships who experience anger and frustration because of a man's lack of emotional expressiveness and sensitivity, which they believe is directed at them personally. A step toward healing relationships would be the awareness on a woman's part that the man doesn't intend to avoid personal closeness with her but has an emotional limitation with all personal relationships because of his masculine socialization. What a woman should never do is pressure or shame a man into being more intimate. Doing so is like prodding a crippled man to run.

What a Man Must Do

A seemingly cynical interpretation of the way gender and the world interact is that men are manipulators of the impersonal world, where they control the agenda and use masks and pretenses to hide their real feelings and motives so seamlessly that even they fail to see themselves doing it, wanting to believe their motives are righteous.

Until recent years, before women and men began transforming the ways they respond and function, women's primary focus was in the personal world, and since men have had the power in the external and competitive world, women have had to learn to manipulate men in order to gain their own power. Women have accomplished this by creating a mystique, a detachment and unavailability that makes men compete for them and feel lucky to gain their admiration, love, and sex.

What a man must do is not deny that in the same way they put on a mask to achieve their goals of success, women do the same thing with men because men have the power to provide the "good life."

This deeper psychological reality and undercurrent is not as apparent or visible in the contemporary world of gender upheaval. And yet, in most of the world, the reality that men manipulate the world while women manipulate men is still true.

Men know they are constantly having to play a game in order to survive, and they must become what others expect them to be in order to become and remain successful.

Women realize it, so they adorn themselves with sexy clothing, jewelry, perfumes, perfect teeth, and beautiful bodies in order to attract and hold on to the men they need in order to fulfill their dreams.

This needs to be integrated into awareness without judgment and without romanticizing in order to cushion this harsh reality.

Men need to see their love relationships for what they are—namely, illusions of whatever men and women need and want to believe—and accept the realistic limits of their relationship with women rather than getting down on themselves for their own manipulative motives and ambitions.

Men must clearly see the underlying basis or foundation of their relationships, asking, "Why does she want to be with me? And why am I choosing her to be my partner?" To the extent that a man is being chosen based on his status, finances, and vocation—a euphemism for being used for the fulfillment of his partner's needs, and the extent to which a man is objectifying the woman based on her physical appearance and her "sexiness" or family history—the relationship will lack a person-to-person foundation and have the potential to become significantly dysfunctional, meaning that it will experience continual crises as the person behind the image or fantasy can no longer remain hidden or disguised.

Men who are particularly vulnerable to the temptation of choosing a partner based on fantasy, image, and projection need to know that the relationship crises and pain they experience are of their own making, not the result of just having made an unfortunate choice in partner. They must also acknowledge that these inappropriate, dysfunctional choices put them in a position of being used and of using their partners in return for ego validation.

6

WHO IS SEXIST? WHO IS LIBERATED?

I was one of those who wrote about the potential of women's and men's gender-role liberation to usher in a new era in women's and men's relationships with each other. This process, however, is clearly not happening easily or without a significant amount of pain, anger, confusion, and rude awakenings. Feminism was supposed to make it possible for women to have it all, to be superachievers in the competitive economy and supermoms at home while sharing equally the responsibilities, joys, and burdens of parenting. Men would be freed from gender-role strangulation as well and, once liberated, could choose to be workers, stay-at-home husbands, or a combination of the two. We envisioned fulfilling partnerships in which the burdens and privileges of a relationship would be shared equally and without concern about who was "supposed to do what" as determined by their gender. It would be an ideal world based on supporting the personal growth of each other.

What seems to have emerged instead, and what continues to characterize the man-woman relationship landscape, is role chaos. Both genders are struggling to find appropriate boundaries while experiencing relationship conflicts. Instead of closeness, trust, and playfulness, women and men seem to be more cautious, distrustful, and ready to do battle and point fingers than ever.

Men feel that prerogatives of liberation are given primarily to women, who can choose to be in the competitive world or at home. They can behave traditionally as they always have, or they can assert their full personhood and autonomy.

Postliberation, the work environment became fraught with new hazards for men. Instead of the atmosphere becoming freer and mutually supportive, it became strangled by a self-conscious political correctness in which men feared accusations of sexism and harassment that could lead to losing their jobs and facing legal consequences.

In the intimate man-woman love relationship, many newly liberated men and women initially came together through their shared philosophies of equality and liberation, and they set about to create their new egalitarianism. However, male feminists, who proudly thought of themselves as models for a new men's consciousness, discovered that within the intimate relationship they still triggered women's rage and accusations of hypocrisy and sexism. With all their well-intentioned supportive efforts and awareness, why were they still seen as the bad guys who deserved women's wrath? Why weren't they being loved, appreciated, and admired for their efforts?

For women, their rude awakening came from learning that the "best of both worlds" (having a fulfilling career while raising a happy, loving child) meant assuming the stresses and exhausting burdens of both roles. Success on the job and being a loving, responsible parent and spouse required large commitments of time and energy, in addition to generating a seemingly impossible juggling act that was damaging their health and shortening their lifespan. Married women complained that at home their husbands still expected to be catered to and were content to put the bulk of the domestic chores on the woman's shoulders. Women's rate of getting what were formerly considered men's diseases such as ulcers and heart attacks showed dramatic increases as a result.

Liberation, which was supposed to lighten the load for both, was creating instead an inflammable and explosive mix. Mutual hostilities and accusations characterized by an atmosphere of ill will and toxic rage took on a soul-shattering intensity.

New attitudes, philosophies, and ideals had surged far ahead of the deeper personal and individual changes needed to sustain and support them. Men and women both had a clear vision of what the new man-woman connection should look and feel like, but the deeper impulses and tendencies of their gender conditioning couldn't keep up with their new philosophies and ideals. While both acted outwardly in politically correct new ways, deeper traditional feelings and reactions still existed. It became a "worst of both worlds" scenario, replete with liberated expectations and traditional reactions, rather than a "best of both worlds" situation in which the romance of tradition and the playfulness of an equal sharing experience could come together. Men still withdrew, turned cold, detached, and intellectualized and were critical and controlling when stressed. Women still blamed, felt abused, and raged against men's "cluelessness" and chauvinistic tendencies, and they continued to accuse men of sexism, insensitivity, and the inability to understand and satisfy a woman's needs.

The ideal of liberation had been an equal playing field between women and men made up of freer communication, equal distribution of responsibilities, a playful sensuality and sexuality, and mutual support. The reality has proved to be much more complicated and volatile. Overturning and transforming deeply embedded, habitual traditional attitudes, responses, and expectations has proved an elusive process. Like in wartime and now nation building, before a peaceful and loving environment can be created, all of the landmines have to be discovered, uprooted, and defused. So it is in the battle of the sexes and the quest for a new cooperation and love. Men and women, instead of creating a gender-free utopia, seem to be in a mode of driving each other crazy with inconsistent and contradictory needs and expectations on the way to liberation.

INSIGHT 50: WHO IS THE SEXIST?

Men who objectify and use women as sex objects, and women who objectify and use men as success and power objects, tend to deny what they do. It is easier to see oneself being used and objectified than recognize and acknowledge using and objectifying the other.

The Conversation

CEO of his own highly successful software design company, Christopher was shocked when he was confronted with accusations of sexism. The woman who accused him and almost cost him his job was his secretary and assistant, who had seemingly flirted with him during the first few weeks after having been hired. Allowing himself to be flirtatious in return was his big mistake.

Christopher: "I have to admit I don't have a clue as to what women really mean when they accuse me of being sexist. 'I shouldn't have asked her to get me a sandwich' or 'I shouldn't have been so selfish and made sure she had an orgasm, too,' or 'I shouldn't have responded to her seductiveness'?"

Dr. Goldberg: "Since men rarely accuse women of being sexist, I think women are just as unaware of their own sexism when they objectify men by how much money they make or their status and power. They don't want to think of themselves as using guys in order to secure a certain lifestyle."

Christopher: "I certainly don't intend to objectify women—and maybe they don't think they're doing it to me. It's just so ingrained that neither of us see what we do when we're accused by the other. All it does is cause defensiveness."

Dr. Goldberg: "Guys don't believe it's really sexist to want a blonde woman with long legs and nice breasts as a girlfriend, and women don't think it's sexist to make judgments about men based on the car they drive or what they do for a living."

The Insight Explained

Feminism has muddled the understanding of what sexism is. Feminists identify and attack the symptoms of sexism and not its essence. Women will judge a man as sexist simply based on a gesture or word he's used, when sexism is really about objectification. The tendency to objectify the opposite sex, however, is not a deliberate, conscious, or evil act, but the result of a lack of personal development. Traditionally, feminine women need to objectify men for their own security, while men are sexist because they don't know how to relate to women as people.

What a Woman Can Do

Most men are bewildered by accusations of sexism. They see themselves as protective and respectful. However, the traditional relationships of our parents and grandparents have deep roots in objectification. Historically, men were attractive and sexy based on their power and as success symbols. Women were attractive based on their physical beauty and ability to please, accommodate, and serve. The healthiest, most viable approach to the gender struggles today, therefore, would be a gentle, nonthreatening, supportive one designed to educate both sexes regarding their objectification tendencies. A confrontational, accusing approach only serves to shut down the dialogue. We are all "victims" of sexism and objectification and in denial regarding their presence in ourselves. Women have experienced sexism more directly. While "they don't mean it" is no excuse, for most men, it is their reality.

Criticizing someone for being sexist is a misguided, counterproductive exercise in moral one-upmanship and self-righteousness. Sexism is an unconscious by-product of traditional gender role defenses and rigidity. Women and men are almost guaranteed to be sexist toward each other until and unless they can relate to the opposite sex as people, not as objects or symbols, needed to fulfill a function they can't fulfill themselves.

What a Man Must Do

In the realm of man-woman relationships, men must be aware that while both men and women objectify each other, men are more likely to be confronted and attacked when accused of being sexists.

When women objectify men by seeing and judging them through the lens of "what does he do for a living and what is his earning potential?" they are viewed as practical and realistic, not accused of being sexists.

When men relate to and choose women based on the woman's looks, her body and her "sexiness," they are likely to be confronted. In the work world, their jobs may be at risk because of an unfortunate, misguided, or ignorant comment or interaction.

Men have to realize that sexism is in the "eye of the beholder" and not in the intention of the person being accused. A man may think he is being playful or humorous, but that will count for naught if the woman he is interacting with experiences his behavior as sexist.

INSIGHT 51: THE LIBERATED MALE

Efforts to become sensitive and liberated in relationships haven't worked for men because they have involved simplistic, one-sided solutions to a complex problem. Pressure on men to take responsibility for improving relationships reinforces the myth and distorted belief that relationship problems are primarily the man's fault because of their sexism.

The Conversation

Warren, an idealistic man in his forties, was in great pain after his seemingly liberated marriage to an attorney ended in a vicious divorce. He had assumed it was a man's job to overcome his sexist ways and prove himself liberated and supportive of a woman's career goals. However, in spite of his efforts in that direction, he found himself accused of not being liberated enough. He was engaging in seemingly endless conversations and arguments, eliminating any kind of spontaneous fun while also killing their sex life. The collapse of the relationship occurred after a weekend of distressing name-calling and insults during which his wife taunted him for being a wimp while he labeled her a castrating, man-hating, crazy-making bitch.

> *Warren*: "How come the sensitive man thing that used to be a feminist ideal and fantasy has turned into just a bad joke for women and a nightmare for guys?"

> *Dr. Goldberg*: "Guys who tried to cater to women every which way found out it didn't work. Either they were treated like girlfriends or, if women actually got involved with them, they were more contemptuous and accusing of them than of the old-fashioned so-called male chauvinist jerks. Men were accused of being phony hypocrites. The women lost interest in them sexually or sometimes raged at them."

> *Warren*: "They can't get turned on by guys who are too sensitive. You know, the so-called nice guys. They like them as friends but don't want them as lovers. It's like guys who say they want strong women but can't get sexually excited by them . . . you know, the Bill Clinton syndrome. He always went after the accommodating, compliant type

when he wanted hot sex. He admired Hillary but obviously didn't get off on her."

The Insight Explained

The gap between what looks good and what feels good is well exemplified by the "sensitive guy" issue. Women who think finding a sensitive man is the solution are usually traditional women in denial of their own tendencies toward passivity and their part in relationship problems. At the gut level they still long for Mr. Real Man. Their fantasy of loving a sensitive guy is a direct expression of their defensive belief that finding this kind of guy is the solution to their problem, rather than growing beyond their own traditional feminine process.

What a Woman Can Do

Most women today laugh at that "so yesterday" idea of being with a "sensitive man." What few women admit, however, is that it's not because sensitive guys are wimps, but rather that they are liberated only in theory. The traditional gender core is still there. Some women may think they want the "new male," but that's because they see themselves as mistreated victims and view traditional men as the problem rather than a symptom of a skewed dynamic between men and women.

The real goal of gender liberation for both men and women needs to be transforming the traditional object-to-object male-female relationship into a person-to-person one that resembles a loving friendship rather than a "hot romance." The process is slow and fraught with denials and misunderstandings, but each step forward brings its own rewards.

The greatest gift a woman can give to a man is to recognize that his "sexist ways" may be unintentional and embedded culturally as a result of his socialization, and realize that a woman's anger, while understandable and justified, overlooks the fact that men and women have been locked into a toxic dance that was traditionally designed to fuel their attraction to each other. That perspective and understanding on a woman's part can be the foundation for beginning the journey toward a lifelong experience of growing and deepening intimacy with a man.

What a Man Must Do

Men tend to have a superficial and mechanical, externalized understanding of how to go about personal change in order to become what many women say they want from men in regard to change.

What a man must do is remember that relationships are always two-way streets, and a man's inclination to feeling guilt, self-loathing, and responsibility for women's feelings causes them to believe that simply by changing themselves, their relationships can be improved. That is largely delusional. Relationships are always an expression of a two-way dynamic, and improving them must be the work of both partners. If the responsibility for change is only theirs, change that is achieved will only be a short-term improvement.

A man who deems himself the sole cause of a relationship breakdown or failure may think his efforts at transforming and improving a relationship can be done alone and that he can solve the problem, but this is a macho illusion and doomed to failure.

INSIGHT 52: LIBERATION—THE REAL DEAL

Authentic liberation is not about gestures or attitudes but about nondefensiveness. When both partners in a relationship are authentically liberated, problems and issues can be discussed without blame, guilt, shame, or self-consciousness.

The Conversation

Thomas had been a "new age" man and an ardent early supporter of feminism. When he came for counseling he was disillusioned, broken, and isolated. Previously married three times to career women he believed were independent, free thinking, and liberated, each relationship had begun with the promise of an egalitarian partnership. He was now angry, disillusioned, and cynical about the possibility of creating a balanced relationship.

> *Thomas*: "I have such a negative gut reaction to feminists and guys who claim to be liberated now. They act like 'born again' religious

people, righteous about what they think and the way they see themselves and the world."

Dr. Goldberg: "For them, it's all about attitude. Their mistake is in thinking having the 'correct attitude' makes them liberated or somehow superior."

The Insight Explained

The disillusionment one so often hears expressed about the liberation movement is that instead of freeing individuals for personal growth, it seems to have made them more defensive. They "own the truth," and those who don't agree with them may be accused of being sexist.

What a Woman Can Do

Gender socialization causes problems by suppressing a wide range of men's and women's spontaneous and authentic responses since they contradict or undermine their masculine or feminine images of themselves. That makes them defensive and rigid, and it blocks their ability to fully express themselves. "Liberation" is about "becoming free of constraints," not making people feel guilty or shaming them for using the wrong terminology or gestures. Guilt, self-consciousness, and shame are the tools of old-time religion, not personal growth.

Many women working hard to create a relationship that does not repeat the dysfunctional patterns of their parents put the focus on externals such as the equal sharing of chores and childcare. Soon, however, the pull of traditional conditioning overpowers the best of intentions, and the relationship begins to assume the shape of relationships from half a century ago.

The power of tradition is deeply rooted and must be changed with inch-by-inch progress rather than overturning embedded conditioning. More challenging is the development of nondefensive communication and a relationship free of blaming and guilt. The goal is to create a good-willed, supportive atmosphere where each partner's experience is seen as valid and a problem-solving approach is taken to resolve conflict. In other words, creating a nondefensive psychological atmosphere is the goal rather than correcting surface mechanics and "politically correct" minutiae.

What a Man Must Do

We are paying the price for superficial understanding of what sexism is and what is involved in the process of change.

Because the common interpretation and focus has been on externals such as the unfortunate or inappropriate use of a word or the expression of the politically incorrect attitude, we have created a "walking on egg-shells" climate where instead of male-female relationships being improved by efforts and support of mutual change, they have instead become more volatile, defensive, and accusatory.

Men must choose a partner who understands the need for mutual efforts at nondefensiveness in which truly liberated relationships that are nonsexist are characterized by mutual support and a lack of shaming, guilt, accusations, and obsessive monitoring.

What a man must do to experience authentic personal liberation is to expect from himself and his partner a generosity of spirit, shared responsibility, and mutual support in the quest for creating a relationship that is devoid of traditional gender strictures.

INSIGHT 53: HER LIBERATION FRONT

Men won't be able to distinguish the difference between genuinely liberated women and traditional women in liberated garb if they assess them based on surface "politically correct" responses.

The Conversation

Oliver, a professor of comparative literature, was profoundly dismayed by relationship experiences with women he had initially been attracted to because they seemed free of the hang-ups he associated with traditional women, whose goals were marriage, children, and being provided for.

> *Oliver*: "I keep getting fooled. I meet a woman who seems to love her job, is involved in politics, and pays half the check, and I think, 'This woman is different. She's not out to just use me to take care of her. She's liberated.'"

Dr. Goldberg: "Most men find it disillusioning when, after a few dates, the conversations begin to sound like the ones with 'nonliberated' women."

Oliver: "I'm always mistaken when I think I can be freer with her to talk about things that bother me in the relationship without worrying that I'll hurt her feelings or be blamed or accused of being a chauvinist."

The Insight Explained

Men are often misled by the symbolic gestures many modern, "liberated" women make. A liberated woman cannot be identified simply by the attitudes she professes. She also must be willing to look at her part of the responsibility for the problems of a relationship rather than act like a victim.

What a Woman Can Do

A liberated woman *acts* or initiates as spontaneously and fully as she *reacts* to what a man initiates. She's clear in expressing what she wants and what bothers her. She doesn't expect her mind to be read. She doesn't treat her sexuality as a gift with which to reward or punish a man. A man in a relationship with an authentically liberated woman will know it by the ease, lack of self-consciousness, and absence of any pressure to be or act "like a man."

What a Man Must Do

In his relationships, a man must focus on "how it feels" rather than what it looks like on the surface in his selection of a liberated woman partner. A genuinely liberated woman is one who has become capable of the full range of human responses that make it easy and pleasurable for a man to relate to her.

A truly liberated woman is not one who focuses on the externals, such as the expression of politically correct attitudes, but rather one who has put her energy into developing herself as a person with a full range of feminine and masculine responses. She will be capable of being both passive and assertive, angry and loving, sexual and sensual, autonomous and interdependent. Her full range of response capability will make it enjoyable and easy for a man to get close to her.

For a man to appreciate a fully liberated woman, capable of nondefensive interaction and conversation, he must do the hard work of developing himself into someone who can relate to a woman as a person, not as a sex object or trophy, and at the same time is capable of expressing his soft and related side. He will naturally not be sexist because being sexist is a constricted, limited, defensive, and unhealthy way of being for him, not simply because "it's wrong."

INSIGHT 54: CAREER WOMAN BLUES

Just because a woman has a career doesn't mean she doesn't want to be rescued and provided for, nor does it guarantee she won't want to give up her career once she gets involved in a committed relationship.

The Conversation

Working for a major corporation, Duke, a divorced man of thirty-five who began his career in marketing at twenty-two and now is vice president of product development, had dated numerous women in the previous fifteen years. He felt a marriage and family was necessary because his heavy focus on work left him feeling isolated, depressed, and questioning why he was doing what he was doing with only himself to take care of. Duke had primarily dated career women, feeling they would best understand his work-centered life. At this stage of his life he was getting increasingly confused and discouraged about what he could expect from and trust in his relationships.

His most recent disappointment occurred with Caroline, age twenty-nine, an executive he met at a networking party. When they first met, Duke believed Caroline had it all. She seemed to be strong, independent, and sensitive. He loved the way she decorated her apartment, and she knew more about jazz, his great passion, than he did. He fell in love with her, and after six months he invited her to move in with him.

Then she began to complain about being stressed out and overwhelmed by her work, feeling unappreciated and exploited by her supervisor, dropping hints that she'd love to be a stay-at-home wife, decorating, cooking, and having babies. This set off alarm bells for Duke because women in previous similar serious relationships wanted to lean on him as they began to lose their career energy. "I don't want a dependent woman who wants me home at a certain time because she cooked a meal or who wants to spend weekends shopping for furniture and throwing dinner parties. I had that with my marriage ten years ago and it was a painful disappointment. The moment we got engaged, my wife started talking about quitting her job. Frankly, I was disappointed and bored," he confessed.

Duke: "Sometimes so-called liberated women wear their careers like some traditional women wear low-cut dresses, to attract and seduce guys."

Dr. Goldberg: "Nowadays, guys like it when an attractive woman seems to have a career she loves."

Duke: "But after they marry or get committed, they hear, 'I'm really starting to feel unhappy with my job; it's so cutthroat,' or 'I'm not feeling fulfilled at work anymore.'"

Dr. Goldberg: "By then the guy feels like he has to support her in 'her new dream' even though he's pissed because he thought he was getting an equal partner, not a dependent wife."

The Insight Explained

The new ideal for women is higher education and a high-paying career. But that doesn't always feel as good as they'd hoped. It's like guys who try to be househusbands and stay-at-home dads. Taking on a nontraditional role puts them at odds with the deeper pull toward "being somebody" in the eyes of the world, and they have trouble feeling okay about themselves. It's hard for both men and women to transcend their earlier conditioning after the initial high of taking on liberated attitudes.

What a Woman Can Do

It's understandable that women, as a result of centuries of conditioning encouraging them to be mothers and homemakers, would struggle with conflict and image concerns as they invested themselves heavily in careers and earning significant incomes. However, many men today want to be involved with women who won't make them feel responsible for support and their well-being. They have been burned and are wary of women who do an about-face and go from assertively pursuing their work passion to losing their career energy and expecting the man to remain enthusiastic and stimulated by a relationship in which a partner who had once been vibrant becomes a stay-at-home kind of person. When children are involved, the man then finds himself in a double bind—still expected to be the provider, yet required to make his marriage and family a priority.

While women are sincere in their initial desire for a successful career, it often turns out to be more of an intellectually ideal "you can have it all" fantasy than something that actually feels good when it becomes a reality. When the opportunity presents itself, they may walk away from careers they spent years working for.

What a Man Must Do

Encouraging women who are ambitious and focused on climbing the success and financial ladder will benefit women and men alike.

In years past, the powerful and success-driven male was envied and seen by women as privileged. Women felt they were left out of the alluring world of power and money. What was rarely noted was the huge price men paid for their success in their personal lives, family relations, health, and the continual stress experienced as a result of "living that dream."

As more women take on the same pursuit, the stressful realities of "making it" in the competitive world will be recognized. That will level the playing field emotionally, and there more likely will be empathy in a realistic appraisal of what climbing the ladder of success actually entails. Men and women will learn that the price for the success trip is high.

The more men and women function equally in all areas of life, the more empathy and compassion for each other's experience will occur. Men must welcome that as necessary for creating the foundation of truly equal male-female relationships that are devoid of ugly accusations and distortions.

INSIGHT 55: THE PRICE OF POWER IS PERSONAL

The person who pursues power must sacrifice the quality, depth, and intensity of their personal life. Some men and women don't know what they are getting into when they take high-powered jobs. They may feel lonely or unrewarded. They may start to feel as though they are missing out on something better.

The Conversation

Benjamin was an entrepreneur who, at forty-eight, was on the cutting edge of developing state-of-the-art video games that were tie-ins to large-budget action movies. As his company became increasingly successful, he was too busy for most of his hobbies, no longer indulging his passion for collecting country-western records and Civil War books. He felt increasingly trapped, bored, and lonely. He had recently begun an affair with a college graduate of twenty-three, realizing it could lead to the end of his twenty-two years of marriage. "I was looking to breathe new life and energy into myself, but knew I was just shooting myself in the foot," he said.

He had started his company with his wife as a partner. After running the company with him for seven years, she decided it really wasn't what she wanted, and so she quit to "raise their young son." "I was jealous and angry," he said, "because I would have liked to do the same thing but felt I didn't have the option. I guess I should have communicated my feelings to her."

Benjamin: "My wife used to complain about the conspiracy by men to keep women out of power positions."

Dr. Goldberg: "The real problem for women is usually that they find out it's not what they thought it would be at the top of the ladder. Working constantly to hold on to a position of power is stressful. Women who scratch and fight their way to the top on their own discover how hard it is to hold on to what they have. Many of them stay single and childless and later regret it. Many women have told me it wasn't worth it, but they realized it too late."

The Insight Explained

Power is not simply a gift given to those who work hard and deserve it. Power must be fought for and requires enormous energy, cold manipulation, and obsessive goal focus to acquire and hold on to. Women may try to retain a more feminine style and way of being, but it's hard to do. Power is the reward for being fiercely competitive, goal focused, and manipulative. Eventually that grates against their core needs to the point at which it sometimes sickens them and they leave.

What a Woman Can Do

Women are increasingly learning about the price of achieving success and power in our society. Prior to feminism, many women assumed men were leading interesting, exciting lives in the work world. That image of men, however, left out the psychological price men paid for their ambitions, competitiveness, and aggressive pursuit of success.

In recent years, as women pursued similar goals, they discovered that the glories of success and power were not what they had imagined. If nothing else, the changes that have occurred in the economic environment will help women understand that there was a major price paid by not only men who ambitiously pursued the brass ring but also the women who chose to commit themselves to and marry ambitious professional men. They pay the equivalent price of the success-driven man who focuses his attention and energy on maintaining his position: energy is withdrawn from his personal life, and his partner may feel abandoned and unvalued, often believing he is purposely choosing to make her second to his ambitions.

Success in any field has to be fought for. It doesn't just happen to the lucky few. To be successful, one must override personal needs that get in the way. It's not just lonely at the top but also cold.

What a Man Must Do

As increasing numbers of women pursue positions of power, they are beginning to realize what men have known all along. The day-to-day reality of being in a position of power is stressful and isolating, and it tends to throw a person's personal life out of balance.

Men married to or dating a woman in a position of power will learn what women in the past have always known. Their partners are often preoccupied, on overload, moody, workaholic, and generally stressed out. Women of power require the same noncomplaining support that tradition-al wives of the past provided for their husbands.

Men must also be prepared to deal with the fact that, particularly when there are children involved, some women of power may begin to express dissatisfaction and unhappiness with their jobs. There will be the clear possibility that such wives will want to abandon their careers.

Dealing with a woman of power will not prove to be a free ride for her partner. Midlife is when a career crisis may likely occur. Men need to be prepared, personally and professionally, for that eventuality.

Being with a woman in a powerful career, however, also provides a man with the opportunity to put his focus on making the family life a priority and allows him to become the support system for his wife, rather than being the primary provider. When increasing numbers of men do that, it will, in the long run, contribute to the rebalancing of male and female roles and provide greater opportunities for both men and women to develop greater empathy for each other's experience by walking in each other's shoes.

7

AND SPEAKING OF SEX . . .

It's hard to fathom that something often acknowledged to be one of the deepest pleasures a person can have could also be the source of so much frustration, anxiety, and fear, with the power to destroy relationships and lives.

Sexually dysfunctional men, particularly men with the unfortunate label of impotence, become obsessive about their erections. After experiencing the initial anxiety and perhaps panic over a disruption of their performance, if they can't resume performing to their ego's satisfaction, they typically become obsessed, depressed, and even suicidal in response to their "dysfunction." They feel they have lost their manhood. Despair and shame sap their energy and may bring on a sense of hopelessness about ever being able to perform again. Before the advent of Viagra-type drugs, men who lost their sexual abilities, particularly if it happened soon after marriage or a liaison with a beautiful woman they had lusted for, were known to experience what psychiatry used to call "homosexual panic"—the fear that one was not really "a man" and therefore unworthy of living. Homosexual panic could lead to suicide if untreated because the fear and anxiety were so severe and overwhelming.

Sexual conquest and getting a woman naked used to be the Holy Grail for men. They thought about and pursued it obsessively and relentlessly. When they succeeded at getting it, particularly from a woman they had fantasized about and craved, the experience could bring them higher than any drug. Not so in today's world—not since feminism liberated women's sexuality. Men found their excitement in the chase and the conquest but weren't prepared to relate to a woman whose desires and needs were as clearly expressed as their own. Much of what in the past had created men's obsessive sexual preoccupation was that women didn't seem to want it, so it was in short supply. Their sexual excitement was based on overcoming her resistance and "scoring." When that element was no longer there and women actively pursued sex, expressing their needs explicitly, what in the past had been pleasure and release became a threat and source of anxiety. The challenge went from getting sex to satisfying her needs.

The modern, younger man, in order to restore the distance and objectification of the unavailable woman, may turn to pornography or other vehicles of erotic fantasy to ignite his desire. Consequently, pornography has become omnipresent, mainstream, and the most popular download option on the Internet.

Traditional men, in the days before feminism liberated women's sexuality, pursued sex with their wives, partners, or dates on a regular basis because sex was resisted. Most traditional women of the past were reluctant and hesitant to display any overt sexual interest, even when they wanted sex, for fear of sullying their feminine image. Before feminism, few women knew or expected orgasms. Most women rarely masturbated, were shy about exposing or exploring their own bodies, and often found excuses to avoid the anxiety and conflicts of sex entirely.

For most prefeminism women, particularly those who were raised conservatively or with religious values that repressed any overt sexual interest, sex was a source of fear and even revulsion. Most traditional men had little knowledge of or interest in providing what a woman needed in order to relax enough to enjoy sex. Men were penis, orgasm, and self-centered about the act itself and out of touch with, disinterested in, and ignorant about the woman's experience. Even if they were interested in learning, their conditioning had made them incapable of satisfying a woman's needs. Being out of touch with much of their personal side, men lacked the ability to be sensually playful, emotionally and verbally communicative, and empathetic about their partner's experience. Grandmas had commonly taught young girls that sex was largely there for men's pleasure, and for women it was a tool or even a weapon of control or power, and young girls were advised not to give it away too easily. It was their primary bargaining chip.

While sex has become readily available, it is still a problematic experience and a major source of confusion and frustration today. In spite of liberation, men and women have different sexual agendas. For many men, sex does not mean or lead to intimate bonding or a desire for extended closeness. To the chagrin and pain of many women, men may lose interest in any other closeness or way of relating after they get the sex they pursued. After orgasm, inwardly they've already left. For most women, however, sex triggers desires for more closeness, love, and even commitment. Some contemporary women may learn to be as sexually opportunistic and compartmentalized as men, but these women are still in the minority and the behavior is usually transitory.

Many men today, even with all the exposure to sexual conversation and dialogue, continue to be unsatisfying lovers for women. It is not intentional selfishness but a lack of growth and fluidity that would allow them to overcome inavoulfno limitations in sensuality and emotional communication. They are, by and large, silent-sex, not intimacy-focused, partners. They just want to be serviced. They want the sex act to be about orgasm and excitement rather than a vehicle for the expression of affection and emotional closeness. We see more and more women turning to other women for the gratification of personal and sensual needs they can't seem to get from men. The label of lesbianism seems inappropriate and meaningless in these experiences. Women are simply looking for satisfaction and the understanding of their needs that men are unwilling or incapable of fulfilling.

What starts off as an exciting and ultimate adventure between a man and a woman often bogs down quickly as the conflicting needs and realities of each other's personalities transform the bed into a battleground and source of stress. Whose needs will be met? What can safely be revealed? Does the other person understand or care enough to make the effort? What are each person's hang-ups or dysfunctions, and how will those become impediments? Are their expectations in sync? And in today's world, can two driven, ambitious, and self-focused individuals maintain a satisfying sex life? Can they safely reveal themselves and not turn the other person off when they do?

The sexual experience drives too many couples into hiding. Rather than enlarging the relationship, it constricts and damages it. It makes liars, cheats, and fakes out of partners even when each initially has the deepest desires to hold on to and grow their love. The sexual journey is filled with hazards. It is not for the timid. However, truly person-to-person sex, rather than self-centered or objectified fantasy sex, has the greatest potential for revealing the deepest truths about both the individual partners and the relationship itself. It is a pathway toward an authentic and satisfying connection, but, if mismanaged, it can become a perennial nightly torture chamber that will poison and often bring an end to a relationship.

The message is simple: The idea of sex may be exciting and fantastic. However, the moment-to-moment reality of sex involves a complex connection between two people who bring different capacities for closeness and communication to the experience. Sex does not have a life of its own. It is an experience shaped uniquely by the personalities of the woman and man in bed together. It can only be what we make it to be. By itself, and without effort and caring, it can quickly fade into nothingness or become a source of conflict, struggle, and pain.

INSIGHT 56: WHEN SHE SAYS HE'S HER BEST LOVER EVER

When a woman says a man is the best lover she's ever had, his ego may be being manipulated. Sexual excitement comes from a woman's feelings and fantasies, not from a man's so-called prowess. Therefore, comparing men to one another is misleading and manipulative.

The Conversation

In a therapy group for divorced and single men, it often struck me how most men were unable to correctly understand and interpret women's sexual response. Men's biggest block or "enemy" once again turns out to be the male ego, which leads men to believe somehow they act or are perceived differently or uniquely in comparison to other men. A woman who tells a man he's her best lover ever is actually comparable to the man who tells a woman she is the most beautiful or her eyes or skin are the loveliest he's ever seen. At the moment men or women make extravagant comparisons, they may very well mean them, but it is an "in the moment" comment, made because of excitement, or something they routinely say to make their partners feel good, endear themselves, and achieve their goals.

Alan was a divorced social worker of forty-two.

Alan: "I knew this woman who talked about some married guy who was her lover. She'd talk about the great orgasms she'd have with him and how innovative and exciting their sex life was. Months later, she revealed that he'd never even gotten it up with her. I was dumbfounded when she told me that just being with him got her wet. She barely noticed his lack of an erection."

Dr. Goldberg: "Then there are the guys who think they've just had the greatest sex ever because they stayed hard for hours and ejaculated several times. They're shocked when the woman cuts off the relationship soon after and shows no interest in having more sex, because they're sure no man could ever match their performance in bed, and positive she'll come after them because she'll miss it. That doesn't happen. Clearly, the 'great' sex was experienced as something completely different by her."

Alan: "In most surveys, when guys are asked to rate themselves as lovers, the majority say better than average."

Dr. Goldberg: "These are the same guys some women say are clueless or disappointing in bed when the women are talking among themselves."

Alan: "That's why when a guy tells me about some woman he went to bed with who said she had the best sex with him ever, I think to myself, 'Yeah, right!'"

The Insight Explained

While for most men great sex has to do with how many times they come, how many different and exotic things they did in bed, or how many times they got her off, most women have a different standard. To them, being in love with a man and feeling he really returns that love and is sensitive to their feelings and needs is what great sex is all about, not techniques or positions. However, most women know that many men have a lot of ego involvement when it comes to sex, so they'll compliment a guy on how great a lover he is. But he better not put too much stock in that because a week later her feelings might change, and she may have no interest in making love with him again.

What a Woman Can Do

Particularly when a man is interested in and attracted to a woman, positive remarks about his lovemaking are likely to be interpreted by him to mean she's bonding with him and will, at the least, want to experience more sex with him. To many men, warm compliments about their sexual prowess have a similar impact as a man expressing ardent romantic feelings and a desire for closeness and commitment have on most women.

Many women already know and understand the power of their sexuality, particularly if the man is really interested in them. They choose to use that power in different ways. However, women who are uncertain about their interest or enthusiasm for a man need to understand that such compliments may create an intense response or connection—even an obsessive interest and fixation—to her on the man's part.

When most women talk about "great sex," they're usually talking about feelings of being in love. Rarely are they speaking of sex as a compartmentalized and gymnastic experience. A woman's feelings are what make the sex feel great. When most men talk about great sex, it's usually about the sex itself. The only time a man can be sure of what a woman means when she says he was "the greatest" in bed is when that sex came along with the equivalent intensity of love, security, and romantic feelings between them. "Great sex" by her definition, however, may not feel that great to him.

What a Man Must Do

Men must understand that when it comes to sex, a woman's experience and that which produces her feelings of excitement and satisfaction are significantly different than for a man.

While it may be validating for a man to hear his partner say he is the best lover she's ever had, the definition of "best lover" is much different for women than it is for men and it is therefore useful for a man to ask his partner what she means—his performance, the way he communicates, his sensitivity to her experience, the fact that he's especially romantic and takes time to satisfy her, or that he verbally expresses his feelings of love and closeness?

A man should also know that just because a woman says a man is her best lover ever, it may not even mean she will want to continue to have sex with him in the future just for the pleasure of it if the relationship apart from the sex doesn't continue to develop.

INSIGHT 57: THE BEST SEX

Trust and attraction are the two basic components of optimal sex. When both exist, the body relaxes and responds at its maximum capacity.

The Conversation

I put emphasis on the term *sex problems* because I personally don't believe most men have them. What they have is a fear of their feelings, painful and seemingly irresolvable conflicts, and a masculine compulsion problem, all of which block, interfere with, and in some cases destroy their ability to make the connection between (1) who they are as a person, (2) how they're feeling in a relationship, (3) the nature of their connection to their partner or mate, and (4) their sexual response. For men to label their sexual response in a negative way is a form of self-hate and rejection. Women don't do that because their egos and self-esteem are not tied up with their ability to perform sexually.

The upside to a man's so-called sexual dysfunction is that it really impacts him, and unless he simply solves it chemically by taking medication, the "dysfunction" arouses anxiety and unpleasant, depressive feelings that might lead him to reach out for help when nothing else would.

Faustus, a computer repairman at twenty-nine, illustrates the issue:

Faustus: "Sometimes I'm with a beautiful woman in bed and I can't seem to get it up. I beat myself up for the lost opportunity and question my virility and sexuality."

Dr. Goldberg: "Lots of guys go through that. They believe because a pretty woman is willing to go to bed with them, a 'real man' should

get excited and aroused. They don't believe sex is connected to feelings or has anything to do with the state of the relationship and the
level of safety and trust they feel."

Faustus: "I don't think that deeply about sex. If I've got a hard-on, I
don't question it. If I don't get hard, I put myself down and obsess
about it. I start to think maybe I'm really gay, or I'll never get hard
again. Then it's panic time."

Dr. Goldberg: "If men could get past that male ego hang-up, their
bodies could be a good barometer of their relationship feelings and a
guide to how they are really feeling. You can't have sex with a woman
you don't trust or to whom you're not attracted without your body
resisting. You may think you want to, but your body's lack of response is telling you otherwise. It's really self-protection, but most
men are too hung up to respect their deeper self giving them messages
about how they really feel. They want that erection at all costs."

The Insight Explained

The masculine compulsion to perform sexually in order to feel like a man
overrides the inner wisdom of the body that knows when a woman is right
for him. Once a man transcends masculine compulsions, recognizing
himself as a person with feelings and not a performing machine, his body
will guide him. If he's truly attracted and he feels safe with the woman
because she's not carrying an agenda that may potentially hurt or endan-
ger him, the sexual response will be there.

What a Woman Can Do

Part of a man's preoccupation and distress when he doesn't perform well
sexually is due to his belief that he will disappoint his woman partner,
that his image as a man will be tarnished, his masculinity put in question,
and he will be rejected because of it, or the fear that he'll never be normal
again. The reality might be quite the opposite. A man's sexual dysfunction can be the potential start of recapturing his personhood—a new
awareness that his penis is not a disembodied piece of machinery, and
that he's a person with feelings and rhythms just like the woman. Women

who understand that would even applaud a man's dysfunction as a sign of the man's personhood emerging, which may allow him to begin to accept himself and lead him to a path where he can discover his true sexuality, not the defensive one in which he believes his penis should always rise to the occasion. Thus, a man's so-called sexual dysfunction can become the beginning of his growing humanness in the relationship and a step leading to an intimacy that would be pleasurable and fulfilling.

In general, men have been damaged sexually by correlating their performance with their self-esteem. The more this unfortunate equation exists for them, the more men will lose touch with the deeper wisdom of their feelings and bodies. When a woman is right for a man, his body will know it and respond accordingly. If there's something "wrong" between them, his body may balk, as it should. A healthy man will appreciate the speed bump his body provides. A defensive man will try to fight the body's resistance, but to his own disservice.

What a Man Must Do

For a man to actually experience the "best sex" for not just himself but also his partner, he must grow beyond the defensive masculine definition of great sex as meaning exotic positions, a prolonged erection, or adventurous experimentation.

Men must know that "best sex" that is not just for the moment requires building a relationship of transparency, authenticity, and great communication. It does not mean sex for thrills, but rather involves sex as an outgrowth of the enjoyment of each other's physical closeness. Once that is created, "best sex" can take many forms and definitions, will be different for each couple, and will be an extension and expression of the whole relationship.

INSIGHT 58: DO YOU THINK SHE'S SEXY?

When women dress or act sexy, it doesn't mean they really want or even like sex. It only means they're exploiting the power they know their sexuality affords them. Authentically sexual women don't need to dress or act "sexy."

The Conversation

Just as authentically generous men with positive self-esteem don't need to flaunt their wealth or success symbols to capture a woman's interest, women who are genuinely comfortable with their sexuality and value themselves as people don't need to use or emphasize their sexuality in order to draw a man's attention. Unfortunately, many men translate a sexy display by a woman as meaning she wants him to make a sexual advance.

Steve, who at twenty-two was a sexually preoccupied man, almost destroyed his promising career as a dental technician by misreading the motives of a newly hired receptionist in his office toward whom he had made a physical advance. His employer managed to defuse the potentially litigious and explosive situation by getting Steve to agree to get counseling and gender-sensitivity training as a condition for keeping his job. He explained this during our first session.

> *Steve*: "I always assumed when a woman dressed really sexy, her breasts practically hanging out, it meant she was looking to get laid. I learned a lesson the hard way when I made a pass at this woman who was totally flaunting it."
>
> *Dr. Goldberg*: "I wonder if women are really clueless about men's responses to them when they expose their bodies in sexy ways. Do they know what they're doing, and what kind of reaction they trigger?"
>
> *Steve*: "It can be dangerous in this day and age to not read a woman correctly. You'll find yourself accused of being inappropriate or harassing her, and it could ruin your life."

The Insight Explained

Dressing sexy for a woman is no more an indication of her actually feeling sexy than driving an expensive car is an indication that a man likes spending money on women. Women know the power their sexuality gives them. Therefore, dressing sexy and actually being or feeling sexy are not necessarily connected.

What a Woman Can Do

While it seems a man is disrespecting and being inappropriately aggressive and harassing when he makes a sexual advance in response to seeing a woman dressed in a sexually stimulating way, the man's motive may be opposite to what a woman may initially believe or interpret it to mean. When he is feeling sexually stimulated, he may act personally interested and attracted. It is distressing and unfortunate for both when signals of attraction go way off course and lead to negative, hostile, and damaging interchanges.

Most men back off when a woman draws a verbal boundary by letting him know clearly when his behavior is making her uncomfortable and upset. They apologize and retreat immediately. Letting a man know he needs serious help in reading and understanding a woman's intentions would also be appropriate.

What a Man Must Do

Sex is men's weak link. Men have a potential for damaging and even destroying the life they have worked hard to create by letting themselves be controlled by their sexual impulses. Jokes about a man's brain being in his penis are a truth that men must come to grips with.

Because most men unknowingly objectify women, attracted to them based primarily on their physical attributes, men must get in touch with what they are doing to themselves when they pursue a woman because she looks and dresses "sexy." Does it mean she loves and wants sex because she dresses that way? Of course not, and men reveal their lack of understanding of women by equating sexy attire and demeanor with an appetite and desire for sex she probably doesn't have. Most women can have pretty much all the sex they want regardless of how they are dressed. The woman who dresses in a way that men read as being sexy more likely is using sexual attraction to draw a man into a relationship.

Pursuing a woman for sex because she is dressed sexy means a man is objectifying her, and it is as much a turn off to a woman as a man feels when a woman is attracted to him because he is wealthy.

Men are vulnerable to life-damaging misjudgments when they pursue a woman based on her sexy appearance, and they put themselves in danger of behaving inappropriately by misreading her intentions.

Authentic sexual pleasure with a woman comes from having an attraction to her as a total person. Sex, when engaged in with a woman based on her "sexy" appearance, will at best be a limited and disappointing experience and at worst create a nightmare scenario.

INSIGHT 59: POTENTIAL FOR RELATIONSHIP DYSFUNCTION

A man who is immediately sexually obsessive with a woman and a woman who obsesses about the closeness and intimacy potential with a man she has spent little time with are polarized. The relationship is already in trouble.

The Conversation

A woman's immediate focus on a man's status or position and a man's focus on a woman's appearance, body, and smile create a powerful initial chemistry. This exciting beginning also creates a major obstacle to developing intimacy and a relationship based on genuine mutual knowing, liking, and caring.

Dave, an affluent, middle-aged owner of a chain of high-end furniture showrooms, found himself repeating the progression of intense romantic beginnings that start with mutual objectification. He was the wealthy, successful, aggressive businessman, while the woman became the beautiful, sexy trophy to be won and displayed. After dozens of these intense beginnings and endings, he became cynically entrenched in his bachelor ways, realizing he was lost and couldn't find his way out of this pattern by himself.

Dave: "What makes dating and finding a relationship that works such a drag nowadays is that it goes to the bottom line almost immediately. She's sizing me up to see if I'm the committing type, and I'm wondering how soon we'll have sex."

Dr. Goldberg: "It's like a business negotiation disguised as 'looking for love.' No wonder folks are questioning what love really is. There's so little enthusiasm for just getting to know somebody."

Dave: "Most of the time when each person gets what they want, they're not sure they even like the person anymore and they question the relationship. It's like each wanted the 'service' or 'function,' but not the actual person providing it."

The Insight Explained

When men think of sex and women think of commitment immediately after meeting, it's not person to person, it's object to object. They both just want their immediate needs met. Probably each already senses they're not really interested in getting to know the other person as a person. Even if they hang on for a while, the relationship will be painful because the choice was not based on knowing and liking the other person, it was based on using them. It makes a mockery of the goal of intimacy.

What a Woman Can Do

It's a seductive trap that has brought down the biggest "winners" of our society; specifically, the men with seemingly irresistible symbols of power and success and the women with the power their physical and social attractiveness provides. Few people want to acknowledge and experience the hard work and many stops and starts that are part of developing an authentic relationship experience. Most seem to repeat the pattern of hot beginnings and painful endings. Breaking that cycle is like tackling an addiction because of the resistance one feels toward giving it up. However, the earlier in life one recognizes this tendency in oneself, the more likely the loving, truly committed relationships most of us want can actually be created.

A polarized relationship is one that is essentially defensive. Neither person really likes the other; they just need the other to fill a significant lack inside themselves. The resulting relationship is shallow and brittle. Animosity lies just underneath the surface and erupts readily. Arguments and ugly fights are easily triggered. Polarized relationships are exercises in intimate terrorism and cannot be improved because neither really likes nor wants to know the other as a person.

What a Man Must Do

Men must learn to translate the language of sexual communication in order to avoid entering into a destructive relationship. When a man is strongly attracted to a woman as a person and potential partner, sexual attraction may be a part of that attraction, but it is not the principal motive. When there is little to no substance to the attraction and a man is bored or mainly interested in a woman to satisfy his sexual needs, his thoughts and focus will turn to sex quickly and obsessively when he is with her, and after sex he will withdraw and want to leave.

Similarly, when a woman's preoccupation and agenda soon after meeting a man involves commitment for a long-term relationship and marriage and she pursues that obsessively, it says she is not attracted to him for who he is as a person but for what she needs from him. Commitment, when it is a woman's obsessive focus early on in a relationship rather than something that emerges slowly and is a natural by-product of a loving connection, while it may seem flattering to an insecure or needy man, indicates that the woman is with him to satisfy her needs for security, not because of the loving feelings she has for him.

Men and women who talk to each other almost immediately upon meeting about sex—for example, "Do you enjoy sex?"—or about commitment—"How ready are you to settle down?"—are signaling a lack of genuine interest in each other as people and viewing each other primarily as candidates to fill an immediate need.

8

THE FAMILY EXPERIENCE

Marriage and family are the ultimate in creating psychological complexity. They are at the core of our profoundest emotions— from deep gratification and joy to intense disappointment and despair.

In spite of the hazardous family journey and experience, driven by multiple layers of each player's personal history and unknowing motives, we tend to believe that if our hearts are in the right place and love is regularly expressed, we can get it right. The shattering of that dream involves a belief and fantasy that won't die. In few arenas is the distressing reality of how one can seem to do everything right yet have it come out all wrong more apparent. Modern dads who do it by the book and make fathering a major priority often still find themselves alienated, disliked, and unable to communicate with their own children. Moms who exude love and who adore and sacrifice for their children may still watch them grow up to be withdrawn, angry, and lost. Parenting, like love and marriage, is an area in which most people believe they know how to do it right, so they resist doing the necessary personal growth work. The painful awakening doesn't come until after the cement of family dysfunction has dried and a sledgehammer is required to make even a small indentation.

I need to share a bias, which comes from forty-plus years in the psychological trenches with parents and families: my belief that it is primarily the family that shapes a child's personality. Most parents, however, don't see the damage they do because the human ego has powerful defenses of denial and repression to protect each person's righteous beliefs, so they blame the children for the problems and behaviors that parents object to but helped create. As a psychotherapist, and as someone who has worked with numerous families and lived through intense family pain myself as a child, there is little that makes me wince and shudder more than when parents, particularly fathers who lack the gift of empathy, criticize and severely punish the behaviors and traits in their children that are a direct result and outgrowth of their parenting. This seems to be most true where the children have serious emotional and psychological problems and dysfunctions.

Family therapy is a complex and often treacherous process. Effective therapy of any kind requires that the patient or client experience and express suppressed, painful, and angry emotions. Parents who pay the bills for children in therapy often object and become threatened when children begin to assert their real feelings, with behavior characterized by rebelliousness, hostility, and a rejection of and healthy movement away from the family nest. When anger at the parents begins to emerge in a child's therapy, the parent's response is often "My child is getting worse and out of control because of this therapy," and they terminate the process. The parents want the child's improvement, but not if it in any way threatens their control. It's similar to how husbands react when their oppressively dependent wives gain strength as a result of therapy and begin to function autonomously, while the husband, who is paying the bill, loses control and power. He will claim she is getting worse and pressure her and the therapist to stop the sessions.

There is so much to understand and explore regarding the family experience, but to me the most important family phenomenon to understand is that healthy families are not simply the result of doing everything right and obsessively worrying about every word or action. The so-called perfect family environment, with seemingly perfect boys and girls, often creates severe dysfunctions in the children when they grow up. The Ozzie and Harriet Nelson family of television's yesteryears illustrates this well. The golden boy/son Ricky Nelson grew up to become a deeply troubled, angry, and dysfunctional drug addict. Many all-American boys and girls from "perfect families" similarly grew up to become deeply troubled, unhappy adults.

What, then, is the best we can hope for in creating the happy family experience? A true measure of the happy family is a child's ability to communicate the full range of emotions and thoughts without being shamed or blocked. Second is developing a realistic and positive sense of self that happens when children are not given an inflated, grandiose sense of self from parents who needed to make them feel they were the "smartest, prettiest, most talented" children in the world because of the parents' own need for ego validation. *A grounded child with a realistic and healthy sense of self who can express the gamut of feelings, thoughts, and interests, and who is also provided support for separating from family to become an autonomous, nonfearful adult, is the recipe for the happy child from the happy family.*

Finally, the "secret" of creating a happy family is growth, openness, and nondefensiveness, with the parents serving as the role models. As one psychologist friend so aptly put it, "No matter how much you try to teach your children table manners, they'll still grow up and eat the way you do."

INSIGHT 60: THE HAPPY FAMILY FANTASY

The so-called blissful, happy families of old generated the many people today who remember their childhoods as having been painful, with their families as hotbeds of dysfunction and their parents as people who should never have been or stayed together.

The Conversation

So many people are tortured by the fantasy that others have had blissful, happy childhood experiences, so why not them? In fact, even the best of marriages and families suffer the consequences of socializing and compartmentalizing male and female to become polar opposites—aggressive performers and selfless nurturers.

Saul, an elderly married magazine writer and publisher, was haunted by the notion that he had "screwed up" his family and witnessed serious unhappiness between his own parents when he was growing up. After months of counseling, he realized his experience resembled most others.

Saul: "One by one, celebrities are talking about their memories of a painful family life growing up—alcoholism, depression, sexual abuse, neglect, harsh criticism, and abandonment. It's the same for most

people. Happy memories of childhood are rare. Celebrities acknowledging their painful early experience of dysfunction are helping people realize that, openly dispelling the notion that some are just lucky to
have been raised in a happy family."

Dr. Goldberg: "And many others who remember their childhoods positively grow up to be dysfunctional anyway, with addictions, broken
relationships, and lack of direction in their lives, and are unaware of
the destructive things that damaged their development."

Saul: "Women remember sexual abuse, men remember angry, unavailable, and critical fathers. Both remember mothers who were depressed, crazy, sick all the time, or just plain miserable. They think
they're revealing something unique, as if their experiences were so
much worse than other people's. The traditional happy family seems
like a cruel mirage."

Dr. Goldberg: "The good part about surfacing the memories is it starts
to debunk false illusions and look at what really goes on. Most parents
start off thinking they'll be different and better than their parents, then
wind up losing their way. Or maybe they're trying to achieve the
impossible. When so many well-intended, educated, sincere people try
and fail, it's time to penetrate the façade and illuminate and make
sense of what we're all up against."

Saul: "I hardly know anyone from intact families who feels their parents were good for each other or made each other happy. More often
it's 'I wish they had gotten divorced. They were a mismatch. They just
didn't like each other.'"

Dr. Goldberg: "Plus over 50 percent of those parents divorced, often
leading to multiple marriages. That can never feel very good for kids.
The failure seems to be built into the gender socialization process of
men and women."

The Insight Explained

Happy or fulfilled traditional marriages and families only seem to work if
people replace their immediate feelings and needs with external structure

in the form of ritualized activities. Living with clear role boundaries for male and female makes things a lot simpler, but the price for living up to the role of the traditional man and woman is too great. When people from these families remember their childhoods positively, it's usually because they're not looking very deeply or they don't know the truth of what their parents' experience was.

What a Woman Can Do

The traditional way of interpreting family dysfunction is viewing it as a dynamic between an emotionally unavailable and critical man and an overly accommodating female partner with poor boundaries who was unassertive, allowed herself to be mistreated, and became depressed. Connecting the dots backward to its origin, that dysfunctional dynamic began in the romance between an alpha male and a woman who was romantically "swept away" and fell in love with him.

Women and men are equal players in laying the foundation for the downfall of the "happy family fantasy," and therefore the remedy lies equally on both of their shoulders. Much progress will be made in family life once people take a closer look at what their socialization has taught them to be, and how that undermines their quest for a fulfilling relationship. Acknowledging the unhappiness that existed at home is a major first step out of denial and into the growth needed to make change.

What a Man Must Do

The notion of the happy family is a seductive but potentially misleading fantasy. The word *family* itself is actually an abstraction that conjures up ideas and feelings about what ideally *should be* rather than what actually is. The often-repeated sentiment that family is the most important thing we have and we should cherish and hold family close means the reality of our family experience will be distorted by guilt, "shoulds," and "have to's." Men shouldn't allow feelings of guilt and responsibility to derail them from realizing how their family experience actually is and makes them feel, how family members really see and relate to them, and the kind of emotional environment that exists.

Men must realize that having and being a part of family is not an assurance of love and closeness. To create and become part of a happy family requires a high degree of emotional health and an ability to relate and communicate in a healthy way. Just being a part of a family, especially if a man participates and relates minimally, will not be a protection against a lonely old age and isolation. Unhappy families are worse than being alone.

INSIGHT 61: WHY FATHERS' LOVE GETS LOST

Men learn the hard way that their children will not bond with or love them because they are good providers. Children don't understand that providing is the way dads show their love.

The Conversation

Like so many other fathers, Marlon received his rude awakening within a year after he divorced the mother of his two young sons. Though he was an acknowledged workaholic, he also worked hard at male bonding activities with his sons, coaching their soccer team and taking them to automobile shows and car races. He was confident that his connection to them was solid, even stronger than the one they had with their mother. It was a profoundly painful shock when they chose to live with her and within a year became attached to her new fiancé. They grew resistant to being with him on the days the custody agreement called for. Holidays were the real wake-up call, when both sons said they wanted Thanksgiving dinner and Christmas Eve to be at their mother's place. After first blaming his ex for brainwashing and poisoning his relationship with them, Marlon began to see the futility of that victim interpretation and instead started to take responsibility for his relationship with them as it actually was.

> *Marlon*: "When I became a father I was proud of providing well for my wife and children financially because I worked my fool head off. My wife complained that I was rarely home, but I assumed my noble intentions would garner me understanding, love, and appreciation. But just like for my dad, it turned out badly for me."

> *Dr. Goldberg*: "Most guys today start off their family lives committed to being involved and caring fathers but eventually become just like

their fathers, always tired, preoccupied, emotionally disconnected, and busy. Or they lose enthusiasm and interest in their family because their marriage is falling apart and they're disappointed in how their kids are turning out. They stop trying to stay actively involved. The bitter lesson comes at divorce time."

Marlon: "I could see how dysfunctional my father was, but I guess I've been in denial about the ways I was like him, if not worse."

Dr. Goldberg: "That should help men stop blaming and being angry at their own fathers. Most fathers start off with the best intentions, convinced that because they 'bring home the bacon,' their families will understand and love them for that. Instead, they get a grudging appreciation. In the process, their connection to their kids gets thin or disappears altogether. The last illusion to fall is their belief that they've done the right thing by their wives, who they believe will love them for that. When the kids grow up and leave the nest, often it turns out wives want to leave as well, or they stay but are unhappy being alone with him again."

The Insight Explained

The traditional family dynamic where the father is the doer and provider has its own inevitable, self-defeating endpoints. Kids relate in an immediate way to their experience. They don't abstract. If Mom is home preparing meals and giving them attention and comfort and help while Dad is distracted, withdrawn, tense, and irritated, the kids will go by their feelings. It doesn't feel good to be around Dad. They may even dislike him. Few people have loving memories of their fathers or feel they even knew them. Consequently, when fathers die, few tears are shed. Their feelings rarely equal the pain and trauma children experience over the loss of the mother.

What a Woman Can Do

Raising children is not a power struggle between a "woman's way" and a "man's way." The kind of empathy, nurturing, and in-the-moment connection that allows children to feel close seems built in to the way most women relate, while for success-driven men, that capacity to develop closeness with their children has to be worked at, slowly gained, and vigilantly sustained because it is fragile and runs counter to the kind of competitive and detached relating pattern men develop. Women who have as their goal preserving their family intact need to be supportive and understanding of a man's efforts as they try to parent counter to their conditioning.

Increasingly, men are realizing there's something wrong with the family picture when it comes to being the diligent providers. At best, when a man is successful and generous, his children will come to him for financial support and say, "Thanks, Dad." After they leave home, their children rarely reach out to be with them. *It is perhaps a man's greatest challenge to transform that self-defeating compulsion to be the family hero by being the workaholic provider and believing he will be loved and appreciated for it.*

What a Man Must Do

Deep disappointment and bitterness will be in store for a man who believes he will be appreciated and loved by his wife and children for being a conscientious provider and a responsible dad who participated in his children's school and recreational activities. *A man must understand that what will determine his actual experience as a father is not determined so much by what he does but on how his wife and children actually experience him.*

A woman may appreciate a husband who is faithful, hard working, and responsible, and his children may appreciate him for his material support and advice, but the family's love and connection to him will depend on the quality and kind of bond he creates. Specifically, it will depend on how family members actually feel when they're around him, and what it's like to talk to and spend time with him. Without a personal and comfortable emotional connection, his best efforts and contributions to the family will get lost.

In most homes, the children's primary (and perhaps only) bond will be with their mother, who does not withdraw, intellectualize, lecture, proffer advice, or get easily distracted when communicating. Fathers must grow beyond their mechanical ways that lead family members to conclude, "I don't think I ever really got to know my dad."

INSIGHT 62: SELF-SERVING MOTHER LOVE

Fusion mothering *is when, under the guise of great love, mothers use their children to satisfy their own needs. A fusion mother can be recognized by her undue closeness to her child, where they become as one, and the child's growth away from mother as a separate, healthy adult is impaired or completely blocked.*

The Conversation

In a group of divorced fathers, Nick commented, "How is it that the limitations, deficiencies, and dysfunctions of fathers are so easy to see while it's so hard to recognize dysfunctional mothers? Whatever they do, it always seems to be more loving and positive. Isn't 'too much' mothering as bad as 'too little' fathering?"

Nick: "I was dating a single mother and it seemed like her attention was totally focused on her children. I don't think she was really that interested in me, except maybe to make life easier for her or give her kids a dad."

Dr. Goldberg: "It's a major self-delusion on a woman's part when she says she wants a man in her children's lives. Usually single mothers are territorial when it comes to rearing their kids. Any guy who moves in will find he's a symbolic substitute father at best, there to fulfill her vision of how he should be with her kids. If he has his own ideas, particularly if he thinks she's too involved and protective of them and he wants to have more say in the matter, she'll likely shut him down."

Nick: "You can't say anything about how they're raising their kids. They'll dump you instantly. Certainly, they won't miss the sex, because that's a low priority compared to the pleasure they seem to get from being with their kids."

Dr. Goldberg: "These women find out too late the damage they've done when the kids approach their teens and start going wild or get hostile and act out in a rage, trying to separate from Mom and establish their own identities. It must really hurt these mothers to see the results of having made their kids the center of the universe."

Nick: "My parents never divorced, but my mom lived for us kids too, and none of us have been able to break away and really have a separate, successful life. We still feel we owe her something."

The Insight Explained

Women who are unhappy over the lack of intimacy, romance, and love from their husbands get closer with their children to get those needs met. It looks like "good mothering" to the outside world, but the seeds of an unhealthy attachment are being sown, and the kids never mature enough to separate and become fully functioning adults. They go looking to replicate that closeness with their prospective partners but are left dissatisfied. Or they marry and repeat the cycle of frustration and fusion with their own children.

What a Woman Can Do

When it comes to parenting, women have the kind of power few men can match. Masculine socialization externalizes men so their way of relating works in the competitive marketplace significantly better than in the one-to-one personal connecting children need and are drawn to. Therefore, changes in parenting models that will generate balanced and secure children will require on women's part the same kind of objective scrutiny and evaluation that is brought to men's role as fathers. Women must allow men to communicate what they see and observe without it being construed as criticism or an attack. The woman who lets that happen will reap the benefits of having high-functioning, emotionally healthy children.

Society recognizes the damage done by an absent or abusive father. The emotionally unavailable, critical, and controlling father is a cultural cliché, but society has a blind spot for the virulent counterpart, the damage done by *fusion mothers*, where the mothering gives the appearance of love but is really narcissistic and self-serving. The kids are starving for a healthy love but drowning under the weight of meeting Mom's unhealthy fusion needs.

What a Man Must Do

The increasing contemporary reality of divorces, frustrated wives, unhappy marriages, and single mothers has resulted in creating family environments where fathers are either an absent parent or a detached and disconnected one. Mother's needs and the needs of the children are therefore prone to being fulfilled primarily within the mother-child bond.

This fusion dynamic between a mother and child, with a disconnected father somewhere on the periphery, may have on the surface an appearance of being a loving and close one. The *content* may seem attractive while the *process* ("the how") that describes the fusion is a toxic one. The damage to the child's growth into a healthy, separate adult may not be apparent until the child reaches an age where he needs to separate.

Men must understand that the extent to which they give the raising of their children over to the mother, their children will grow up with significant problems as they struggle to become separate adults.

When divorced fathers become passive parents, children seek out their mothers to fulfill their emotional needs and vice versa. Once the fusion between mother and child is created, men may never again be able to break in and have an emotional bond with their children. However, whatever problems the children will have will be as much a product of his doing and the consequences of his detachment, passivity, and outsider behavior.

To avoid the consequences of self-serving mother love, men must make and continuously nurture their bond with their children. For most men that will probably require professional assistance and a therapeutic commitment to overcoming their mechanical or disconnected tendencies that act as a wall separating them from their children.

INSIGHT 63: ROBO-DADS

The way children bond with and feel toward their fathers has little to do with how good a parent he is, but by what he's like to be with and how it feels to be close to him. Externalized male processes produce "mechanical fathers," who go through the motions of good or even "perfect" fathering, but with an endpoint result no different, if not worse, than had they been indifferent or not present at all.

The Conversation

At thirty-eight, Philip, a sociology professor, was bitter about his experience as a father. When he first became a dad, resolving to make fatherhood a priority, he changed his work schedule, took parenting courses, read books on the subject, and shared equally with his wife the responsibility for day-to-day childcare. The results were disappointing. As his son entered the early teenage years, they barely spoke, and Philip was shocked to discover his son was abusing alcohol and drugs. While he still maintained he was doing the best he could, doubts had begun to creep in as to how he was parenting.

> *Philip*: "My dad was so 'not present' it left me with a lifelong feeling of emptiness and low self-esteem. So I resolved to pay a lot of attention to the kind of dad I would be. I sense there's something wrong. I'm trying to say and do all the right father things, but it doesn't feel like it's working."

> *Dr. Goldberg*: "All your 'perfect fathering behavior' and good intentions may not be getting through to the kids or be enough to create a strong, loving bond. I call 'modern' dads 'mechanical fathers' because their responses seem so programmed, intellectualized, and controlled but not emotionally connected. Underneath it's the same old disconnection as in days gone by. The kids are conflicted, confused, and in a double bind: 'Dad seems to be trying so hard, but I still don't feel as if he cares.' So the kid winds up taking advantage of the dad's need to see himself as a great dad and his overcompensating behavior, and manipulates him because he's such an easy target. Dad's buttons are easy to read. They say, 'Please tell me I'm doing a great job and I'm the world's best dad.'"

> *Philip*: "I wish this weren't resonating with me! I guess I've also found myself feeling pretty smug about how great a job I'm doing. I want to believe I'm coming across differently than my dad did, but maybe I'm just kidding myself."

The Insight Explained

When men consciously set out to design a "good-father strategy" by reading and educating themselves and simply going in the opposite direction of their own dads, rather than growing as people to become nondefensive and nonintellectualized, they often don't see that they are still relating in an externalized, disconnected way, no different than traditional men. All they've changed is their outward behaviors. Sadly, they may incur even greater resentment in their kids. The mechanical father's relationship with his child may be no better than the relationship he had with his own father, whom he remembers so critically.

What a Woman Can Do

Since fathering and coparenting is a fairly recent role change for most men, when making a sustained, conscious effort not to be the workaholic, detached critical father, the results are often disappointing to him, learning that some things can't be easily mastered simply by setting his mind to it. Women can be important to men's efforts at change and growth by helping them learn about themselves, specifically in terms of what their actual impact is and whether what they are doing is or isn't effective.

Healthy fathering involves the capacity for generating a nondefensive, loving, emotional bond. It is not achieved by forcing himself to do or say the right things or merely carving out extended quality time for his children. Most fathers have weak or absent bonds or attachment with their kids but don't see or know it until divorce or when the kids grow up and drift away.

What a Man Must Do

The robo-dad or mechanical father, with whom no bond or deeper emotional connection is possible, from my work and observations as a psychologist, is a common reality. In past generations, children experienced that as a feeling of having no real closeness with their father, even when they may express appreciation of him as a "nice guy."

To understand why and how their connection to their children fails, men must realize no matter how hard they try to become the new kind of loving, empathic father, their deeper externalized, goal-focused, and obsessive, responsibility-oriented, and intellectualized way of being will cause them to be experienced as robotic. They may actually feel an intense love for their children, but that feeling won't be transmitted because of their externalized way of being.

The children may never express it. His wife may hide or cover her frustrations with her husband, but the absence of an enduring bond isn't based on how much time he devotes or the activities he participates in. It is revealed by how the children find it a strain and struggle to communicate with and show love to their father.

INSIGHT 64: A MAN'S BABY BLUES

The new mother whose attention and affection move away from her partner and focus on the baby is like the man who withdraws after sex and turns his attention to the football game on television after he's gotten what he needs.

The Conversation

Carl, a father in his twenties, came for counseling at his wife's insistence when she discovered he'd been spending a great amount of time looking at Internet porn. She felt hurt because it had begun during her pregnancy with their first child, when she was feeling less than sexually desirable and attractive. When it continued after their child was born and she had worked hard at making herself sexually desirable again, she became infuriated and demanded he seek help. Not wanting to lose her, he agreed.

> *Carl*: "I wasn't ready and didn't want to be a father, but I deferred to her pressure. I thought giving in to her desire for a baby would cement our relationship and make her love and appreciate me even more. Man, how that backfired!"

> *Dr. Goldberg*: "It's a rude awakening for many guys when the mother-to-be turns away from them after the baby comes or makes them feel they're selfish and immature for complaining that they don't get enough attention or sex."

The Insight Explained

Once some men get what they want from women, their real feelings come out. If they are just selfishly interacting with her for their own gratification, they withdraw and shut her out until they need her again. A woman may act very loving and caring to a man while she's motivated by a goal, like marriage or children. Once that goal is reached, her attitude may change abruptly, her true feelings emerge, and she may begin to close him off.

What a Woman Can Do

A woman's desire for a child makes it hard for her to know how she really feels toward a man she's decided to marry because he'd be a good father and provider. Men sense the reality of a woman's feeling after she's achieved her goal of becoming a mother, and that may be a factor in their turning to porn as an outlet for their frustration and discontent. A woman who doesn't take as personal rejection his interest in porn after a baby is born can preserve and grow the relationship by not viewing this in a judgmental and harsh way, focusing instead on the underlying feelings she may have communicated toward him that are pushing him away and causing him to seek gratification elsewhere.

What a Man Must Do

The consequence and price of being in an objectified relationship in which a man was chosen because he was "good marriage material" or had "good dad potential" is that once a woman "has gotten what she wants"—namely, marriage and motherhood—she may pull away from her partner and focus almost exclusively on the baby.

In the case of a woman's change of feelings after a baby is born, she may rationalize her loss of sexual interest under the guise that she is experiencing a "mothering instinct." Men are commonly blamed when they fantasize about new sexual partners or have an affair after their partner becomes pregnant or gives birth, and they are told their behavior is a reflection of their immaturity and inability to tolerate their partner's diminished attention. Mutual blaming may occur as each partner is in denial of his or her original, deeper motive.

Men must recognize that they may actually be sensing the unfortunate emergence of their own and their partner's lack of feelings for each other as people.

More important, men must recognize the distressing downside of building a relationship based on objectification, choosing a woman because of her physical attractiveness, and being chosen because of his willingness to be a provider and father a child.

These objectified relationships are relationship nightmares waiting to happen and the ones that can seriously damage (and even destroy) a man's life.

INSIGHT 65: FOODAHOLIC WOMEN

Programs for adult children of alcoholics are everywhere; yet there are no programs for adult children of mothers with food addictions.

The Conversation

Terrence, an attorney who at fifty-five is obese and has a cigarette addiction, came for counseling after experiencing a near fatal heart attack. He'd been in a twelve-step program for alcoholism for ten years. While he stopped drinking, he found himself "always eating," particularly when he felt stressed, which was most of the time. He was always thinking about food and what he would eat for his next meal. Though he was almost one hundred pounds over his ideal weight, he felt like he was starving at mealtimes. He remembered as a young boy growing up that most of the conversations in the house were about money (his dad's concern) and food (his mom's preoccupation). Mealtimes were particularly stressful, with his mother pushing him to eat more while his father said he ate too much. Most discussions seemed to revolve around food, including its expense. "I don't think my mother knew how to relate to us or my dad in any other way besides feeding, and when we didn't eat a meal she prepared, she made us feel guilty." Terrence recognized that he ate and drank not out of hunger or thirst but as a way to reduce his anxiety and inner tension.

Terrence: "As an ex-alcoholic I was always lectured and warned, but I noticed that women who have eating addictions are rarely confronted, probably because they don't cause fights or automobile accidents. They have a lot of health problems, but their disorders aren't noticeably dangerous or destructive to others."

Dr. Goldberg: "That's right. Since everybody eats, addictions to food are rarely recognized, and the impact of those who have them never gets properly explored. Food addictions usually go unidentified by the health care system, except for women with bulimia, anorexia, or other diagnosable eating disorders. These have a negative effect on family members. People with food addictions are like all other addicts: self-absorbed, manipulative, and secretive."

Terrence: "That was my mother. Everything was about eating, dieting, and arguments about that. It had a negative effect on her ability to nurture and take care of us kids the way we needed her to. We had to take on the parent role because Mom was too needy and focused on her preoccupation to mother us right."

Dr. Goldberg: "Whether the addiction is to drugs, gambling, work, food, or whatever, addictions destroy people. Family members suffer. Kids shouldn't be expected to understand their mother's problems. Obesity is rampant, and eating is the way many people structure their lives, entertain themselves, and calm their anxieties. Every other ad on television seems to be about some new food product."

The Insight Explained

It is women who are most likely to have eating disorders. But because food is associated with love, nurturing, pleasure, and celebration, eating disorders are commonly overlooked. Mothers with food hang-ups transfer those obsessions in some form to their children by conveying an inappropriate emphasis on food and eating, along with destructive emotions such as guilt, self-hatred, and shame for not eating right or eating too much or too little.

What a Woman Can Do

Eating disorders in our society are easily disguised because food and eating are considered expressions of love, security, comfort, and celebration. It seems to be psychological nitpicking to focus on the relationship of eating patterns in the house to the problems children have when they enter adulthood. But just as it's the courageous man who can recognize the effects of his drinking on the family, it is the courageous woman whose role is that of feeding the family who is able to recognize and acknowledge that the excessive and urgent emphasis she places on the importance of what each person is eating negatively affects her children.

Children of mothers who have eating disorders and food addictions must recognize how that connects with their own similar issues. Too often these addictions and disorders are kept secret and denied, so their consequences and effects on children don't get worked out.

What a Man Must Do

While a man must learn to recognize his proclivity to addictions such as alcohol, porn, sports on television, working, or the many ways in which a disconnected man distances and escapes his personal relationships and expresses his intimacy dysfunction, he also needs to recognize what these addictions are telling him about who and what he really is in his relationships.

At the same time, a man must recognize that while his addictions are readily visible to others and may cause him to be blamed for his family and relationship problems, women have addictions that are equally damaging but more difficult to identify, rarely acknowledged, and often vigorously denied. The preoccupation with food in our culture is so widespread that it is seen as normal. Eating disorders are elusive and difficult to identify because eating for fun and the preoccupation with food and dieting are so embedded.

Food becomes an addiction when it is used to sublimate cravings for dependency, a childlike hunger for love and affection, an escape from depression, anger, and boredom, as well as from an inner emptiness resulting from identity issues and low self-esteem. All of these underlying creators of food addiction have ramifications for family and intimate relationships, including those with a partner, children, and their own mothers. The existence and impact of food addictions on the family, and the need to acknowledge and transform them, must be seen as equally critical as other addictions, and they are one piece of a total puzzle and dynamic that create family dysfunction.

9

WHY, WHEN, AND HOW IT GOES BAD

Becoming a father is entering a situation replete with double bind, no win conflicts, particularly for those men who are trying to transform themselves into the perfect modern and liberated man.

The 1970s and 1980s were witness to the emergence of large numbers of men who came out of their personal caves to reveal and confront the pain of having been deprived in one form or another of a loving father. They gathered together, many under the umbrella of a men's support group. These kinds of groups spread rapidly, as did men's retreats into the woods and under tents, where they bonded, expressing and sharing their pain as they grieved their history of father loss.

For some, father loss happened through straight-out abandonment. Dad faded out of the family and disappeared. For others, Dad stayed, but he became a cruel, critical monster, remembered as punitive, emotionally unreachable, alcoholic, unpredictable, violent, unfaithful, and irresponsible. The men remembered their dads with a combination of rage, hatred, and longing. In the face of traumatic memories, they were aware of the hole inside of themselves that needed to be filled up by a loving male figure.

Other men were raised by single mothers who had divorced their fathers and remarried. Dad left the house, perhaps got behind on child support, remarried, and created a new family and faded away. These dads could no longer handle the conflicts of noncustodial fathering in which constant resistance, accusations, arguments, and myriad obstacles eroded their desire to father and created a psychological climate that was no longer tenable.

There were the weak and dependent fathers who, once remarried, fathered more children and found themselves pressured by their new wives to spend less time with their children from the previous marriage. They had to deal with resentments and accusations between present and past wives and the financial struggles of trying to be responsible for two or more families. Not wanting to fail again, and wishing to appease and mollify their current spouse, they found it easier to just pull away from the children of their past marriage, almost as if they never existed.

In the mildest of these father-loss experiences and pain, Dad never actually left the house physically but was emotionally absent or unavailable. He was either "always working" or "impossible" to hold a personal conversation with. When he died, his friends and family were prone to say they never really knew him or what he was thinking or feeling. Perhaps they understood he loved them by his actions as a provider or perhaps as an occasional companion, but not much beyond. They ached to know him in the way they knew their mother but couldn't find a way to make that happen.

Only the fortunate few, perhaps from families of men who had done significant psychological prep work on themselves, could remember a loving and communicative father. Others perhaps remembered a father who took them fishing or to sports events, but Mom remained the go-to parent. That became most evident after growing up and leaving home, where most of the communication was with Mom. Having a conversation with Dad by phone was always a challenge, characterized by brief, practical, to-the-point conversations. Dad didn't know how to or was too uncomfortable to carry on any kind of sustained personal conversation.

It takes a perspective on gender conditioning to fully understand the history and binds men find themselves in today that ate away and eroded their potential as parents. In the traditional home of the past, Dad's role was the provider and fixer-repair person. That wasn't enough for most men. They also wanted to be successful in the competitive marketplace and admired in a worldly way. However, worldly competitive success and being a seamless provider are costly, because a man's energies have to be obsessively goal-focused outside the home and immediate family. While becoming a hero in the outside world, he was also becoming an absent parent who, when he was present, was tired, probably preoccupied, irritable, and unknown. The invisible sign on his back read, "Leave Dad alone. He needs to relax in peace and quiet."

Today, we have new generations of enlightened fathers, many of whom understand the need and feel the desire to be fully participating, caring, and interactive dads. But many of them have not done the psychological work to become emotionally connected and are simply following an abstract model of good fathering. Their fathering behavior on the surface is sensitive and excellent, but something key is profoundly missing—namely, a deeper, genuine emotional connection. Consequently, the bond with their children, while outwardly good, lacks adhesion and easily splinters and flakes away.

If they are stay-at-home dads who are either secondary or nonproviders, with the wife as the primary support, they must wrestle with the sense that in the eyes of others they are weak, effete losers. Only the rarest of men can avoid self-condemnation, depression, and self-hatred. They must also deal with the feelings and resentment of wives whose dreams of an ideal marriage and family life have been tainted and compromised.

The most tragic of contemporary fathers, I believe, are those men who long to be active, participating fathers but are being blocked by angry ex-wives, and because of limited economic resources, they have been unable to wage successful custody battles. Some claim their ex-wives have promoted their alienation from their children. Some find themselves having to defend themselves against accusations of abuse. Other painful scenarios may involve the inability to make child support payments, which then justifies the mother's refusal to provide access to the children and jeopardizes the man's work situation because of the current laws that punish men who are untimely with child support by withholding professional licenses and even driver's licenses.

The bottom-line problem, however, is that the masculine socialization of men that has severely externalized men to be efficient achievers and performers has severely damaged their ability and capacity for creating close, authentic loving and caring personal bonds. Unfortunately, few men are able to recognize their disabilities when it comes to developing intimacy. In denial, they put no priority on the long-term work of healing themselves. Only the exceptional few truly grasp and begin the difficult journey out of their masculine vacuum. Ultimately, however, most men really have no one else to blame for continuing to remain stuck in a fathering nightmare.

INSIGHT 66: CUSTODY BATTLES

A man may believe his children will appreciate his fighting for the right to have custody, but he is mistaken. What the child is more likely to feel and believe is that Dad is a jerk who is being mean to Mommy.

The Conversation

Sanford was a "victim" of a custody battle, having victimized himself by engaging in a protracted struggle that cost him over $100,000 in legal fees. After well-intentioned wrangling on issues such as holiday schedules, pick-up times, and more, in which he "won" by getting most of what he fought for, he discovered he had "lost the war." Though he proved he cared enough to fight aggressively for equal access and guarantee that his ex-wife could not "poison the waters" of his relationship with his children by controlling and dominating custody, in the end he was embittered by the discovery that once the fighting was over, the children withdrew from him emotionally. When they were with him, they would go silent, hostile, and passive, and say they wanted to get back to their mother's apartment. The disappointment left him angry and bitter.

> *Sanford*: "Any guy considering a battle with a wife he's divorcing ought to stop and learn from guys like me who've spent fortunes on court custody matters. You may succeed on paper, gain more weekends or extra evenings, but then the reality hits—you won the battle but lost the war. I got everything I fought for, with one small hitch: My kids are now so angry at me for what they believed I was doing to their mother that they hate me. When my time to be with them comes, they make my life hell. I can't believe it. I thought I'd be a hero to them by 'fighting the good fight.'"

> *Dr. Goldberg*: "Guys don't understand this. They're used to responding to personal problems by turning them into challenges and arguments over right and wrong. A relationship with one's kids, unless they're tiny babies, is not something you 'fight' to have. It develops through attaching, bonding, and relating. Once that's done, even when you're not around, they'll still be thinking about you and looking forward to your next visit."

Sanford: "I knew a man who won total custody and had his kids exclusively for two years. Their mother had a drug problem. One day she shows up at the kids' school after not seeing them all that time, and they go running to her, screaming with delight, 'Mom! We missed you, Mom!' and started crying the tears they'd been suppressing. They went off with her that day and refused to go back to live with their dad. The custody he had didn't do a thing to attach them to him. Their heart was with their mother."

Dr. Goldberg: "There are so many variations on that theme. Dads need to understand that if kids are closely bonded to their moms, fighting her in court will only make them hate him for what he's doing to her, particularly if they see her in tears. Most guys should concentrate on making themselves open, nondefensive, and connected in order to become a person their kids will long to be with. Then, if Mom tries to block access, the kids will make her life hell and she'll be glad to send them off to him."

The Insight Explained

Most children, especially younger ones, are closer to their mothers than to their fathers. They identify with her emotions, so if Dad is in a legal battle with her, they'll hate him for it, just like their mother does. During divorce, mothers have the power to poison the children's feelings toward their father, to show him he can't continue to control her. Parenting is about creating a loving, attached, and positive relationship, not fighting legal battles to secure more access and time.

What a Woman Can Do

As a matter of principle and "father's rights," many divorcing fathers enter into distressing and destructive legal battles over custody.

Between a build-up of resentment over feeling that their husbands had been controlling, hurtful, and dismissive in the marriage, and a sense that their husbands are dysfunctional people, women often want to limit the father's influence, impact, and exposure to the children.

So they jump fully into the fray to prove they will not allow themselves to be "controlled" again. Besides draining the family finances, fighting also creates rifts and damage to the family atmosphere, with the children both torn and upset by the family war.

Many contemporary men are sure the legal system favors women when it comes to custody. Their defensive response is to wage an expensive and destructive war with their wives without examining their own relationship with their children and what the children feel, want, and believe. Those are the realities that ought to guide men's approach and actions. Self-awareness and growth will trump legal victories. The bottom line is that if there is a close relationship between Dad and his kids before divorce, he won't have to "fight" for visitation because the kids will express their desires to the mother and she will willingly grant more visitation rights to avoid their hostility.

Most custody battles are short sighted, stressful, and unnecessary. The children's growing-up years are ones of major change for the parents as well as the children. New partners will enter the picture. Employment and financial pressures will alter the family dynamic. Fighting for a fixed and rigid custody program is misguided. The issues are altered continuously by time and circumstances. Any agreement is by its nature temporary. Parents' energies should be used to work out differences and find ways to be supportive of each other in the efforts to be the best parents possible and to fulfill the needs of the children and not their own.

What a Man Must Do

Men turn their relationship problems into "issues," arguments and battles over right and wrong that are off-putting and self-defeating. What a man must do when divorcing and confronting custody struggles is recognize a misguided tendency to believe he must fight for access to the children to prove how much he cares.

A man in a custody battle must first and foremost discover the truth of what his child or children feel and want, and recognize that as something that is non-negotiable and must be respected. To deny his children's experience is to thicken the wall that may already exist between himself and them. If they express or have a preference for being with their mother, his emphasis should be on patiently improving and building his bond with them, and he should avoid forcing them into a relationship with him that they are resisting.

A man must also recognize how his own workaholism and tendency to be emotionally unavailable are the key elements that negatively impact and damage his bond with his children. Fixing that will be what changes how his children feel around him, rather than focusing on the amount of hours and days he will have access to them.

A man must recognize his tendency to deny the negative ways his children feel about and see him. Money invested in personal therapy and self-improvement will be much more productive than money paid to an expensive attorney.

From the time his child is born, a man must recognize his tendency to let the mother be the primary and available parent while he busies himself outside of the family, which sets the stage for the bitter and disappointed feelings he will have in later years when their lack of closeness, attachment, and desire to be with him are revealed.

INSIGHT 67: A MAN AS A "GOOD CATCH"

What is a mother conveying to her daughter when she counsels her to marry well? Or when a son is urged to stay with a woman because she is beautiful and comes from a good family? They are being taught that images and symbols supersede everything else. They are being taught to objectify the opposite sex.

The Conversation

Leon, a well-known talk show host, had hit a relationship wall. After three marriages, two live-in relationships, and countless others had caused him great emotional pain and a large portion of his money, he realized something was seriously wrong. All started with magical beginnings and felt like drug highs but lasted less than a year. None turned into friendships once the romance was over. "I can barely remember their names. We used to tell each other we'd always remain friends."

Leon: "It feels good being successful and attracting women. It's a lot better than being unemployed and invisible, that's for sure. But it becomes obvious it's really my success, and not the real me, that is the attraction. I go along hiding my true self and magnifying my symbols in order to keep their love and adoration, but knowing it won't last."

Dr. Goldberg: "You mean eventually she'll begin to see who you really are underneath your image of success."

The Insight Explained

Women are in touch with the frustration of being loved for their looks and not for their inner essence. Similarly, most men know they're only lovable based on the strength of their ability to provide and be a man. The moment they can't perform as they should, their self-esteem plummets and their personal world begins to collapse.

What a Woman Can Do

A woman's physical beauty and a man's successful career may have an initial magnetic effect, but they also make one vulnerable to the kind of objectification that leaves one feeling the person they attract doesn't see them beyond the surface. To love somebody is healthy and good. To use somebody as an object is offensive, if not pathological.

At some point, women and men have to confront the stark reality of their choices, which is that they've been loved and valued for their symbols and they are trophies for their partners' egos.

What a Man Must Do

While trading on his professional and educational credentials and image may be tempting and may lure some women into wanting him, a man must know he is displaying his feelings of personal inadequacy and low self-esteem when he hides behind his image.

He is trading short-term conquest and appeal based on a seductive image and fantasy in exchange for the hard work of building an authentically loving relationship by being his real self.

When men as fathers push their daughters to choose a husband based on what he does for a living and his earning potential, they are colluding with the unfortunate tendency to objectify a man based on externals that may have no connection to who he is as a person. Knowing that, a man who uses his status and success to attract a "beautiful woman" must realize that he is setting the stage for a dysfunctional relationship that will inevitably go into crisis.

INSIGHT 68: THE ILLUSION OF TECHNIQUE

When things go wrong in his intimate relationships, a man may look to find the reasons for the crisis in something he did or didn't do or say. He doesn't see that it's the way he is, based on his role as a man, that produces the inevitable end results.

The Conversation

Sawyer seemed destined to be a winner. He was the "perfect boy": focused, smart, competitive, uncomplaining, goal oriented, and someone who always got the job done. "I was the one everyone could count on, the one girls wanted to take home to Mom and Dad." It was a shock to Sawyer, therefore, when his "perfect marriage" to the cheerleading captain of his high school football team began to fall apart soon after their wedding. She became profoundly depressed following the birth of their child, and then she announced that she wanted a divorce. She accused him of being controlling, emotionally abusive, arrogant, and critical. "I didn't see it coming. I was the same guy when she dumped me as when she married me."

After a year of soul-searching in a support group for divorced men, Sawyer began therapy. He learned that it was not so much what he'd done that ended his marriage, but rather what he was all about as a person acting out the role of the perfect man for which he had been praised while growing up.

> *Sawyer*: "You read relationship books that create this impression that there are right and wrong things to say or do to make a relationship work. So if it goes bad and a guy gets dumped, then it must be something he did or said. But I've known plenty of guys who actually did everything right, and it still didn't work."

Dr. Goldberg: "I call that the 'illusion of technique,' meaning there's a formula for everything people strive for, such as being popular, a great lover, or successful."

Sawyer: "When guys fail, they think, 'Why didn't I bring her flowers more often?' Or, with the kids, 'Why didn't I work less and get more involved?'"

Dr. Goldberg: "Those are the hindsight things that seem to ring true, but if the guy actually had a chance to do it all over, and did it the so-called right way, he would wind up with the same result for two reasons. The first is every problem is a combination of his-and-her issues. It's not just him. Second, when it comes to relationships, it's more how a man is as a person to be with than anything specific he did or didn't say or do."

The Insight Explained

Men try to solve their relationship problems with the same self-defeating process that caused them. They relate in an externalized way, trying to understand and fix the problem using the same flawed process that created it. It's hard for them to look beyond the external mechanics and focus on their personal impact.

What a Woman Can Do

How many women can see that what they come to resent in their husbands after years of marriage are expressions and extensions of the very same characteristics that made a man initially so attractive? A man's confidence, assertiveness, fearlessness, goal-focused ambition, intelligence, and take-charge attitude are the characteristics that morph into her feelings that he is controlling, out of touch with his feelings, self-centered, and arrogant. Women who can see that reversal in their perceptions are more likely to be able to see the relationship breakdown as the product of both people. Instead of being angry at him, a longer-range psychological perspective will allow a woman to be more inclined to see the social conditioning that shaped both partners as the real problem, and that the solution is a joint effort at change. The interpretation that a woman was the victim of a hurtful man may be consoling, but it will only lead her to repeat the same pattern and dynamic until she decides all men are the same.

What a Man Must Do

To improve himself as a father, a man must change his belief that there are external and facile ways to overcome his personal deficits and limitations. In his desire to change himself easily and avoid the difficult and elusive work of overcoming his disconnected, externalized tendencies, a man will be attracted to "how-to," quick-fix solutions.

Becoming a good father, a good husband, and a person who can bond and relate in a personal way isn't a matter of reading the right books or learning relationship strategies and techniques, which are an escape for the disconnected, externalized male who wants to avoid getting in touch with his deeper motivations and lacks the patience required to begin the process of becoming a person capable of authentic bonding and relating.

It's easy for a man to fool himself into believing he is being the good guy and loving father by saying, "I love you," and eliciting flattering comments as to what a good father and husband he is, believing that means he's created a genuine bond and loving relationship. A man must know that he needn't continually reassure others of his loving and concerned feelings, and he can draw boundaries that may even make him appear to be the "bad guy" when necessary, and yet still create a loving and close bond.

Genuinely intimate relationships cannot be created by using techniques and strategies. The latter may produce short-term results but will lack an enduring substance. Disconnected and heavily externalized men have their work cut out for them if they want to avoid the negative relationship endpoints created by masculine socialization. There are no shortcuts, and while techniques of relating and communicating love and caring may help him jump-start the process of transformation, the struggle to connect personally requires patience, vigilance, unsparing authenticity, and continual effort.

INSIGHT 69: MEN'S DELUSIONS OF TRUTH

Professional men who are exemplars of "rational thinking" find themselves in the most painful and out-of-control irrational conversations with their partners because their externalized, goal-focused, logical way of being grates on their partners and triggers responses of resentment and frustration.

The Conversation

Humphrey was an esteemed physician and published author. His private practice flourished with celebrity clients. By forty-three he was a total workaholic. "I can't stop working. I get too antsy." In truth, when we first spoke over the phone he confided that he worked all the time because it was too stressful being at home with "my crazy wife." "She's impossible to reason with. I think of divorce all the time, but I'm afraid of her and what it might unleash. She's accused me of robbing her of her best years, ruining her life, and being a phony. Her favorite insult is calling me a 'hypocritical Hippocratic.' I've never felt this helpless and hopeless."

> *Humphrey*: "It's a pathetic irony when a highly educated man who prides himself on the power of his rational mind and ability to solve any problem with logic tries to use that objectivity and rationality with his wife and children. All he succeeds in doing is arousing resentment in them."

> *Dr. Goldberg*: "In total frustration, men end up calling their wives crazy or criticizing their kids for being spoiled, ungrateful brats. The harder men try to get through to them by using logic, the worse it gets."

> *Humphrey*: "It's like some kind of payback I'm receiving for being deluded. I've always believed any problem could be solved with facts and information, and truth can be found using logic and reasoning."

> *Dr. Goldberg*: "It's what I call the 'masculine delusion.'"

The Insight Explained

Extreme rationality and the belief in the power of the mind to solve all problems are part of the defensive and externalizing process of masculinity. While it may work in the physical and static world of science and mechanics, men discover that same way of answering questions, when used in the personal world, alienates, frustrates, and infuriates family members.

What a Woman Can Do

The smartest of men have a blind spot when it comes to the way they relate personally. As they spew their wisdom and truths, family members withdraw.

It's difficult for women married to these highly intellectualized, "know-it-all" men to see past their resentment over feeling talked down to and having their feelings and sensibilities dismissed as irrational. What gets a man's attention is the communication of confidence and independence on the woman's part. Being challenged to change by a woman who makes it clear she will otherwise leave is the best approach to bringing out the dependent and insecure boy that lives inside of a man, behind his hyperactive intellect.

What a Man Must Do

A man must realize that the value and importance he places on truth, logic, and rationality is not necessarily shared by his wife, children, family, and others in his personal circle; in fact, emphasizing such values may alienate them and generate underlying feelings of resentment. Secretly, they may actually wish for him to shut up.

During conversations or arguments within the family, a man's impersonal and logical way of communicating is a powerful manifestation of his disconnection. Though superficially impressive, it is ultimately a factor in preventing the development of authentic relationships, causing others to withdraw out of frustration and feel as though they are not getting through.

Men must recognize that belief in the logical power of the mind to solve and manage personal problems and experiences is inappropriate and toxic.

The epitome of irony and self-defeating male cluelessness is seen in the marriages and intimate relationships of highly intellectualized, rational, and professorial men who try to use their "reason" to control, teach, or persuade family members while the communication during an argument escalates.

Instead of pointing a finger at those who are close to him and labeling them as "crazy," "stupid," or "irrational" because they don't communicate the way he thinks they should, men need to point the finger instead at the intellectualized relationship idiocy they deny.

INSIGHT 70: HIS RELATIONSHIP DEMONS

Men's three relationship enemies are their egos, resistance to doing the hard work of personal change, and denial of their personal isolation and dependency.

The Conversation

When his partner of three years suddenly left, Bradley crumbled, though he confided that he sensed it was imminent.

When I asked why he hadn't done something to preempt and prevent the break-up, he acknowledged that he arrogantly assumed his partner couldn't survive without him, he was too busy with work to worry about the relationship, and even if she left, he could replace her with somebody better. He was unprepared for the unexpected harsh reality—that he needed her more than she needed him, and he would feel suicidal and paralyzed with fear after she walked out. He tried self-medication, drinking a bottle of wine each night to fall asleep. He was on the verge of becoming an alcoholic.

> *Bradley*: "I kind of laugh when I hear guys say women are so difficult to figure out or relationships are such hard work. In relationships, most men make zero effort besides showing up and doing the guy thing of dinner and a movie."

Dr. Goldberg: "Men don't seem to learn when it comes to their relationships how unaware, vulnerable, and blind they are. They are convinced they understand women, when they really don't. They believe relationships are easy. If men built buildings that way, those buildings would fall apart."

Bradley: "I used to think women were simple to understand and the fragile sex. I was out of touch and couldn't admit or see how I was the needy baby, afraid to be left alone."

Dr. Goldberg: "During the beginning and end of relationships, men are fragile. They get in too quickly, and when it should end, they hang on and make things worse for themselves and their partners. At neither time do they learn anything, so they keep hopping from the frying pan into the fire."

The Insight Explained

The first blind spot blocking men's relationship growth is the belief that they're perfect as they are, they know everything, and a woman who gets to be with them is lucky. That leads to the second blind spot, which is that by finding the right woman, a good relationship will just happen. Third, because men are cut off from their feelings and personal selves, they don't see how they become putty in the hands of a woman who happens to be physically attractive and pays them extra attention. Instead of choosing a woman who will challenge them to grow, they choose a pleaser who'll tell them what they want to hear.

What a Woman Can Do

Men's relationship experiences won't improve until they can see who they are and how they go about relating. More than anything, men need to acknowledge the work they must do to overcome generations of conditioning that have severely disabled their relationship skills. Women have changed because they worked hard at it, using vehicles such as therapy, support groups, assertion training, and making themselves vulnerable and open to personal change. That's the model men need to imitate.

Once women see clearly the sad underbelly of the seemingly invulnerable and independent man, they can gain an appreciation for their own *actual* and latent power and competence in their relationships. That they can function better without men than vice versa is seen by the greater resilience divorcing women demonstrate when balancing jobs, family demands, and education, while divorcing men lock themselves into a new relationship as soon as possible. Knowing this and keeping it in focus can help women hold fast to their life vision and bond with a man based on what he's like to be with rather than his provider potential.

What a Man Must Do

The enormous changes in women during the last fifty years resulted because they have been willing and able to acknowledge their vulnerabilities and feelings of unhappiness and frustration, reach out to others for help without shame or embarrassment, and develop and maintain support systems. For men to survive and thrive and not become the disposable gender, they must learn to emulate women.

A man must be wary of the need to hide and deny his vulnerabilities, fears, and weaknesses while being able to fix his problems by himself and acknowledge what he's been taught about life as a man is making him sick and isolating and killing him.

A man must learn that he has a right to put a premium on the quality of his personal life and experience, his well-being and growth, and acknowledge what needs to be done in order to transform himself. He must acknowledge that he can't do that by himself and realize that playing the part of the lone wolf who is in denial of his personal needs in order to maintain an image of being indestructible is sick, crazy, and unnecessary.

To overcome his enemy, the masculine ego, a man needs to identify his many blind spots and the damage they do to his relationships by causing him to always need to be right and to win while maintaining an attitude of self-protective distance. Listening to what others who are in his life have to say about him is also a necessary step.

Committing himself to change and growth means a man must overcome his compulsion for quick change, his avoidance of appearing vulnerable, his resistance to listening to others, and his need for concrete, logical, and immediate solutions.

Finally, a man must get in touch with the child part of himself that knows it hurts to always go it alone and to deny his need to feel close and be known by others for who he really is inside of himself. The prescription for curing the personal sickness that his masculine socialization has created must be part of a lifetime program of slow but steady transformation toward becoming a total human being and not just "a man."

INSIGHT 71: THE PERFECT ALL-AMERICAN COUPLE

The myth of the football hero and beautiful cheerleader as a perfect couple is a cruel fantasy that has created pain, feelings of inadequacy and failure, self-hate, depression, and the erroneous diagnosis that childhood trauma is identified as the cause of the relationship failure, rather than the gender conditioning of men and women being the root.

The Conversation

Mark was an All-American collegiate football player when at age twenty-four he married the homecoming queen and cheerleading captain of her college football team. The hometown newspaper covered their wedding on the front page, and the local television station filmed the event.

After three years of trying to cope with Mark's drinking and his wife Bette's addiction to pills for her chronic depression, they ended the relationship. Mark realized later that they both had fallen for the false surface of each other's image because they had the competitive desire to stand out, when in reality they had little in common and even less to talk about.

Mark: "I see all these couples that fall under the category of 'look great, feel terrible' relationships between a pilot and stewardess, doctor and nurse, star athlete and cheerleader, businessman and secretary-assistant, or film director and actress. The chemistry may be hot initially, but I can't imagine these couples spending any fulfilling time together. What do they really have in common, except for looking like a 'hot couple' in the eyes of others?"

Dr. Goldberg: "The myth that these two are a lucky match is deeply ingrained culturally and almost irresistible."

Mark: "It's hard enough to make it work when the man and woman are not gender archetypes. The expectation and beliefs are powerful, seductive, and unattainable."

Dr. Goldberg: "Makes me think of those twentieth-century perfect and irresistible couples like Joe DiMaggio and Marilyn Monroe. They were examples of relationships that looked great from the outside but played out like nightmares."

The Insight Explained

The "perfect" masculine male and feminine female archetypes are examples of individuals who from a distance seem so attractive and enviable but are actually "gender defensive" extremes. He's cut off from his personal side. She struggles to repress her power side by resisting being assertive and aggressive. Because of their polarization, they experience the world in opposite ways and will only get along if she accommodates his vision and beliefs and suppresses her authentic self. When the relationship collapses, childhood issues are seen as the cause, when, in fact, even if their childhoods had been ideal, the breakdown in the relationship would have occurred.

What a Woman Can Do

The perfect couple is embedded in our cultural fantasies. Why does society do a collective swoon when two mismatched people who look like a hot couple marry? Such fantasy couples are made out to be larger than life and then become a source of pity and cruel jokes when their relationships come apart in public view.

What a Man Must Do

Overcoming the heavily reinforced fantasy that the perfect American couple exists is extremely challenging because the media continually promotes it and people have a need to gain their families' and society's approval. Unfortunately, people tend to learn the lessons and hard truths of realistic relationships and love only after experiencing the trauma of repeated failures in their efforts to accomplish it.

Even those who have damaged their own lives chasing the all-American fantasy continue to promote the belief that it can be made real. We see it in the smiling wedding photos and the responses of parents and family members who applaud its pursuit.

The challenge for men is to overcome and see beyond the damaging illusions about relationships they were fed early in their lives, before repeated relationship failures and traumas cause them to shut down and falsely conclude that they are failures in not accomplishing what they were told others have done.

INSIGHT 72: WHY TRADITIONAL RELATIONSHIPS MUST FAIL

Even if a man and a woman seem to have much in common, it means nothing if they view the world in opposite ways. Polarized thinking erodes and destroys the best of relationships and causes them to feel the same frustrating feelings over and over again.

The Conversation

Truman, an elegant, handsomely tailored, silver-haired man of fifty-three, epitomized the perfect gentleman. He learned from his childhood and in prep school how a man was supposed to treat a woman.

Truman tried valiantly to keep up with and support the changes his wife began going through seven years after their marriage. However, he couldn't help feeling he was responsible for his wife's emotional pain. There was always a voice inside of him saying it was his fault whenever she was unhappy. He tried to become whatever she needed him to be, but he often worried he was "being a pussy" and not the man he should be. After nineteen years of marriage, his wife, Marguerite, announced that she had to leave him as her only hope of saving herself. It tore him up and paralyzed him. He couldn't understand what he had done wrong.

Truman: "I thought that relationships were supposed to become much better now that we got away from the traditional roles."

Dr. Goldberg: "Only the outward appearance has changed. Men and women still play the same games with each other and have the same old expectations, and that's what creates the emotional distress. Men and women today are not interacting much differently than grandma and grandpa did. Only the façade has changed."

Truman: "Looks that way to me, too. Most men still initiate relationships, pay the bills, and strategize to get sex. Many women still wait for men to take the lead and continue to find men attractive based on their success symbols."

Dr. Goldberg: "Little has really changed for most people. We thought we had it solved. Men and women today seem to have so much more in common, like staying fit, investing money, enjoying sex, cooking, and watching sports. Both can be good money makers and have interesting careers. Still, relationships aren't more lasting, and, in fact, divorces are uglier than ever and happen sooner, and custody battles are more vicious."

Truman: "I know lots of people who, in chasing that dream of compatibility, understanding, and love, have gone through multiple relationships and marriages. It's good for a year or two. After that, the same old issues come up and divide them. Then they realize they see things so differently."

The Insight Explained

The changes in men and women over the last fifty years have come from working on themselves individually. The way they interact with each other and what turns them on, however, isn't much different than before. Many men are still focused on how a woman looks and whether she's going to be good in bed. Some men still want to have their cake and eat it too; they want to play and make no commitment. Most women still want to know what a man does for a living and how successful he is. The way they interact is the same as always, and often women end up feeling diminished and controlled, blaming men for that, while lots of men end up feeling misinterpreted, angry, guilty, and like confused failures.

What a Woman Can Do

Many women feel men are clueless about them and don't get what women are all about. That assessment has validity, but it is equivalent to the belief of many men that women are crazy and no reasonable dialogue with them is possible. I use the term *gender polarization* to describe the problem in which men and women use opposing gender defense mechanisms. It results in men and women experiencing realities in opposite ways. What is exaggerated in one gender (e.g., autonomy and separateness in men) is blocked in the other (e.g., the drive for closeness and the avoidance of conflict). This situation generates an extreme breakdown in communication once women stop accommodating, by acting as if they agree with the ideas and activities of men that they find repugnant. Women who want to have a satisfying, workable relationship with a man need to begin with the premise that *we're both defensive in opposite ways and there's no point arguing over who's right; it won't get us anywhere.* The challenge is to reduce both partners' defensiveness so they can hear each other accurately and reach a middle ground. That effort requires good will and acceptance of the fact that there's a problem on which they both need to work.

When it comes to man-woman relationships, we've accomplished the easy, nonthreatening part but not the hard, painful one. Men and women on a deeper level still see the world and process reality differently. They use the same words but give them different meanings and blame the other for the problems that arise.

Two things have to take place for things to really change. First and foremost, the emphasis in problem solving in a relationship needs to shift toward changing oneself, rather than pointing at the other. Second, both partners have to be willing to do the hard work of seeing patterns and responses in themselves that are defensive and alienating. Both need to question entrenched beliefs and philosophies to discover the defensive roots that cause them to experience and perceive things differently. They need to stop seeing themselves as "right or wrong," because in gender polarization there is no right; there are only opposing realities that need to be worked through.

What a Man Must Do

Growth and change are hard; going back to the ways of tradition is always a seductive temptation. Men must see through the clichés of tradition—namely, that opposites attract and the sparks and friction built into such relationships are a healthy and inevitable part of life. They aren't.

The traditional relationship between the "manly man" and the "womanly woman" is a recipe for relationship pain and torture. Traditional relationships are promoted in spite of the obvious dysfunctional consequences we witness daily. They are in fact relationships characterized by brittle, lonely men who believe they failed and angry, self-denying women who feel they have been controlled, exploited, and misled. Yet it is hard and threatening to have a discussion about this. Only behind the cloistered walls of therapy do women and men try to authentically identify and explore their real feelings as they try to heal their wounded relationship selves.

A man must overcome the inflated belief that he can do as others have done in the past and achieve a different outcome. Almost every traditional couple vows to each other that they will not repeat the dysfunctional behaviors of their parents and grandparents. Every couple that makes that vow will fail to fulfill it. Tweaking and surface efforts to change will never be enough to avoid the relationship traumas of generations past. The couples who try and fail despair as they witness their relationships becoming even more toxic than those from whom they sought to distinguish themselves.

A man must realize that the opposite ways of experiencing, thinking, and responding that characterize men and women in traditional relationships are not fixed and can be transformed. However, it requires continual self-awareness and courage, plus an ongoing long-term vigilance and effort.

We live in a world of seductive imagery that keeps pulling us backward. The opposite ways traditional men and women perceive, interpret, and respond to their experience must be recognized as the cause of the destructive breakdowns in communication and the antipathy and wariness that exist between the sexes. They include the women who have given up on men and the men who have become fearful of women's power to derail and bring down a man's life.

Men must overcome the ego-driven belief that they can do things the way they've always been done and achieve a different and better outcome. On the contrary, men's efforts have actually resulted in worse results than the generation's before. Today's less traditional relationships are less resilient, prone to greater destructive outbursts, and lacking in the endurance and willingness to go along than previous ones.

The greatest challenge for men is acknowledging and identifying the reality of their inner selves, their feelings, conflicts, and the defenses and rigidities that continue to control their behavior. Men must do their share in depolarizing their relationships so ultimately both genders can experience reality similarly and in a nondefensive way, and not perpetuate the rationalization that men and women are just made differently or come from different planets. Indeed, while their biological make-up and genetics may be different, the psychological tendencies to communicate defensively, be unable to recognize and understand the experience of their partners, and recognize their relationship issues and their separate distortions are not biological or genetic.

INSIGHT 73: INEVITABLE ENDPOINTS

The progression in traditional relationships is from romance to boredom to rage. "Trying harder" cannot change these inevitable endpoints—only depolarizing the relationship can.

The Conversation

With each new thrilling encounter, always including hot sex, Waylon vowed to make the relationship last and not end painfully like his previous romances. "How were we so in love but now can't stand to be in the same room together?" he asked. He'd learned to identify the clues. "I could tell by my gut when the romance was over. I'd find myself getting distracted and bored when I was with her."

Waylon: "When I'm feeling euphoric about a new woman, I always think it's going to stay that way forever. When it ends I tell myself I've learned important lessons and won't repeat the same mistakes."

Dr. Goldberg: "It's amazing that in relationships so little carry-over of the hard-learned lessons happens. Most relationships still demand an initial excitement and high that men and women should have learned to be wary of."

Waylon: "For me, that high lasts about six months, although it seems it gets shorter with each new experience. Then there's that lull before the storm, where it gets boring and predictable. We're trying to fabricate the original feelings and hold on to the vestiges of the initial high, but it's forced. Finally, the true frustrations emerge and the arguments, sniping, and miscommunications begin. With so much invested, this painful stage usually goes on much longer than the initial romantic one. Finally, one of us throws in the towel."

The Insight Explained

The progression of romance to boredom to rage occurs inevitably in relationships that begin with traditional romantic fantasies of having found the "perfect partner." With the ideal man/ideal woman combination it happens quickest, although the "trying hard" and denial may keep things going for a while because neither partner wants to face failure and start over again with someone new.

What a Woman Can Do

There are different ways to gauge the underbelly of a romance. "Does the relationship make sense in the real world, or do you need to isolate yourself from others in order to survive it?" If it's too high, it has to come down, and that's to be expected. It's okay to be in sober reality and work things out rather than strain to keep it going artificially. Acceptance of the demise of that initial drug-high feeling and not bemoaning its loss as something catastrophic is a sign of growing up.

When relationships that start off on a romantic high begin to stagnate and become boring, couples already have hopes, dreams, and perhaps a lease in both of their names. They begin to try harder to revive the initial romance, but since they no longer observe the niceties of dating behavior, including whitewashing of their darker personality aspects, no improvement occurs in the relationship. To alter these dynamics, men and women have to change the initial expectations and interaction and work on self discovery and mutual responsibility, with an acknowledgment that the expectations of initial excitement and euphoria are warning signs rather than indications of magic.

What a Man Must Do

The couples who are now at each other's throats were once romantically enthralled. Before the rage and after the initial euphoria, they probably experienced a period of boredom. Though they did all they could to avoid ugly battles, the relationship spun out of their control.

Men must realize that despite their proclivity for seeing themselves as unique and different from other men, there are psychological and relationship dynamics and realities that have inevitable endpoints more powerful than they are.

A man must be aware that the arguments, outbursts, periods of boredom, and relationship breakdowns he experienced and witnessed in his own life were not just because of his and his wife's separate dysfunctions but also a built-in inevitability. He must see that once he enters a seemingly compelling relationship with the all-too-common *actor-reactor*, or macho-hero male with an adoring, accommodating, selfless, eager-to-please female or a disconnected and externalized male with a needy, emotional female dynamic, he will be swept into and later become a statistic of the all-too-common male-female relationship progression of *romance* to *boredom* to *rage*.

A man must forgive himself for having been in denial or unaware of the red flags he sensed early on in a courtship that was too powerful and alluring to resist: (1) we didn't have much to talk about; (2) we always had to have something to do as a distraction from the deadness and boredom; (3) even though we knew something was missing and wrong, we chose to deny and ignore the signs and not do anything about it; (4) mainly guilt and a sense of obligation caused him to continue; and (5) we lost interest in sexual intimacy early on and succumbed to mainly eating and watching television.

The deeper dynamics are too powerful to harness.

For the man not yet in a committed relationship, he must first acknowledge that relationships are not magical events, it is safer to be alone than to try to escape aloneness in a toxic relationship, and good relationships are the consequence of each partner working to become a fully responsive and responsible person capable of avoiding blame and guilt in a relationship.

A man must not block or deny the early warning signs of instant romance and commitment followed by the need for distraction and a growing sense of deadness and the futile, round-robin arguments.

INSIGHT 74: WHY SHE CAN'T BE YOUR SOUL MATE

The error of projection is when a man assumes a woman will experience the personal elements of their relationship the same way he does.

The Conversation

Douglas described his sense of magical closeness when he first met Fiona: "In the first six months we were together I had this sense that she understood everything I was saying exactly as I meant it and shared all my attitudes and opinions. What a relief, after my marriage where it seemed we bickered and disagreed about everything. Before the year ended, that perfect compatibility with Fiona started showing cracks. Eventually, even the slightest word could lead to a raging battle. It was as bad as my marriage."

Douglas: "When we first met, I said, 'Look, I need a certain amount of space and freedom in a relationship,' and she seemed to instantly 'get me.' Boy, was I excited! We had sex that night and I told her, for me, having great sex was like having a great meal, something you do for its own sake, and for the pleasure of the experience. She said she couldn't agree more."

Dr. Goldberg: "In other words, you believed you'd found this magic woman who had the same responses to things like freedom, closeness, and sex as you did. It was like having run into a female version of yourself and you believed it was genuine."

Douglas: "I thought I was the luckiest guy in the world to come across a woman who knew exactly where I was coming from because she was coming from the same place."

Dr. Goldberg: "Women often put themselves in sync with men's wishes and tastes just as unknowingly and automatically as men do when they automatically take control of a relationship and start making all the decisions."

The Insight Explained

The denial of the deeply rooted differences in the way men and women experience things, due to their different gender socialization and childhood experiences, is a common blind spot for men as well as women, and it results in dangerous misreading and misinterpretations. If a man has a carved-out way of seeing things, he believes everybody who is reasonable and intelligent will see it his way. He may not find that very often, but when he does he believes it is real.

What a Woman Can Do

A woman who has learned to be a tuned-in reactor to a man, and mirror perfectly what he's thinking, saying, and feeling, can induce in men a magical sense of being fully understood. This is particularly true for a self-centered, insecure man who felt frustrated in past contentious relationships. It turns the usually level-headed man into an obsessive pursuer. While it gives women who understand how this works an enormous power, the power may be short lived and onerous because most women tire and get turned off by the intense dependency, false idealization, and love they trigger.

In general, it's an age-old major breakdown in communication between men and women when each thinks the partner can sense and feel things exactly as they do. The partner who wants the love and acceptance more simply mirrors the other, reinforcing this illusion. Once the relationship moves into a committed phase, not only will the naïve male who believes this to be true be disappointed, but he may also be shocked to discover the other person actually sees things completely differently.

What a Man Must Do

To avoid the dangerous distortions involved in falling in love with a woman because she seems to be a man's perfect fit—someone who feels and sees things exactly the way he does, shares his worldview and his cynicism, resonates with his preferences and choices, equally loves the sports he follows, shares his views on family and the rearing of children, and is so much like him that she seems to be his "soul mate"—a man must recognize that because of the different ways men and women are socialized and brought up to be, such a magical compatibility is impossible and not to be trusted.

A man must recognize how women are raised to please and accommodate, and that the needier a woman is and the lower her self-esteem, the better she will probably be at reading a man in order to give him what he wants and thus get what she needs. Her "amazing" ability to be "just like him" is a temporary accommodation, much like a good salesperson's ability to immediately bond and become best friends with a customer deciding on the purchase of an automobile or a new home.

To avoid the tendency to believe the unbelievable, a man must overcome and heal his own defensive ego that causes him to seek out a partner who is "just like him" because of his inability to share control and relate to someone who sees things in a different and challenging way.

A man must inoculate himself against the self-defeating tendency to believe the unbelievable—namely, that the woman for him is a clone or replica of himself. He must work on his issues so he can reach a point at which he is refreshed and positively challenged by a partner who can stretch him, not just please him by becoming his "magic lady."

INSIGHT 75: IS HE MR. WONDERFUL OR MR. HORRIBLE?

A man is neither as wonderful as a woman wants to believe he is in the beginning nor as terrible as she tells him he is in the end.

The Conversation

Bill had experienced, even welcomed, the excitement a woman had when she first met him. He particularly loved hearing that he was different from other men, a refreshing change. In his heart, however, he sensed she was projecting her fantasies of a dream man onto him. Still, it felt too good to challenge. And he never got used to the extreme reversal that occurred at the end. When it's over, "the most special man I ever met" transforms into "you're an asshole—just like all the other men."

Bill: "I used to love it when a woman I just met would put me on a pedestal and gush about all my supposedly great and special character-istics, how unusually nice and thoughtful I was. Every little thing I did was 'great' or 'fabulous.' If I bought her a gift, it was the best she'd ever received, and if I'd take her somewhere, my choice was wonder-ful. The operative words here are 'I used to,' because now it turns me off when I hear that over-the-top stuff. I've learned not to trust it because it's just what she needs to believe about me and doesn't have much to do with the real me."

Dr. Goldberg: "I think you're being too critical. What's wrong with a little romanticized fantasy? It kind of gets the relationship motor go-ing. A woman needs to feel the guy is 'Mr. Wonderful' to let her guard down and fall in love."

Bill: "That might be true except for the inevitable downside. At the end of the relationship I'm seen as this monster, this piece of shit who's worse than other guys and who misled her into believing I was different."

Dr. Goldberg: "Maybe you were on your best behavior in the begin-ning, which is why she thought you were so great."

Bill: "I don't think I'm that different. It was all going on inside of her—what she needed to believe I was. Besides the downside, I also came to realize it doesn't really feel that good to be seen as Mr. Wonderful when you know it's not who you really are. It sets the expectations way too high. It's like when you're a kid and your grand-ma tells you you're the most wonderful child there ever was. You'd like to believe it was true, but it also makes you feel uncomfortable and kind of weird because it's not who you know yourself to be."

The Insight Explained

Particularly in romantic beginnings, many women need to overcome their gut resistance and fear of men by creating a fantasy that they are completely different than other men in order to feel safe and comfortable. It suggests she's a traditional woman who can't handle conflict and reality in her relationships and therefore needs to see a man as perfect in order to open herself up and become vulnerable. The reality of the man she experiences is a projection of her own needs, with little to do with who he really is.

What a Woman Can Do

Men are not that different from each other in the way they relate because of masculine socialization that levels them all. The major differences are temporary surface ones at the start of a relationship. A woman who believes the perfect man is somewhere out there needs to ask herself why she is placing such importance on finding a man who is entirely different than all of the others, and what that says about her deeper responses and feelings about men in general.

Men are half of the problem, because their egos want to believe it when women tell them how unique and special they are. It feeds their competitive urge to be seen as better. However, both the giver and the receiver of the illusion will be deeply disappointed. The search for "uniqueness" suggests that there is in fact an underlying resistance and negativity toward men.

The man who is the object of a woman's initial adoring and over-the-top, positive response may be tempted to believe the woman's euphoric illusions because it feeds his need to see himself as special and different. By doing so, however, he is colluding with and contributing to her distortion of reality, which will create the foundation for a painful backlash when she realizes the difference was an illusion.

What a Man Must Do

To avoid the distressing outcome of a relationship where a man who is first put on a pedestal only to be told he is the extreme opposite when the relationship goes into crisis and is ending and that he is a terrible and traumatic disappointment and the epitome of everything negative, a man must (1) become secure enough to not need the kind of flattery and ego strokes that initially tell him how special and wonderful he is; (2) recognize that there is no such thing as a man who is completely unlike all other men; and (3) identify in himself the personality characteristics and issues that he does share in common with other men, such as the need to succeed and be seen as a winner, independent, strong and unafraid, in control, and able to perform well sexually.

Knowing who he is as a man and a person is the best prevention for entering into a relationship with a partner who initially insists he is unique, superior, and wonderful. Once the relationship begins to fall apart, a man needs to understand and recognize that his partner's personal issues, defensiveness, and way of responding were equally at play in generating the deterioration.

Further, he needs to avoid playing into his partner's need to believe that he is different from all other men initially by having the courage to show his real self, warts and all, and not accommodate her unreal fantasies.

Undertaking therapy as his relationship begins to fall apart will be an antidote to being blamed and blaming himself and being seen in an awful light as a horrible person for who he supposedly turned out to be.

In general, a man needs to recognize that the "wonderfulness" a woman sees in him at the beginning and the "horribleness" she sees at the end are both projections reflecting whatever a woman needs to believe in order to enter a relationship and later in order to leave the relationship and feel vindicated and free of responsibility for its demise.

10

WHEN A RELATIONSHIP IS POISONED

We have a physical body, and physicians tend to its needs when we become ill. We also have a "social body," which is our personality. Mental health professionals tend to it when it ails. Relationships are mainly the product of this "social body" that, like our physical body, has needs that must be fulfilled if it is to remain healthy and thrive. When those needs are not met, relationships sicken and become painful. If never attended to and worked on, the relationship becomes poisonous. If allowed to continue in that poisonous state, it threatens to destroy those in it. It reaches a point of irreversibility, or *last-stage toxicity*, when it can no longer be saved or improved, even though many couples continue to soldier on because the alternative of being alone seems to be a worse prospect.

Poisoned relationships also become a form of Russian roulette. Who will self-destruct first? An indicator that one is in a poisoned relationship is the occurrence of fantasies in one or both partners of an accident or violent episode suddenly and unpredictably taking the life of one's partner, thus leaving the surviving partner to continue on without the guilt, confusion, messiness, and ugliness of a separation and divorce battle. The onus of responsibility is avoided.

What does a relationship require in order to build an immune system that will protect it from becoming poisonous? Relationships, like physical bodies, have needs that must be met in order for them to remain energized and vital. They need *nourishment* in the form of good communication, mutual caring, and loving support. They need *exercise* in the form of mutual engagement, interaction, and shared activities. They need *fresh air*, which in relationships means enough separation and space to allow both to breathe individually and maintain a separate identity alongside the "our" or "we" identity of the relationship. They need *physical warmth and closeness* in the form of sensual and sexual intimacies. They need *water*, or the psychological means with which to cleanse and refresh themselves and retain fluidity. When a relationship has all of the above, it can build a strong immune system that allows it to resist and fight off trauma and the stresses of everyday living.

When deprived of what it needs, much like with one's physical body, a relationship may survive for an extended period of time while it progressively weakens. Rather than two people energizing each other, the partners begin to drain and exhaust each other. Spending time together becomes enervating and fatiguing. The only safe and viable way to be together is during activities that have a built-in "escape" from closeness, such as watching television or movies, eating, and maintaining a crowded calendar of busyness that makes it possible to avoid an intimate connection. Being together is tiring because the interaction doesn't produce a transfer of energy. The relationship is dying or already dead. That doesn't mean it will necessarily end, even though it's barely alive. Ending the relationship requires enough personal security and self-esteem in one or both partners to keep the capacity for self-care alive and the ability to act on the sense that one is better off alone.

One can keep running from a relationship, but, with time, there are fewer places to hide from its deadness and toxicity. Unnourished and unattended relationships have no immunity to allow them to heal themselves.

There are hallmarks by which to identify a poisoned relationship. Arguments and conflicts are characterized by *blame* and *guilt making* and *denial of responsibility*. Benign conversations readily inflame and become explosively hurtful, cruel, cold, and frustrating. Each partner seems only able to see what is or has been done to them, but not how they participate in creating and perpetuating the agony. The other person is always seen as the problem. There is no good-willed motivation to focus on one's own share of the responsibility.

Poisoned relationships have the characteristics of complete gender polarization. Men display their worst relationship tendencies, such as emotional coldness, cynicism, lack of affectionate sensuality, criticalness, withdrawal and the refusal to communicate, raging outbursts, and aggressive violent displays. Women who blame relentlessly portray themselves as victims, lose their ability to carry on a calm conversation, and are provocative; they are unable to stop or limit their emotionally charged accusatory tirades and are seen at their worst. Perhaps, in a hopeless and desperate bid to elicit a response from their partner, they push and provoke until they trigger destructive behaviors that confirm and validate their notion that they are in a relationship with a hurtful male monster.

Surprisingly, or perhaps not so surprisingly, when one considers the psychological sickness of the relationship, the partners often continue to cling to each other in a dance of hate, unable to let go, even though regular threats to leave are made by both. Instead, the relationship awaits a final crisis that will liberate both from their toxic nightmare. Even then there may be a reluctance to make a clean break. The impulse to remain in the relationship and punish one's partner causes them to stay. How else to explain the fact that the relationship continues to drag on even at a point where the slightest word or gesture can bring on a raging interchange followed by days of cold silence and hostility?

A poisoned relationship lacks the health and tools with which to facilitate a constructive, self-caring end, even though it is beyond rehabilitation. Relationships characterized by blaming, perceiving oneself as a victim, extreme emotional withdrawal, and continual hammering and insults cannot be rehabilitated. They are codependent relationships of the worst sort and require therapeutic intervention so they can be brought to a nondestructive and final conclusion.

INSIGHT 76: FATALLY POISONED RELATIONSHIPS

When a relationship has deteriorated to the point where the woman sees herself as an abused victim and the man has become stone cold and silent, the relationship is poisoned, and it is time to put it to an end.

The Conversation

The opposite end of the romantic euphoria continuum is one of bottomless rage and contempt. Tyrone was experiencing that extreme downside, living the potential for destructiveness that the poisoned relationship atmosphere had created. This being the third time he'd gone through this, he desperately wanted to avoid a repetition of it. The initial high no longer seemed worth the dreadful endpoint.

> *Tyrone*: "I strung out my last relationship until the bitter end before I threw in the towel and acknowledged it was beyond repair. I was the last one to see what had been obvious to my friends for a long time."

> *Dr. Goldberg*: "It's hard to face the painful truths that signal the end. So couples go round and round with repetitive, even vicious fights, followed by sentimental promises to work harder for change. Usually the guy is apologizing for being hurtful, and the woman is either holding it over him or being 'understanding.' Finally, they arrive at the classic end state where she's crying and acting deeply wounded, and he's cold and withdrawn and has given up trying to apologize, explain himself, and have a rational, problem-solving conversation."

> *Tyrone*: "When I'm at that stage in a relationship, it feels painful even to be alive. I feel like I'm walking through a minefield, just waiting for the next word or gesture that will ignite another explosion."

> *Dr. Goldberg*: "When the last vestiges of good will are gone, what is left is a woman in unbearable pain, flooded with low self-esteem, frustrated and hungry for love, and convinced that her partner is deliberately doing all kinds of terrible things to her, and that she has been the abused, patient, and loving one. By then her partner has realized that saying anything to her is hopeless and risky, so he goes completely silent. He would like to lash out but accomplishes the same thing by totally ignoring her."

The Insight Explained

Similar to how the physical body deteriorates when it is diseased, relationships can reach end states where they become sick and poisoned. Men and women become caricatures of the worst of their gender. The man is in perpetual rage, uncommunicative, cold, and uncaring, while the woman is constantly on the verge of tears, with feelings of helplessness and self-pity. This relationship end state is characterized by a lack of good will, mutual blaming, and an atmosphere so volatile and explosive that a single word or gesture can trigger a massive eruption of hostilities and a breakdown in communication that may go on for days.

What a Woman Can Do

A relationship environment can become toxic in the same way as the physical environment. A poisoned relationship is one in which both people have become fully defensive and good will has disappeared. At this point, positive change is no longer possible, while remaining in the status quo becomes a form of self-destruction and an expression of fear of change.

Because men seem able to compartmentalize their negative feelings as they endure the cold contempt of poisoned endings, it generally falls to women to create the final break and put an end to a fully toxic relationship atmosphere. Doing this is not "giving up." Rather, it is a courageous way of facing a relationship climate that has moved beyond the possibility of healing due to the absence of good will on both sides. Men, because of their ability to distance themselves from their emotions, are prone to disconnect and hang on out of habit, and to find private ways to escape from their painful situation.

What a Man Must Do

Particularly when there are young children involved, men and women, out of the misguided and well-intentioned belief that children are better off when their parents stay together, may want to continue to try.

In deciding whether to end the relationship, and in the process of shaping its termination, which ideally should be done with good will and avoidance of blaming and denigrating, a man must recognize that (1) guilt and a sense of responsibility are not healthy reasons to continue in a toxic relationship; (2) the fear of being alone is not a reason for remaining in a toxic relationship; and (3) in the ending of a relationship usually one person has to play the part of the "bad guy," who draws a boundary and initiates the ending.

Recognizing when to end a relationship is a complex task best done with the help of a seasoned, fair-minded therapist. The best way to measure the degree of a relationship's toxicity is by how easily the slightest word or action can create an explosive misunderstanding and an ugly encounter that results in icy distance for days, with neither partner willing or able to reach out to the other.

Good will on the part of both partners is necessary in order to repair a relationship. When ill will exists and a need to punish and destroy one's partner overrides everything, the relationship is probably poisoned and nonfixable. Repairing a relationship requires that each partner have good will, meaning they both want to work things out and there is willingness by both to place major emphasis on their own contributions to its condition. When the wish that one's partner would die as a way out exists and is felt by a man to be a solution, the relationship should probably end.

Before finally deciding whether a relationship has to end, counseling with a well-trained and licensed therapist should be attempted. This works both to get an objective reading on the potential of the relationship and hopefully to soften the relationship's atmosphere, so that if an ending is to take place, it can occur without the need to hurt or destroy the other.

Once it is clear that a relationship is irreversibly damaged, ending it as quickly as possible is best, with a clear sense that termination is important for the health of both partners. Placing blame and seeking vindication and support for one's belief that the other person was at fault are wasteful and untrue. My experience as a therapist has taught me that when relationships end, it is the will of both, even though it may appear to be primarily the will of one.

INSIGHT 77: KNOWING WHEN YOU'RE BEING USED

When a man feels afraid to be himself, say what he thinks, and show himself as he really is, thinking he would then disappoint and antagonize the woman and face her rejection, it suggests he's being used.

The Conversation

As Wesley reflected on his relationship history and search for a true and lasting love, he became aware that, at forty-seven, he had never really trusted his gut reactions.

Wesley: "When I'd meet a woman toward whom I was having that 'head over heels, this is definitely the one' feeling, I'd become so anxious that I only focused on whether she was into me and not what my own gut responses to her were. In almost every case in my dating life and my search, my gut was telling me something I didn't or couldn't process, that if I was obsessing about everything I said to her and whether she was still into me, there was something wrong. What I think I'm finally learning is when a woman really cares for you and loves you as you are, you don't have to continually preoccupy yourself with whether you did or said something that somehow caused her to not love you anymore. When you're really loved, you have a sense of security that whatever you say or do, she won't just say it's over. It's only when you're an object to be used that you can be easily discarded. I'll hear a woman say how much she loves me, and that she wants to be closer, but when I communicate with her honestly instead of just trying to be who and what she wants me to be, I can feel her anger and disappointment."

Dr. Goldberg: "While it looks like she's loving you, she's really only loving her fantasy of what she needs and wants you to be. Love and intimacy can only be real and solidly founded if they're based on each person disclosing themselves. If being real means being rejected, how can that be love?"

Wesley: "But what if I'm not very lovable when I'm showing my real self? I feel like I'm damaged and hostile, so why would a woman love the real me?"

Dr. Goldberg: "That sounds like male self-hatred."

The Insight Explained

If you are genuinely loved, you feel safe letting yourself be fully expressive spontaneously, without fear of rejection. If a man or woman has to be what they think the other wants and needs in order to feel loved, it isn't true love and, as such, can end at any time.

What a Woman Can Do

What most women don't realize is the immense control and power they have once a man attaches himself. When men become vulnerable and commit emotionally in a relationship, they have a fear of rejection. For both women and men, when one partner is self-centered and only in the relationship to get their own needs met and ready to leave unless they're getting what they want, the relationship is on borrowed time, and no matter how good it might feel at any given moment, it can collapse suddenly. The way to recognize that potential in your relationship is by observing whether you are experiencing a chronic sense of insecurity and fear that produces an obsessive self-monitoring. The message being in-tuited is that "if I'm not exactly what my partner wants and needs, they're going to reject and abandon me."

I suggest that if couples plan on creating a long and lasting relation-ship, it is important for them to risk disclosing as much of their real selves as possible regardless of the consequence. Having to monitor and check oneself out of a fear of rejection not only is an indication that you are not really being loved but also becomes increasingly unbearable. Setting the goal of only presenting yourself honestly creates a foundation for a satis-fying and lasting relationship, even when it feels risky to do so.

What a Man Must Do

It is crucial for a man to be able to distinguish genuine love and caring from the mere appearance and illusion of love created by a partner who is feigning love in order to disguise an exploitative motive.

A man may think he is being loved when a woman responds to him passionately, but if in order to get and keep that response he feels he must always provide what his partner needs or be what she wants him to be, and fears that when he says what he really thinks or feels it creates tension and a response of anger or disinterest, it isn't love.

A man who is not truly loved can sense by his fear or anxiety of being unself-consciously just as he is when he is not with his partner. A man who is being used will tend to be paralyzed by a fear of saying or doing the wrong thing for fear that the woman will stop loving him. Truly being loved means not feeling one has to hide important parts of oneself in order to maintain the love.

A man can recognize when he is being used if his partner always brings conversations back to whatever she needs and wants, and she becomes bored or distracted when most anything else is being discussed. Most important, a man must avoid a woman's passionate response that feels extreme and unreal, in the sense that it doesn't seem as if she is seeing him for who he is and how he knows himself to be but seems to be projecting her fantasies and needs onto him.

INSIGHT 78: WHEN YOU'RE JUST AN OBJECT TO HER

When a man is being used by a woman, she acts most lovingly toward him when he is doing something for her. When he is not giving her what she wants or is not doing things for her, her "love" and attention diminishes and disappears.

The Conversation

Clifford, an old-fashioned guy (as he described himself), in reviewing his relationship history, said, "I used to think doing for a woman was the way you showed her you cared. It took me a long time to realize two important things. First, doing for someone to please them is a bottomless pit; it never ends. The moment you slow it down, stop, or do less, she'll think something is wrong. Second, this approach makes her the matador, maneuvering the charging bull.

"She learns how to push your buttons whenever she needs or wants something. 'Oh darling, it would be so nice if you could take my car to the mechanic, I'm having trouble with the steering,' or 'Would you be a dear and pick up my dry cleaning?'"

Clifford talked about how this pattern made him feel like an object, never really loved but used. Even worse, when these relationships ended, the "doing for" seemed to carry only negative weight. When she was walking away, she'd say things like "Yes, he was a nice guy, but he didn't know how to relate. His idea of relating was to do things, when what I really wanted was a guy I could just be close with and talk to."

Other men have made similar comments.

Clifford: "I had this girlfriend, and it seemed like when I was doing something for her, like spending money or making plans for the future, everything was great. But when we were just being together without my doing for her, we seemed to get lost. There was no energy."

Dr. Goldberg: "By doing, you mean giving her gifts, fixing things, helping her solve her problems, or running her errands?"

Clifford: "Yes. The times when I wasn't doing for her, she'd be pouty and miffed, and things between us seemed boring and dead, and she'd find something to fight about to push me away. She'd lose interest in sex as well."

The Insight Explained

When a man objectifies a woman as a sex object, he "loves" her most when they're having sex. When they're not, he tends to lose interest. Women who objectify men see them as there to provide for and take care of them. They're no more interested in the personhood of the man and his needs and feelings than a man is interested in the personhood of the woman who he relates to for sex.

What a Woman Can Do

One of the primary factors that turns love into hate is when partners realize that they are being used rather than loved. The using may be mutual, though individuals can rarely see or acknowledge themselves doing the same thing they see being done to them.

Early in a relationship, a man can recognize when he's being exploited as an object because he feels a continual pressure to do things for the woman, and when he's not, she barely responds. It's the equivalent of when a man is using a woman primarily for sex and seems uninterested in her otherwise.

The traditional relationship was all about the chivalrous man who could do for his wife and family and the loving wife who showed him appreciation by taking care of him. That compartmentalization hardly fits today. It frustrated women in the days of traditional relationships to not be with a man who could give them what most women really need, which is someone who can communicate, empathize, and be enjoyable to be with. While it may seem charming initially to be with a man who is eager to be helpful and plays the gentleman, ultimately these relationships reach a point of stagnation because interaction is the sign of life in a relationship, not doing for the other.

What a Man Must Do

A man must learn to recognize when he is being objectified by his partner. When he is, there will be a constant focus on his performance and status, and he will feel the pressure to stay in his role. Whether he is a doctor or an actor, a military man or a car mechanic, his partner will move conversations to what he does and the functions he plays in order to reassure herself that she has made the right choice to be with him and avoid negative feelings she may have about him as a person. Put simply, a man being objectified will feel a continual pressure to show off to his partner because she relates to him and "loves him" based on his function, not who he is as a person.

A man who is being objectified may be introduced to friends and family by his title or occupation, accomplishments, and status. As a man it is tempting to allow oneself to be objectified—"Donald wrote such and such a book" or "Michael is a great singer"—because it may make him feel good about himself. The downside is that the love he receives will be contingent on his continuing to perform successfully. Should he fail or no longer be able to perform, he will be distanced. Coolness will replace passion, with the possibility that he will be rejected.

An objectified male is also vulnerable to criticism for what his partner feels he can't or doesn't want to give her or be for her—"Gary is always working on his books, and I feel like I am not even there" or "Marshall is so absorbed with his work I feel that he doesn't even see me."

INSIGHT 79: MR. POISON

Men who get stuck in their anger and are unable to see the toxic effect of their disconnection and coldness vent against attorneys, courts, the sys-

tem, and women. They lack the ability to see the impact of their alienating
behavior, which is their contribution to the rupture of their relationships.

The Conversation

Eduardo was "Mr. Poison" personified. As a family man he had terrorized his wife and children, systematically destroying their self-esteem and
ability to relate in a confident, open way. Whether it was physically or
with words, his way of expressing displeasure or loss of control was to
attack. After an ugly divorce, in which his wife walked away with almost
nothing just to get away from him and end the nightmare, he spent the last
third of his life with women who had a slave mentality. Even when they
gave him whatever he wanted, he was quick to insult them with terms
such as "idiot" and "dumb shit." They stayed with him because they
wanted to be included in his lifestyle of expensive cars, vacations, dining,
and luxury apartments, which they had no way of getting for themselves.

When things go wrong in his relationships, "Mr. Poison" is quick to
blame. He lacks the ability to see how he affects those close to him, who
inevitably abandon him. The only ones who remain are those whose sense
of helplessness and worthlessness is so great that they absorb the abuse in
return for being taken care of. A conversation I had with a mental health
worker whose specialty was working with these "poisonous" men when
their lives were falling apart expressed it this way:

> *Salomon*: "Maybe guys don't acknowledge their personal needs be-
> cause if you act like you don't expect or need anything from anybody,
> you'll never be disappointed or feel like you've been betrayed or hurt.
> Instead, they just walk around pissed off at everything—parking lot
> attendants, waitresses, 'the system,' women, their kids, 'foreigners,'
> politicians, and so on—even though they'd probably deny all their
> free-floating anger."

> *Dr. Goldberg*: "The saving grace for most men is they don't even
> know how lonely, desperate, or isolated they are. They've replaced
> their personal need and vulnerability with free-floating hostility, arro-
> gance, detachment, distrust, or paranoia. In their minds, everything
> 'sucks' or is 'bullshit.'"

Salomon: "Exactly! They are equal opportunity haters but don't know it and can't admit it. Progressively, over time, no one talks to them and vice versa. They truly believe it's because nobody is worth talking to. They barely notice that even their own kids hardly bother to spend time with them. If they could acknowledge their loneliness or desperation, they'd have to look at how their own cold, analytic, controlling, and distancing way of relating has cost them everything personal. They try to satisfy themselves with money or pleasures that don't really require connections or closeness to anybody else. Eventually, even that doesn't work. It all gets old and they go dead because there's no energy coming in from others."

The Insight Explained

Men transform and rationalize the dysfunctions caused by their externalization into abstract philosophies or arguments about "truth" and reality. That way they can distance themselves from seeing how their disconnected way of relating progressively destroys everything personal. They're good at seeing through other people's "bullshit" but can't see through their own. They don't make the proper connections that would allow them to transform their experience from one of generalized hostility into one of acknowledging their own intense but denied needs. Instead, they use rationalizations like "We're all born alone and we all die alone" and have cynical beliefs about how love and caring are just illusions.

What a Woman Can Do

"Mr. Poison" is every woman's nightmare. While these men, through their self-centered aggressiveness, may accumulate a modicum of wealth, they feed on the insecurities and dependency women of low self-esteem struggle with. Once in the relationship, women become empty vessels, unaware of their own feelings, because in their desperation to hold on to the poisonous man, they've incorporated all his attitudes and ideas and have none of their own. The trade-off is the total annihilation of a woman's self, and while it seems initially scary to end such abusive relationships because of a woman's decimated self-esteem, the price of not doing so is having to live in a nightmare world.

As for men themselves, their abstracted ways of processing make it hard for them to see how they're continuously creating and amplifying the impersonal reality they live in. As a result, they lose the opportunity for self-awareness and growth. Until men acknowledge the pain behind their personal reality, whether resulting from inadequate or abusive parenting or simply from societal expectations, they'll continue to chase intellectualized illusions about so-called meaning and truth, as if that existed somewhere "out there" and were something they needed to struggle or wrestle with because of the way life and the system supposedly are.

What a Man Must Do

A man can recognize the poisonous blamer inside of himself by the fact that those close to him relate in fear of displeasing him because they need him and are fearful of his lashing out. When things go wrong or he is displeased, it is always the other person's fault.

A man must recognize the poisonous blamer inside himself by his repetitive and accusatory outbursts and his inability to apologize or say, "I'm sorry." When things go wrong in his eyes, his impulse will be to rage and punish. When not criticizing those in his life, Mr. Poison may rage against authority and the restrictions he labels as "stupid."

In a relationship, it may be difficult for a man to recognize the poisonous blamer in himself. Indirectly he can recognize his impact by the fearful and anxious way his partner or children relate to him and the urgency with which others apologize and take responsibility.

A man must know that, as an aggressive, critical, accusatory, controlling male, while he may be treated with kid gloves and deferred to by intimates and friends, below the surface he will be hated and abandoned once those close to him no longer need him. While his ego may not allow him to recognize the true feelings of those who flatter and defer to him, he will increasingly become the isolated male, whose only intimates will be those with low self-esteem who are fearful of drawing boundaries because they are dependent on him. Their responses to him will be manipulative and duplicitous.

As his children grow, they will have as little to do with him as possible. His wife or partner will only remain with him out of dependency and insecurity, and his friends will progressively remove themselves as thcy tirc of his ncgativity and his nccd to always be right and prove himself superior.

Because the only ones to remain with him will be those of low self-esteem and personal insecurity, and their responses will be limited to false expressions of caring, the poisonous male will sense that and, out of boredom and contempt, increasingly respond with sarcasm and denigrating remarks, often in a loud tone, which will exacerbate the toxic atmosphere he creates to the point that those around him will fantasize about his death.

INSIGHT 80: WHAT MAKES HIM MR. POISON

The toxic man thinks he listens but is easily distracted by his own inner prejudices. He thinks he loves, but he responds positively only when accommodated and stroked. He thinks he is open, but when engaging in anything except what he wants and can control, he is bored and negative. He thinks he is reasonable, but reasonable to him means his logic rather than the other person's experience.

The Conversation

While most men cannot see the poisonous elements existing in their own personalities, they can see them more easily when they remember what it was like to try and relate to their own "poisonous" fathers. Pain around frustrating, absent relationships with their fathers is common among men, and the fathers they describe manifest the poisonous components of masculinity.

Joe: "So many times I've resolved to have a closer relationship with my dad, but something about being around him just repels me and seems to make that impossible."

Dr. Goldberg: "Many men and women have this fantasy that there's a way to get closer to their dads and get them to respond if they could only find the right button. But you can't have a loving relationship with someone simply by working at it by yourself. There are real limits based on the way the other person is in return."

Joe: "Yes, my dad would say the way he is was just fine. When you'd try and tell him otherwise, he'd say you were feeding him 'psychobabble.'"

Dr. Goldberg: "Well, make sure your expectations of closeness with him aren't unrealistic. Also be sure to appreciate the positives about him and the way he relates, since appreciation and approval, not condemnation, is the only way to achieve any degree of positive change with him."

Joe: "My dad really doesn't listen. He's got a very short attention span. Other guys I've spoken to have had the same experience. My dad thinks he's the most open and caring guy in the world, when, in fact, if he can't do things his way, he withdraws. I know he thinks he's a real loving person to his family and the people at work. But most of the time, you don't even get the sense that he knows anyone else is around. Unless you do all the work and ease him into relating by being real nice to him, he's in his own world. After a while it grinds you down and you just want to give up trying because you realize how impossible it is. What makes it all feel so hopeless is the monster-size gap between the way he sees himself and the way he actually comes across."

Dr. Goldberg: "Maybe the way to tell how toxic a man is, and to best protect yourself from being hurt by him, is to focus on the size of the gap between what he believes and how he comes across. When the two are on opposite ends of the spectrum, you should give up trying."

The Insight Explained

What makes a man toxic is a combination of his lack of self-awareness regarding his effect on others and the fact that he seems so sure that the only way to be is the way he is.

What a Woman Can Do

Many women in relationships with toxic men have the mistaken notion that their love and patience will soften and heal the man. The opposite is true. Such men respond well or at their best when their woman partner demonstrates power, sets strong boundaries, and gives them the clear message that she will leave the relationship if she is treated abusively. That message, however, needs to be followed through, not made idly. If a woman fails to follow through after she's been treated abusively, it begins a progressive decline. Lack of follow-through is seen as weakness to be taken advantage of. She becomes someone to dismiss and ignore.

What a Man Must Do

A man who fits the definition of Mr. Poison is only likely to consider change or point a blaming finger at himself after he has been distanced and abandoned by those he believed loved him. Until then, so long as he can have his way and with little consequence, Mr. Poison will resist self-reflection, change, apology, or recognition of his hurtful impact, and he will continue to believe he is anything but poisonous. In fact, he may even think he is very much loved, and he may rationalize that those who don't like him are just jealous of his superiority.

Men must see that they are vulnerable to evolving into poisonous people because of their early socialization as a male that sanctioned aggressive, ego-driven, competitive, autonomous, controlling ways of being. Specifically, men must know that they are vulnerable to becoming poisonous and being hated because of their need to dominate and win. In order to not acknowledge vulnerability, they won't apologize when they are wrong or have been abusive. It will be easier for a man to recognize his poisonous impact by the many relationships he's had and lost and by the absence of people who reach out to him. His phone never rings unless it is for a reason, and nonobligatory social invitations rarely occur.

A man's tendency will be to resist seeking out therapeutic help that he is willing to commit to because of feelings of negativity and criticalness toward therapy and his therapist and his cynical belief that it is a waste of his time and money. However, not doing so means no change will take place and his personal world will shrink and finally dissolve and disappear completely.

INSIGHT 81: MS. TOXIC

The toxic woman is a blamer who sees herself as a victim and her partner as the cause of her unhappiness.

The Conversation

Ken: "I discovered a way to quickly identify a woman who's dangerous and hopeless to be around, no matter how distracting her beauty may be. I simply get her talking about her ex-boyfriends. If she tells me horror stories about how they lied to her and cheated on her, makes negative generalizations about all men, and tells me that's why her relationships failed, insisting it had nothing to do with her, then it's time for me to make a polite exit. If she's really gorgeous, I have to make sure I don't get seduced by that."

Dr. Goldberg: "People repeat their relationship histories. Whatever they've done before, they'll do again. It's only the fantasies stirred up by romantic beginnings that obscure that fact and make guys believe that choosing the wrong men was her only problem in the past. When a woman can't acknowledge her defensiveness or personality dysfunctions, and recognize that she's a blamer and a victim, any relationship with her will have to be totally on her terms. Even then she'll find something to feel hurt or disappointed about, and it'll be the guy's fault."

Ken: "I always used to get fooled by a pretty face and a sweet, pleasing manner. When I'd hear a woman's stories, I'd think all the guys from that woman's past were losers, and that with me, it'd be different."

The Insight Explained

The women who block negative feelings and never acknowledge anger, and who can't see how they contribute to the difficulties and problems they experience in relationships with men, will inevitably see themselves as the injured party. When a woman is unable to see her dysfunctional patterns and responses, her impact will be destructive and poisonous.

Worse still, many men will buy into her victim interpretation and believe that the problems actually were their fault. Then they'll experience the self-hate that comes with trying to improve a relationship without help . . . and failing.

What a Woman Can Do

As a psychologist counseling a wide range of couples over the years and working with them on a deep level, I've come to understand and believe that healthy, fulfilling, nontoxic relationships are those in which both partners focus on their own contribution to the relationship's problems, where the blaming finger is not used. While blaming may give the blamer a sense of vindication and righteousness, it inevitably means the end of growth for the relationship. Blaming blocks the kind of meaningful dialogue required to keep a relationship alive in a healthy way. Growth itself begins when blaming ends, along with the full realization that whatever happens in the relationship is created by both partners.

What a Man Must Do

Men must recognize the toxic woman in order to avoid closeness and interdependence with her. She can be identified through her moral righteousness and her spiritual, yet judgmental, pretensions of being a loving and caring person that cause her to believe that every negative relationship experience she has is caused by the less evolved other person.

Ms. Toxic must be recognized by a man in order to avoid the hopelessness of developing a caring relationship because she is unable to see and acknowledge her contributions to and share in creating its problems. Behind a surface disguise of "niceness," Ms. Toxic builds up intense inner rage and a sense of being mistreated and abused. Everything that happens is seen as the fault of the other. The ending of a relationship with Ms. Toxic, while inevitable, will usually be horrific. Men must not deny the obvious signs early on in how she describes, blames, and denigrates her partners in past relationship failures, how she cries in pain when arguments break out, and the way she acts wounded and then righteously forgiving of the other person. Unexpected raging outbursts increase with time, and comments of "I hate you" occur more frequently.

Improving and changing a relationship with Ms. Toxic is impossible because of her self-righteous blaming and her victim rage, which make her unable to self-reflect and point a finger of responsibility at herself. She is always the victim in every relationship failure.

11

MAKING IT BETTER: IT'S IN THE HOW, NOT THE HOW-TO

When it comes to fixing and improving a relationship, the "how-to" approach is a seductive blind alley—the "magic key" illusion that seduces you into believing there is an objective answer or solution to your relationship problem "out there" and someone else has it. "How-tos" are sleight-of-hand tricks, which explains why the appetite for the latest book and theory seems to be bottomless. Countless new ones come on the market regularly. Each season has its own version of a "how to fix a relationship" book containing the newest and latest belief system that will supposedly and finally create that elusive sense of satisfaction, peace, and fulfillment.

Think about it. If "how-tos" actually worked beyond the initial morale boost and spurt of energy and optimism one gets from feeling inspired by a charismatic writer or preacher, much in the way a Sunday sermon can create a short-term "feel good" experience, would there be hundreds of such books published with competing prescriptions and claims that contradict the content of the other books?

Why, then, do intelligent readers continue to follow that siren call? I see it even in my profession among the PhD graduates who have been rigorously trained to be critical thinkers and discriminate, detect, and reject unscientific and unproven answers and solutions. The temptation to slip into an instant "here's how to fix the problem" mode seems irresistible even to the highly educated, although a cardinal rule that clinical psychologists learn in their training from day one is to avoid giving advice or "how-tos."

Why is the "how-to" advice approach the wrong way to go, and why is it tempting and irresistible? The answer is simple yet harsh. The belief that there is a "how-to" answer "out there" gives us permission to take a pass on our own responsibility in creating the dilemmas, conflicts, and problems we face. "How-to" solutions give individuals permission to tell themselves the problem was created because they didn't know the right thing to do at the time: "Now that I know what to do, I can fix it and make things better." For example, a woman having problems with her sex life might conclude, based on her reading, that "I should wear sexier clothes to excite him, or I need to touch his penis in a different way," or "I need to be less available, and make him pursue me more," or "I need to lose weight to turn him on." He in turn might tell himself the problems of sexual disinterest on his partner's part are because "I need to be more romantic and do little things like bring her flowers or candies, or leave her love notes," or "I need to take more time for kissing and foreplay before I penetrate her," or "I need to tell her what I need, and what I feel, and ask her what she needs," or "I need to stimulate her clitoris more energetically and for a longer time."

Each proceeds to do the "how-to" they have learned and believe will make the difference. These "how-to" techniques may work . . . temporarily. They work, like the distraction technique of a magician, by allowing momentary escape from the real issues and emotions of the relationship. Soon, however, things revert back to the way they were before, and the problem becomes worse because the struggle now has developed an overlay of defeat and hopelessness: "I tried different things and nothing seems to work."

"How-to" solution writers are not to blame for misleading the reader. They are catering to people's need to believe there are concrete and easy answers and solutions to their difficult personal problems, solutions that allow one to put the focus of the problem outside ourselves and avoid the scary work of asking oneself the following: (1) How and what does my problem tell me about who and what I am all about in my relationship? (2) How am I being perceived by my partner, and to what extent is the problem we're having caused by the way my partner feels about me and my personal impact? (3) How do I really feel about my partner, and to what degree does my response reflect that? (4) In what way is my present problem in this relationship part of an ongoing or longstanding pattern I have that was already in place before this relationship began? Was I like this in past relationships, and did it contribute to their end? Did I choose my present partner because I fell into the trap of believing I could change my experience by finding somebody new?

Putting the focus on one's own patterns, processes, and unknowing defensiveness is threatening, certainly much more so than following the advice of a "how-to" expert. Intellectualizing a personal problem by reading a book about it that pretends to give the answers or listening to charismatic speakers, even when they are credentialed professionals, is comforting and inspiring, but, like all easy answers to difficult problems, they mislead. We embrace them *eagerly and uncritically* because we want to believe a "how-to" will save us, and we want to avoid putting the spotlight on the "who we are" of the problem. The external content solution seduces us by allowing us to avoid confronting the painful truths of our own processes. We pay the price by trading short-term escape for the build-up of long-term defeat and hopelessness. The price for the "instant" solution is the buildup of bitterness, cynicism, and a sense of defeat that comes from repeatedly trying and failing. Nothing worthwhile and lasting when it comes to relationship problems comes easy, and when "how-to" solutions magically seem to appear, the consumer must beware.

INSIGHT 82: HOW SHE JUDGES

When a woman wants a man, he can't do anything wrong; when she doesn't, he can't do anything right.

The Conversation

Toby, a product engineer of forty-one, had just experienced an excruciatingly painful relationship ending, in which he found himself regressing to stalkerlike behaviors.

> *Toby*: "There I was beating myself up and wracking my brain going over all the details of my relationship after I'd been dumped by this woman I was stuck on. 'I should have done this or that,' or 'Why

didn't I tell her such and such?' or 'Looking back now, I can see the turning point when it started to go south with her.'"

Dr. Goldberg: "Men don't see it, but what they're doing is engaging in magical thinking. They'd be the last to acknowledge that they're totally irrational in the way they're going about making sense of what went wrong in their relationships."

Toby: "When I was feeling really desperate, to the point of wanting to kill myself or somebody else, I was begging this woman who'd rejected me, 'Just tell me what it is. I'll fix it, I swear. Just give me one chance. I'll go to therapy. Anything you want, just say it and it's done. I really mean it this time.'"

Dr. Goldberg: "That's when the woman tries to get through to a desperate guy just to get him off her back, but he doesn't believe her. She'll say something like 'It's nothing you did. You were great; it was me. I can't exactly explain it. I just can't be with you anymore, even though I still care about you. And please don't go to therapy to try and change for me. Do it for yourself if you want, but please not for me.'"

Toby: "The funny thing is the flip side—how at the beginning of a relationship a guy can act like a total jerk or even an abusive asshole, but if the woman wants him, she doesn't seem to notice that at all. Or a guy might obsess about what he's wearing, what restaurant to take a woman to, or getting his car perfectly polished and clean before he picks her up. He's convinced it'll make a difference."

Dr. Goldberg: "He'd be shocked to discover that it barely matters what he does or how he does it if she's already fixed on being with him. If she's not, then he can do everything perfectly and it'll be a waste of time."

Toby: "I know exactly what you mean. I've been a lying, callous idiot with some women and they still wanted me. Other times, when I was the one obsessed, I'd go over every detail of a date beforehand to make it perfect and still wouldn't get to first base. In fact, she could be treating me like total shit and I'd be like a dog at her feet, hoping she'd pet my head and smile at me. That'd be enough to keep my little fantasy going for a while longer, until I finally got the message that I was in a 'no win' situation."

The Insight Explained

When a woman attaches romantically and intensely, it's because she has a driving need to fulfill. It could be her need to be rescued, validated, married, supported, or whatever, and the man she attaches to seems to be someone she believes could perfectly fulfill her need. If she's convinced he's the guy, her blinders will pretty much go on to everything negative about him, sort of like a guy who's sexually hot for a woman and can't see anything real or negative about her as a person. Likewise, when she's done with him, either because her need has been met or because she concludes the need can't be satisfied by him, she closes herself off. The man becomes invisible to her. Once that happens, all the fancy dancing in the world won't change anything. While a man's agenda may differ from a woman's, the same basic dynamic occurs. When a woman desperately promises to make whatever changes the man desires, she only paves the way for his abusive and contemptuous behavior, and while out of pity he may act as if things might be worked out, a woman's desperation will only succeed in creating the opposite effect.

What a Woman Can Do

Because men tend to express their caring by doing, they readily buy into the erroneous notion that when a relationship ends, it was because of specific behaviors they did or did not do. With that logic they believe they can resurrect the relationship and bring back love with the correct "how-to" formula. It's difficult in these instances for women to convince the man that "this time it's really over and nothing can be done." To avoid stalking behavior, women need to set and maintain strong boundaries and not waver or succumb to feeling sorry because of the man's pain by giving him false hope that there might still be a way to get the relationship on track.

What a Man Must Do

To avoid agonizing over what to do in a relationship he is in or trying to make happen, a man must recognize that a woman's feelings in a relationship are not simply the product of what he says or does or his ability to find the exact or correct way of responding. To avoid beating himself up when relationships are not happening as he wishes, a man must recognize that a woman in a relationship may have her own agenda that is independent of anything specific that a man says or does. If she wants him, she will tend to overlook or minimize almost anything negative. If she doesn't, she will overlook and be unresponsive to even his best efforts.

Just like a man who is pursuing a woman he desires, women tend to know what they want ahead of anything specific that may occur, and just like a man who desires a woman will continue to pursue her even in the face of her obvious disinterest or lack of response, a woman who wants to be with a man will tend to overlook, deny, and turn a blind eye or deaf ear to a man's negative shortcomings and offensive or insensitive remarks.

Contrariwise, once a woman has decided she is not interested or attracted to a man, there is little to nothing he can do to change it. It is wasteful and hurtful to himself to believe he has the power to make something happen when in fact he doesn't. In the seemingly most hopeless of situations, a man can try to wait, persist, and hang on in the face of painful rejections in the slim possibility that a woman's life circumstances will change and a window of opportunity will appear. That, however, will be based not on what he does so much as on her own changing needs.

INSIGHT 83: CHANGING A BLAMER'S MIND

"A blamer is a blamer is a blamer," and there is no way to improve things in a relationship with people who see themselves as victims of their partners.

The Conversation

Jonathan was a self-described rescuer of forty-nine. He loved the buzz and romantic excitement that accompanied a new relationship with a woman in trouble, be it her stalking ex-boyfriend, an abusive husband, or extreme financial distress. He enjoyed the feeling of being desperately needed. After a number of these experiences that began on an incredible high and ended suddenly and unexpectedly, usually after the woman's ship had been righted, he discovered that he went from being the hero to being the bad guy, and it left him blindsided. The latest pain from being unexpectedly dumped brought him to his knees. He described his experience with Joanne.

Jonathan: "When I met Joanne I liked her openness in telling me about her past relationships. She described the guy she had just broken up with and how she'd spend weekends bored while he'd be watching sports, and how he was selfish and quick during their lovemaking, and how she tried everything to make the relationship work before she finally gave up. I felt protective toward her. She seemed kind and sweet. I felt she deserved so much better. My other reaction was 'The guy sounds like a classic jerk.' I decided I'd do my best to make it all up to her."

Dr. Goldberg: "The protective impulse and wanting to make things right for a woman is a romantic turn-on for guys. Showing a woman that you're different and better than other guys may be what that's all about. It gives you an opportunity to play hero!"

Jonathan: "But I found out the hard way that the hero thing is a delusion and trap. I never stopped to think, 'Hey, she's blaming everything on the guy. If she's doing that with him, she'll probably do it with me too.'"

Dr. Goldberg: "When did you come to see that?"

Jonathan: "After a few months. I wasn't playing superhero anymore and we started having arguments and conflicts. According to her, every argument or problem we had was my fault. When I asked her, 'What about you? It takes two to tango, don't you think?' she'd stare at me coldly, as if to say, 'You're turning out to be no different from my ex.' At first I let it go, but after the tenth fight in which I was being portrayed as the bad guy and she was taking zero responsibility, it clicked that this was her pattern and I gave up. I sure wasn't going to spend my life apologizing and explaining."

The Insight Explained

Because they believe them to be true, women are convincing when they describe the injustices of past relationships and how they were hurt and betrayed by previous men. This may be recognized as an indication of the way they interpret their personal experiences, particularly when all the past men are seen negatively and as having been at fault. Then it becomes clear the woman is out of touch or in denial of her part in creating her experiences. Since it's unlikely that any relationship's breakdown is solely or primarily the fault of one person, the woman's sense of herself as a victim is being displayed by her blaming interpretations.

What a Woman Can Do

Because a chief complaint and fear of many men in committed relationships is that sooner or later they're seen as responsible for the decline and conflicts in their relationships, when a man finds a woman who does not blame him for relationship issues, and better still acknowledges her own flaws and contribution to its problems, it has the potential to create the kind of intimacy most women would hope for. The sense of fairness it generates in men tends to release the best of their relationship behaviors. Inviting a man to provide feedback on matters of who is responsible while listening and accepting his reality is the kind of loving response most men long for from a woman, who can then be seen as someone who knows how to be a best friend and buddy.

Romantic beginnings and a strong initial attraction between two people tend to obscure the fact that in intimate relationships people repeat their patterns and histories. This is particularly true of blamers because they feel righteous and like victims and therefore lack a motivation to introspect and change. Their blaming behaviors are their way of making sense of what happens to them generally and will continue across the board in other matters as well. The inability to see one's own issues, flaws, and defensiveness tends to grow, to the point where the relationship eventually is interpreted in a black-and-white fashion, with the blamer always the innocent, injured party and the partner portrayed as the spoiler.

What a Man Must Do

Men must recognize a situation or relationship that has moved beyond the possibility of change or will always feed on his tendency to feel guilty and take responsibility, and when he is with a woman incapable of seeing her 50 percent contribution to the problems. Once in such a relationship, a man will always be made to feel that in any conflict or argument he is at fault.

A man must recognize his powerlessness and the futility of his attempts to show a woman otherwise. His attempt to prove or point out her distortions of perception by using facts and logic will only infuriate her more, as she sees it as denying what (to her) is an obvious and correct perception.

A man must see that his lack of psychological understanding will prevent him from recognizing the tendency and need to blame her partner, and recognize that a woman's need to see herself as the blameless injured party is embedded in her personality, not just a simple one-time response to a specific situation.

Men in such relationships must look at what it is about themselves that made being in them acceptable or attractive. Only a man's insecurity or low self-esteem would allow him to enter a relationship in which he is always blamed and where he is not setting a boundary or refusing to take sole responsibility when the problems are actually the product of their mutual interaction and communication.

INSIGHT 84: HER RELATIONSHIP SUPERIORITY

Because many women express feelings more easily and are more focused on the personal side of life than men, it is assumed that they are more in touch and aware. This is one of the relationship illusions that retards the growth and development of male-female relationships and closeness. The relationship cluelessness of men is considered a given, while the lack of awareness in women is harder to see but every bit as impactful.

The Conversation

After several years of therapy, at forty-four Terry arrived at a profound awareness. After years of believing that he and other men were clueless in comparison with relationship-focused women, it occurred to him that women had massive blind spots that produced distortions and defensive reactions when relating to men and were every bit as great as men's.

Terry: "When I was younger I believed women understood relationships far better than men and were more loving and tuned in to the personal stuff. I was convinced I was a relationship moron. But since then, I'm beginning to think women's so-called relationship intuition and superiority is an illusion. Yes, women may be more focused on the personal and relationship issues, but they don't understand them any better, because if they actually did, relationships would work better than they do. I really don't believe women know themselves any better than men do."

Dr. Goldberg: "Many women are convinced relationship problems are caused by men's personal denseness. These women believe they're always ready to do whatever it takes to make things work, but the ways they go about it are as distorted as what men do. On the surface it may look better, but it really isn't."

Terry: "How do you work things out with someone who's sure that it's the other person that needs fixing?"

Dr. Goldberg: "Women may be right in saying men have serious problems with feelings, closeness, and commitment. I wouldn't argue with that. What they don't acknowledge is how their relationship hang-ups, such as romanticizing stuff, crying instead of negotiating, failing to set boundaries, not recognizing their own shortcomings, and getting overly involved and emotionally fused, are as destructive as what men do."

The Insight Explained

A woman's investment in her relationships and making relationships her priority creates the illusion that she's the loving and healthy one, while the man who is preoccupied with external concerns and ambitions is thought of as the selfish or clueless one. Just because she's more focused on relationships doesn't mean hers is a balanced focus. If women truly were better at relationships, they would recognize and work on the changes they need to make. They would never let relationships deteriorate to the point where they became abusive or destructive, and they would never be blamers or victims because they wouldn't allow things to get to the point where they'd find themselves in that kind of position or situation.

What a Woman Can Do

It can be both liberating and exhilarating for women when they realize that their relationship frustrations and disappointments with men are not simply due to men's deficiencies. While the latter may be true, it is important to acknowledge that women have their own defenses, and these defenses create overreactions and distortions in their relationships with men. While this may sound like criticism, I believe, to the contrary, it contains the potential for new and great hope that when women acknowledge and work through the gender prisms shaping their relationship perceptions, their experience of intimacy will become qualitatively new and improved.

What a Man Must Do

Because a man's sensitivity, emotions, and needs are commonly less visible than a woman's, and because they were taught as boys that being a man meant controlling and hiding their vulnerable inner life, men who are filled with caring, tender, loving, and sensitive feelings, thoughts, and impulses must remember that what they experience inwardly must be expressed outwardly, lest they find themselves misunderstood and misinterpreted.

Men must understand that just as women are increasingly displaying their aggressive, powerful, autonomous, sexual, and assertive selves without inhibition or masking, in other words the parts of themselves that used to be hidden because they were considered unfeminine, men must take the cue and understand they can and must increasingly and confidently acknowledge and make visible their softer side. Specifically, they must learn to openly show their vulnerable and sensitive nature and their capacity for love, affection, loneliness, sadness, and selflessness, and to freely and happily display their total humanness in order to challenge and destroy negative stereotypes of men as being the clueless, animalistic, and insensitive gender.

In other words, men must take equal responsibility in the same way women have, to liberate the world of stereotyped gender assumptions and break ground toward the evolution of a fully humanized, balanced, and nondefensive gender world.

INSIGHT 85: THERAPY IS FOR HIM, NOT HER

Women who see themselves as abused victims don't see their equal participation in the downward spiral of their relationships. Instead, they think relationship therapy is about getting the man to change and become more loving.

The Conversation

As a therapist with over forty years of experience as a couples counselor, as well as in working with men in crisis, I've found that when relationship therapy is initiated by a woman who seeks out couples therapy for the purpose of fixing her man, the potential for meaningful and enduring change is small. I begin by asking each partner what percentage of the relationship problems they believe is the product of their own issues. How much of the relationship struggle do they see as the consequence of their own behavior and problems? If the answer comes back, "I believe it's mainly the other," I can predict that enduring, constructive change will not happen.

Dorin, the father of two young boys at forty-four, made an unsuccessful attempt at relationship improvement through counseling.

Dorin: "When a guy finally agrees to go for counseling, how is he going to get through to a woman who's been crying and begging for hugs and conversation, and never seems to get angry, that she's also a contributor to their problems?"

Dr. Goldberg: "Clearly, that's an issue that hasn't been solved at all or even managed reasonably."

Dorin: "Women don't seem to ask themselves why they chase hugs and conversation from a guy who seems disinterested in that. Hopefully, counselors are trained to see beyond what it looks like on the surface."

Dr. Goldberg: "Why are they with these men? Why do women eagerly pursue commitment and marriage with guys who are supposedly insensitive jerks?"

Dorin: "They'd probably say the men were a lot different at the beginning, and they probably were."

The Insight Explained

Many women think they want to make their relationships work and will do whatever it takes to make that happen. But once the dialogue begins, it's obvious that it's all about maneuvering the men to take responsibility and make the changes. Many guys are so self-blaming and guilt ridden they do try to fix it all by themselves, just like they took responsibility initially to make the relationship happen. Inevitably, they will fail, because relationship problems are about how two people relate to each other, not about what one person supposedly is doing to the other.

What a Woman Can Do

When it comes to relationships, men are vulnerable to self-blame and guilt because it's been drummed into them that they are relationship idiots. While this may seem to many women to be a vindication for the pain they've experienced and leaves them feeling largely not at fault, such an interpretation is a way to win the battle while losing the war because the vindication comes at the price of "no meaningful change possible" for the relationship itself. For women who truly feel they want their relationship to survive, this kind of interpretation will not take them where they think they want to go. The hard work for women is to reject such an easy analysis in order to find the fifty-fifty core of responsibility that exists buried beneath.

Women may pay lip service to the idea that when there are problems in the relationship, the relationship itself is dysfunctional rather than just one person's fault. But in the final analysis, they often believe that it really is the man's fault. When a relationship fails, what many women rarely see but need to focus on is how they've facilitated, contributed to, or even provoked the responses and behaviors they hate.

What a Man Must Do

Because men tend to be seen as the destroyers of personal relationships, they are also seen as the ones who are most in need of psychological help. Unfortunately, men tend to be more resistant to therapy than women, even though the original creators of psychotherapeutic treatment were men.

Men must increasingly avail themselves of personal therapy to demonstrate their willingness to take equal responsibility for the relationship issues in their lives and acknowledge their need for help with their vulnerable personal selves.

Men must tell their partners and others in their lives the way they experience things, and then go about trying to repair and improve their close relationships. Rather than become defensive when told they need therapy, men should embrace the suggestion and seek out other vehicles for opening themselves up so others can see what men traditionally have hidden from the outside world.

Women usually feel men are the spoilers of intimate relationships, and that they should get help for themselves because they are seen as poor communicators and advocates for their inner and emotional selves. Men should agree but let it be known that their partners need to participate as well if relationships are to be improved.

INSIGHT 86: HER FEELINGS ARE HER REALITY

Trying to prove to a woman that what she feels is not true is impossible and alienating. What a woman feels cannot be negotiated or even changed. Her feelings create her reality of the relationship and guide her actions.

The Conversation

It took Marx, a heating and air conditioning engineer, two failed marriages before it began to dawn on him that men and women process reality differently, and he couldn't use his customary linear and logical way to talk women out of their feelings and their intuitive, emotional responses, which seemed to him to be irrational, if not outright crazy. When he began to have severe communication problems with his two children as well, both of whom seemed to avoid having any personal conversations with him, he began to consider the possibility that there was something flawed in his approach.

Marx: "Under the categories of 'hopeless pursuits' or 'why waste your time?' I would definitely include trying to explain to a woman that what she feels doesn't make any sense, or attempting to change her feelings with logical arguments."

Dr. Goldberg: "More than just a 'hopeless pursuit,' I would add, 'unless you want to kill the romance in the relationship and make her really resent you.' It makes the woman feel that the man doesn't understand who she is, and that means he can't possibly really love her. For the man, it makes him want to withdraw out of frustration because he starts to see the woman as stupid, childlike, or irrational."

Marx: "When a woman says she's afraid to do something, I see guys trying to convince her to get over her fears with statements like 'There's nothing to be afraid of' or even saying something like 'That's ridiculous.' Or when she's worried about something, a man might respond, 'There's nothing to worry about,' or 'Worrying won't solve the problem.'"

Dr. Goldberg: "When it's just between him and her, like when a woman tells a man she doesn't feel he loves her like he used to, or the comment he just made was hostile and intentionally hurtful, or he never seems to want to be with her anymore, men will try to prove her feelings are wrong by giving her some idiotic facts or examples."

Marx: "I've fallen into that trap myself, but now when a woman tells me something she feels about the relationship that makes no sense to me, I just listen and try to understand where she's coming from. Occasionally, I might ask her to get specific, but even that is usually a waste because she just sees that as my way of trying to negate her experience or belittle her. So mostly I'll just say something like 'If you see me that way, how can you still be in love with me?' or 'You must really be questioning our relationship. It sounds like you don't like me very much.' That usually brings the conversation down to a tangible level where we can talk, but without pissing her off."

The Insight Explained

Because men apply logic and the need for concrete evidence or proof to most of their discussions, arguments, or confrontations, they have a false and defensive sense of being "right" and on higher ground. But what the man is really saying is "I don't care if I lose the war, so long as I win this battle." And that's exactly what tends to happen with his relationships with his kids, wife, family members, and friends. He comes across to them as having a "you're just a dumb shit" attitude. They don't really hear his so-called logical arguments. Instead, they respond to his put-down attitude and air of superiority.

What a Woman Can Do

If men are to break the pattern of systematically destroying their personal lives, they first need to recognize and acknowledge how the ways they relate are alienating, and that personal relating is not just a matter of using logic to prove something is right or wrong or by informing others as to what to do and how to do it. It's about letting people be who they are, not negating their experience, and being supportive, empathetic, and sensitive to their feelings as well as recognizing the validity and reality that their emotions are as meaningful as his logic.

Men need to hear from women that their automatic, so-called logical solutions to family and marriage relationship problems are both off-putting and weird sounding in the way that they minimize the personal elements of a problem. Men need to be confronted in a supportive way about how others are made to feel when personal issues come up. Women need to overcome their concern that a man's feelings will be hurt if told the truth of the responses of others. Men who minimize and deny the significance and meaning of emotions need to be educated as to the damage they are doing to their close relationships.

What a Man Must Do

It is only chauvinism that prevents men from recognizing the validity and value of women's feelings. In particular, they must realize the futility of trying to talk women out of their feelings.

Indeed, if men's logical approach to personal and life issues were a superior way to live, they ought to be living higher-quality lives than women. Clearly they aren't. When men's personal lives begin to unravel or they are abandoned by their partners, most men, using their logic, are unable to figure out what's going on. Consequently, their response and approach exacerbates and usually makes matters worse.

Men's compulsion to win and not show vulnerability by asking for help, and to override their fear and fight at all costs, is not only stupid but also borderline insane—and proof that men are their own worst enemies.

If a man is to have a working relationship with a woman, he needs to be able to read, translate, and learn from her feelings. In addition, men need to question the very idea that their so-called objectivity or logic is even productive and trumps women's emotions and empathies. If it did, men would not be prone to doing the many things that make no sense at all, such as using aggression and violence to solve problems, self-destructively entering into relationships because of a sexual craving, or becoming addicted to mind- and body-altering substances that destroy them because they can't manage their emotions.

Men need to not only not deny women's feelings but also acknowledge the possibility that the woman's way is worthy of learning from and emulating.

INSIGHT 87: HOW *NOT* TO FIX YOUR RELATIONSHIP

Problem-solving "how-to" couples advice that doesn't take individual personality issues into account can lead to despair about never "getting it right" and a premature giving up on the relationship. Simply put, it leads to the feeling of "we've tried everything and nothing works; we must not be right for each other." This may not be true at all.

The Conversation

Cal, age twenty-three, had tried the quick, easy ways to handle the problems of his marriage by telephoning radio-shrink programs, reading advice columns, and Googling, receiving tips that initially sounded helpful and persuasive and almost always worked, but only for a brief time. He realized he had to do something more substantial to save a deteriorating relationship with a woman he was in love with but who was driving him crazy because he couldn't understand her moods and responses.

> *Cal*: "I've stopped talking to so-called experts and even to well-meaning friends when I'm having a problem with a woman. They want to help, but their advice usually sounds like it has more to do with them than with me. They hardly know what's really going on and they're telling me what to do and how to fix it."

> *Dr. Goldberg*: "Like the advice column industry or the talk show shrinks who come up with answers and 'how-tos' after listening to somebody's problem for a few minutes, who are bright enough to make the answer sound good and pump people up, but they've basically got to be boilerplate solutions."

> *Cal*: "When I was in the middle of my first major love affair and really scared because my girlfriend seemed to be losing interest in me and may even have been cheating on me, I talked to anyone who'd listen. Everybody had a different solution."

> *Dr. Goldberg*: "A lot of professionals who are supposed to be experts do the same thing. They dispense advice quickly, and because these people have degrees or some supposed expertise, people take them seriously. What would you do looking back now?"

> *Cal*: "I wouldn't have searched for easy answers or solutions. Today, I'd get my girlfriend to tell me what her ideas were and I'd tell her mine, and then I'd shoot for small changes, not a big miraculous makeover."

The Insight Explained

If nothing else, "how-to" advice in relationships overlooks and denies the reality that each partner's personality issues are a relationship's bottom line. You can't fix a relationship if you don't take these into account. Short of doing that, it's best to do nothing at all because "how-to" answers are sure to fail, at which point there'll be a desire to give up trying.

What a Woman Can Do

If "how-to" solutions to personal problems really worked, there wouldn't be a "flavor of the month" in relationship advice books. The occasional good advice book would suffice for years. The fact that there are so many different and contradictory solutions offered, and that people are continuously looking for new ones, suggests that there is something fundamentally missing or wrong with the simplistic "how-to" approach. It's surprising that more people don't recognize the fallacy, but perhaps it's because people want hope but without personal change. "How-to" answers allow people to believe quick and simple solutions exist. With these "how-to" approaches, people can avoid looking at the deeper conflicts, feelings, and complexities in the relationship that would be very threatening to talk about.

Professional experts in the media develop seductive and manipulative ways to make others believe they have the answers. These are essentially cons, because no solution to personal problems can be meaningful without knowledge of the history, personality issues, and idiosyncrasies of the people involved. All such advice givers should be viewed as entertainers at best, con artists at worst, or deluded misleaders if they really believe what they have to offer is valid.

What a Man Must Do

Even the brightest and most educated of men tend to be lost when responding to and dealing with relationship crises.

In trying to understand and repair a failing relationship, men are prone to looking for answers in the wrong places and asking the wrong questions. The fact that men have major blank spots in relationships results in their vulnerability to being blindsided by their partner's responses. They didn't see the breakdown coming. They had no clue that their partner was unhappy or their child had a substance abuse problem or was suicidal. As a result, when a crisis occurs, men tend to overreact and look for a concrete and immediate solution. This makes them likely to do and say the wrong things, mismanage the situation, and then finally give up.

Fixing a relationship requires an awareness of process, which means a deeper understanding of oneself and one's impact on others, and an awareness of who the other person is and why they respond as they do. It is about how one communicates and the impact that has.

Because men tend to look for "how-to" solutions, their problems don't get fixed, instead deteriorating even more. "How-to" solutions provide generic one-size-fits-all answers that oversimplify complex human interaction.

Looking for quick and concrete answers tends to give rise to alienating solutions, such as concluding that their partner is crazy or being influenced by other people. Instead of seeking counseling to understand themselves and their problems better, men tend to look for answers outside of themselves by focusing on "what should I do" instead of "who and what I am, and how that brought this situation on."

Men must realize that the masculine way of solving their personal problems does not work, and they must focus on the way they've contributed to creating the problem because of who they are instead of combing the minutiae of everything they've said and done to solve the problem.

INSIGHT 88: WHEN NOT TRYING WORKS BEST

By not trying to satisfy a woman's needs, a man may make her frustrated and angry. But if he tries and fails to satisfy her needs, she will feel hopeless and possibly contemptuous of him. Therefore, it is better for her to fantasize about what might be if he only tried (hope remains) than for him to try and almost surely fail, at which point hope dies.

The Conversation

Sidney, a statistics professor at a community college who formerly thought of himself as a progressive male feminist, had a rude awakening after a brief marriage to an academic colleague who was also editor of a campus feminist periodical. Prior to the marriage, Sidney fashioned himself as enlightened compared to most of his "male chauvinist" colleagues, and he believed he understood and knew how to genuinely fulfill a woman's needs by being a sensitive, egalitarian, nonsexist partner. When the relationship ended in a brutal name-calling battle with his liberated wife, he was sobered and brought down to earth, realizing he wasn't who he thought he was, and that trying to be the perfect man who was tuned into women's needs was just an illusion he had about himself.

Sidney: "Sometimes I wonder if trying to make a relationship work is some kind of a no-win situation because, no matter what you do, it doesn't seem to help. I've tried the active approach, where I really made it a point to find out what the woman needed, and set out to satisfy her. I've also been with women where I knew what they needed, but I didn't care enough to try. Funny thing, but looking back I think I caught more shit from women when I tried than when I didn't."

Dr. Goldberg: "Maybe it's as simple as the fact that when you tried, you were forcing yourself to be something that wasn't really you or do something you weren't really into."

Sidney: "It could have been that, but I also think when I tried hard it came across to these women as unmanly behavior or weakness. I was giving my power to the woman and a deeper part of her didn't like it."

Dr. Goldberg: "When it comes down to it, even though some women will deny it, if a man demonstrates power, it turns them on, while giving up power by trying too hard to please turns them off."

Sidney: "I could see how I was coming across like a wuss when I was eagerly trying to please, and how unattractive that must have seemed, even while it looked like I was being thoughtful and trying to make sure I was giving her what she needed."

Dr. Goldberg: "In the bigger picture, though, what happens is that much of what women and men call their needs turn out to be bottomless pits. Like when a guy says he needs space. How much space does he need? Can a woman ever give him enough space? When either sex tries to fill a bottomless need in the other and they fail, then the other person starts to feel like 'this is never going to work, so I ought to leave.' Or sometimes they just get angry because they feel frustrated."

Sidney: "If I don't try to fill her needs, at least there's still hope in her heart that at some point I will try, and then she'll be happy. However, if I make strong, clear efforts to give her what she wants and she still feels unfulfilled, then I've deprived her of hope and it starts a major downward spiral."

The Insight Explained

For women as well as men, deeper feelings in a relationship emerge from the dynamic between the two people. That is, the rhythm or the flow of a relationship, such as when one person always controls while the other complies, creates the emotional atmosphere, rather than the specifics of what people do, like whether the man is thoughtful and brings her flowers or the woman greets him at the front door in a negligee every night. If a woman has a deep-seated need for reassurance, love, closeness, or support, these are needs that may be impossible to ever satisfy. The type of man who is willing to struggle to satisfy such a woman may be a man whom she experiences emotionally as giving up his personal power. The negative effects of this are compounded by the sense of hopelessness that comes from seeing one's partner trying and failing miserably.

What a Woman Can Do

It is not an insensitivity to women that causes me to counsel men to be cautious when they set out to give a woman they love everything and anything she needs. Rather, what I point out is the *content/process paradox*. Specifically, it means that even though a man may be doing everything right (*content*), it is *how* he delivers that message (*process*) that will determine the woman's feelings and response. If his pleasing behavior is experienced by her as motivated by a need to see himself as better than other men, or by weakness and through an accommodating personality, or because of low self-esteem, or if he believes he is being the perfect nonsexist man but is out of touch with his underlying controlling ways, or does it in an intellectualized, disconnected manner, it is the latter that will determine his partner's feelings toward him.

Men who never intentionally try to please a woman may intuitively sense it's a futile effort. While the woman may feel some resentment toward him over his seeming lack of concern to make her happy, she is at least left with the belief that if and when he does try, things will be much better.

What a Man Must Do

Men must overcome the notion that to solve a problem one must work at it and try harder. They think that if their partner is unhappy, they must do something to make her happy. Or if she is sexually frustrated, they must find techniques and ways to satisfy her.

Men must understand that their compulsion to fix problems and make things better often reinforces the belief that they are responsible and at fault when a partner expresses frustration and unhappiness, and that they must do something to make it better. If they don't read the situation correctly or efforts fail, things will be worse than had they done nothing at all.

The only time it makes sense for a man to try to fix a problem with his partner by himself is when she asks him to and clearly indicates what she needs from him, and she accepts the fact that he may not succeed at it.

When a man attempts to fill a woman's needs—"I need you to be closer to me" or "I need you to do certain things to show you love me"— he may believe that since he's actually tried to do what the woman says she wanted him to and it didn't seem to work, the situation is hopeless. If he then tries harder and fails, it may cause his partner to conclude that she will never get what she wants from him. However, if he doesn't try because he sees the futility in the attempt, she can continue to hold on to the fantasy that if he only tried harder things would improve.

INSIGHT 89: FROM "MONSTER" TO PERSON

Once a man catches a glimpse of the monster his process has created and how it has driven everyone and everything personal away, then he must begin the hard work of reconnecting and incorporating the lost and de-

nied personal parts of him in order to become accessible, "in touch," and connected.

The Conversation

Clint, age sixty-seven and a divorced father of two who never remarried but had a long string of very accommodating lovers seduced by his wealth and charm and subsequently terrorized once caught in his web, would fit the definition of "the monster" male. He prided himself on the fact that since age twenty-two, when he first left home, he had never been in a relationship where he wasn't totally in charge. The "monster" in him took the shape of seducing needy, dependent women and then insulting, criticizing, controlling, and manipulating them once they let themselves get locked into the relationship with him. His cold and disengaged personality protected him from seeing how most people really felt about him. As he got older, he realized his children rarely spoke to him or showed affection unless they wanted money from him. After a heart condition and a stroke mellowed him somewhat, he became aware of how alone he actually was. At the recommendation of his doctor, who also warned him about his growing alcohol addiction, he reluctantly came for psychological help. He even tried to control his therapy. I placed him in a men's group, where he was affected by the following dialogue I had with one of the members.

> *Dudley*: "I like to call them the 'macho moments of truth': those powerful, scary moments when a man gets an unvarnished glimpse of the person he is that other people experience when they try to relate to him. In essence, 'the monster' he's become is someone who doesn't listen, always has the 'right' answers, is continuously measuring, competing, and intellectualizing, and is totally wrapped up in himself. In denial about this, he sees himself as someone who cares and loves."

> *Dr. Goldberg*: "Clearly there's something off-putting behind the veneer of masculinity; an essence that is unbeknownst to a man who repels others and makes it hard to observe himself objectively. He can't see who he really is and what he's all about. What he sees is what he'd like to believe. What he is, however, is visible through the many ways he is distanced by others. He can barely recognize that his

only relations with others are because of an activity or goal. There are no spontaneous, unstructured, intrinsic, personal moments with him because he has become incapable of them."

Dudley: "I see that developing in guy friends of mine, and periodically I have my own moments of truth when I catch a momentary glimpse of the disconnected 'monster' I'm becoming. I can see that I only come out of my enclosure for specific reasons or to meet specific needs, then after I get what I want I retreat back."

Dr. Goldberg: "What disgusts you in yourself is the 'masculine ego,' which without the standard bells and whistles to disguise itself is offensive or even creepy."

Dudley: "How many guys would be able to look at themselves clearly, especially once they get older and have so much invested in their illusions? Suddenly there's the realization that they blew it and lived a lie about themselves, and they aren't in any way who they've told themselves they are."

Dr. Goldberg: "That's very painful to bring into focus because when a man does that, he's also at a loss about what to do about it. The only way he'd want to change is if it could be done quickly and without the internal dredging he's spent his life avoiding. So change for all but the totally determined isn't possible."

Dudley: "Maybe they're jumping the gun. Before anything is going to happen realistically, a man needs to keep the monster he's become in focus long enough to penetrate his walls, to see how he's actually his own victim, because nobody else really cares if he destroys himself. The road back to his personal self involves removing the defensive layers in order to reconnect with the personal human being he blocked off and abandoned years before. He can't do it by himself, so his first hurdle is overcoming the resistance to reaching out and asking for help."

The Insight Explained

Masculine socialization in the young male launches a slow and steady erosion of everything personal until nothing is left, and he ends up disconnected, out of touch, and out of reach. The end state of the externalized masculine process is personal oblivion, which is a condition of disconnection or the inability to make authentic personal connections, but he doesn't know it and wouldn't acknowledge that he even cares about it. He has evolved into an impersonal ego monster. The road back is not a matter of doing something but a gradual reclaiming of feelings, vulnerability, and needs, which will then revive his capacity to listen, empathize, and care while recognizing the continual ego chatter that encloses him in pursuit of his abstract goals of superiority, omniscience, and even omnipotence.

What a Woman Can Do

Women who find themselves deeply involved with a "male monster" who is alcoholic, insulting, critical, and brutal need to give up the fantasy that they can love him into becoming more human and caring. Instead, women need their own moment of truth to identify their reasons for wanting to remain in a love relationship with such a damaged and tyrannical man. Is it low self-esteem, fear, and dependency, or the need to hide behind a strong man who will take charge, support, and take care of her, or the desire to live the provided-for life? If that kind of choice is made, women need to realize that the price is prohibitive and they are sacrificing their psychological integrity, self-esteem, and growth potential. They need also to accept the fact that the men will never change.

As for the man himself, in those macho moments of truth when he realizes that there is nothing authentically personal left in him, that no one really cares about him, nor does he care for anyone, he is facing the monster that his defensive and extreme masculine conditioning has created. Those moments of truth usually happen at times of personal crisis when his guard is down and he is vulnerable. There is no on-off switch, and the process of change will be a lifelong commitment. The upside of it is that even small changes can make a big difference in his personal experience. The downside is that he's facing an experience similar to the struggle of an addict working to master and overcome a horrendous end-stage addiction one day at a time, and whether he will succeed remains in doubt.

What a Man Must Do

Men who come to realize that the way they are and how they are experienced, mainly as scary to be around, are the primary causes of a negative condition of their relationships. Men must face the fact that the relationship breakdowns and traumas are not the fault of others. They then are faced with the challenging and daunting task of humanizing themselves as they begin the journey of transforming the off-putting "monster" within that they have become by fulfilling the role of being the man.

Men must not blame or hate themselves for what they've become but instead understand that masculine conditioning has created deep roots; therefore, becoming a less defensive, more expressive and connected person will be a long-term struggle characterized by small victories.

Initially the changes men make may be threatening to their self-image, and a man may believe he is losing his power in making himself foolishly vulnerable. Therefore, he must remind himself regularly as to why he needs to change, because not changing will resign him to personal oblivion. The only people remaining in his life will be those with a materialistic or security agenda.

Indeed, many men will feel they'd rather be respected and feared than loved if changing means giving up personal power and control.

12

HOW GOOD RELATIONSHIPS
ARE LIKE PIECES OF FRUIT

Often the sweetest, juiciest, and freshest fruit at the farmer's market where I shop is also the ugliest. It may even have blemishes. I'm drawn to it because its unattractive outward appearance assures me it hasn't, in all likelihood, been messed with by the professional growers who use various processes, chemicals, waxes, and pesticides to ensure that the fruit is pretty enough to attract buyers in the larger markets. Most people don't seem to want to buy fruit that is ugly or has a blemish, no matter how delicious it might be. They equate the appearance of it with its value. But if a piece of fruit is supposed to be organic, the blemish or lack of obvious outward beauty tends to reassure me that it is.

Contrariwise, at the high-end expensive market where I occasionally shop, the beautiful, perfect-to-the-point-of-unreal, blemish-free fruit I buy is often tasteless. In a blindfold taste I probably couldn't even tell you which fruit it is because it also has no smell. To me that indicates the fruit is probably lifeless. It might as well be in a can. It is not fruit I want to eat, much less purchase at a premium, even though it looks as perfect as fruit can look.

The metaphor for me is apt as we think about how to recognize a good relationship and the traps to avoid in order to not create or pursue a relationship that may look good in the eyes of others or even one's own eyes but is essentially dead, if not, in fact, poisonous. In this matter, you're not likely to get much helpful input from family and friends who tend to applaud and encourage one to be in a relationship that looks good without regard for its moment-to-moment vitality. They may even try to shame you for not pursuing or remaining in such a relationship, accusing you of being too picky, critical, or hard to please. Or they may tell you that you have a fear of closeness. The phrase *fear of closeness*, in my mind, is one of those voodoo phrases that can promote the destruction of a healthy survival sense when a voice within is urging us to avoid or get out of a relationship that may look very good on the outside but is actually soul and life destroying.

Contrariwise, healthy relationships may not look very good to others, even to some mental health professionals, because the partners may engage in what seems to be rough, insensitive, or politically incorrect conversations and interactions. Outwardly, the relationship may even look "ugly"; yet it is actually full of life, deep caring, and love, while the perfect-seeming relationships are often dead in the water or drowning in a sea of self-conscious politeness, appropriateness, and political correctness. They may look like good relationships but turn out to be fragile, lifeless façades with a great public face, like the ones a politician uses to hide his emptiness, toxicity, and callousness. Behind the smile and outward appearance is a relationship that can easily disintegrate and disappear.

How does one recognize or create a good relationship? It's not an entity or thing that can be characterized with a content description of the sort that one might find in a singles advertisement that lists a set of characteristics in which the person describes who he is and the kind of partner he is looking for. If it were truly possible to find or create a good relationship that way, computers probably would be the best tools with which to make that happen. The track record of websites that use such content descriptions to pair people off has not been very impressive.

Good relationships are not a matter of being "lucky enough" to find the right partner or someone who is referred to as a "soul mate." In relationships, the partners we tend to attract, and the ones to whom we find ourselves attracted, reflect who we are. "You are who you attract or are ready for" might be a better way to understand the process.

As a psychologist and psychotherapist, my major criterion for the creation and sustaining of a healthy relationship is one's own lack of defensiveness, which makes it possible to be drawn to and attract others who are equally nondefensive. Nondefensive people are not attracted to defensive people for the simple reason that the defensive person will be made uncomfortable by the authenticity and openness of the nondefensive person. Contrariwise, nondefensive people who value their own transparency and spontaneity will be repulsed by the judgmental uptightness of the defensive person.

Of all the layers of defensiveness that need be worked through and dissolved in order to achieve a good relationship that is resilient and has the capacity for a continuous lifetime of growth, *gender defensiveness is most important*. A lack of gender defensiveness means neither he nor she will be restrained, confined, or constricted by a gender conditioning that socializes us to block, repress, and deny certain feelings or responses due to our gender. The nongender-defensive woman is capable of "unladylike" abilities to acknowledge and work through conflict, express anger, assert needs clearly, take responsibility for her sexual pleasure, and maintain a comfortable separateness as well as a capacity for closeness and intimacy. Similarly, the nongender-defensive man can express his vulnerabilities, fears, and dependency and the whole spectrum of his emotions. He does not disconnect, withdraw, intellectualize, and abstract in the face of conflict, stress, and an exchange of strong emotions.

The good relationship is something to grow toward, not look for. In fact, the cultural fantasy that guarantees continuing personal unhappiness is that good relationships are a matter of having the luck of finding "the right one." That notion reinforces the content fantasy, where the perfect content is much like the perfect fruit described earlier. It has *nothing* to do with a good relationship. The fantasy involved in pursuing it may have everything to do with preventing a person from ever experiencing it.

The good relationship does not exist in its *what* but in its *how*. It is not achieved by trying to be or finding the perfect person. Rather, it exists in the ongoing process of becoming an open and nondefensive person to the point where one's relationship can be authentic, expressive, and a form of playfulness. Its hallmark of personal responsibility is opposite to the traditional, primed-to-become-toxic relationship characterized by *blaming*, *guilt making*, and an inability to acknowledge and work through one's own responsibility in the creation of whatever frustration and unhappiness one finds oneself in.

The message is a hopeful one, and the analogy to pieces of fruit is accurate. Luck, good fortune, and outward appearance are largely irrelevant in the creation and maintenance of a genuinely good relationship with the power to endure and the ability to grow and become better and more deeply satisfying with time.

Personal growth, the development of nondefensiveness, and the ability to recognize, work on, and eliminate the many ways we block and distort our experience and create our own relationship unhappiness is the key. It is a key that with sufficient effort is within the grasp and capacity of everyone willing to do the work required to attain it. It's worth every ounce of effort that one puts into it.

INSIGHT 90: A WOMAN TO CREATE A RELATIONSHIP WITH

The relative absence of a distorting and defensive feminine process is what determines the real, loving woman. She hears her male partner objectively as he intends, is not a blamer or a victim, recognizes the relationship problems as a two-way street, and shares responsibility for creating as well as fixing them.

The Conversation

After years of trying to find the perfect partner, Martin realized it wasn't a woman's education, looks, or politics that brought out his most loving feelings, but rather the way she related to him.

Martin: "I've really changed when it comes to my idea of the perfect woman. I used to think a loving woman was one who was loyal and helpful to her man, easy to get along with, and who understood and accepted him for the man he was. I've had close relationships with several women who were exactly that way, but it didn't work because somehow I wound up always feeling I was the bad guy doing something hurtful or wrong, while she was the good and caring one."

Dr. Goldberg: "Clearly, if the traditional ideas of what a loving woman is were all it took, many relationships would be close to perfect because there are already a lot of women like that. What's missing from this idea, however, is the ability for a man to see himself as a key factor in the formula of how a woman responds. The defensive traditional 'ideal' feminine woman is a selfless pleaser who is actually blocked in a way that initially makes her seem to be someone she really isn't."

Martin: "That helps explain what I experienced. The 'perfect' women I've been involved with always turned out to be the ones who wound up resenting me for giving less than they were, making me feel guilty, and blaming me for their bad feelings about themselves. Eventually, I discovered that what I thought was their total acceptance and understanding of me was an illusion. When I'd express my thoughts or feelings, they'd misconstrue them or tell me I was being insensitive or rude, and I'd feel blindsided by their reactions."

Dr. Goldberg: "Most men's ideas of the perfect woman are actually very traditional: a variation on the biblical idea of a wife who is a faithful, loving shadow of her man. The fantasy is more like an abstraction of a pure, sweet, noncompetitive, and beautiful woman. It turns out that in the real world of relationships, she has a major downside. That is, she blames the man when there's a disagreement, accuses him of saying and doing hurtful things, and does not see herself as an equal creator of their issues and conflicts."

Martin: "Right. Nowadays, I don't expect or even want to be with a woman who is 'perfect' in that feminine way. What I look for is a woman who expresses who she is and what she wants, acknowledges the not-so-nice parts of herself, and therefore makes it okay for me to express mine as well. I can tell in my gut if I'm with a real, loving woman because I never have feelings of being the bad guy, nor do I ever feel I'm the sole cause of any problems we have. I accept the fact that we'll have fights. In fact, I welcome them if it means we both get to display ourselves to each other honestly and without judgment."

The Insight Explained

Due to their externalized, linear way of experiencing relationships, men tend to have an abstract idea of a loving woman as being someone who exists apart from the moment-to-moment give and take of a relationship. By assuming that who a woman is remains fixed and exists apart from the dynamics of her relationship with a man, men re-create their relationship nightmares to the point of concluding that women can't be trusted and are unpredictable, manipulative, and not at all who they pretend to be. In fact, the real, loving woman can only be seen by how she experiences and responds to her partner as the relationship is in progress.

What a Woman Can Do

Men's growth in relationships can be measured by the degree to which they perceive love and caring in terms of how a woman relates to them, and vice versa. The real, loving woman can be recognized by her lack of traditional feminine defenses, meaning she communicates her preferences and boundaries clearly, sees herself as an equal creator of whatever happens to her in the relationship, does not portray the man as guilty of destroying her, takes responsibility for her moods and self-esteem, and loves him for who he knows himself to be.

A woman's focus on her physical appearance or being the supportive wife, keeping the perfect home, or dressing and acting sexy, regardless of what the man might say, only minimally generates or triggers his loving and committed feelings over the long run. What men need, even when they can't articulate it, is a relationship in which they can fully be their authentic selves, knowing they will be accepted. A woman of strength, with clear boundaries and solid self-esteem, is what assures him that he will not be cast as the heavy or made out to be the love spoiler. That is what men want.

What a Man Must Do

Men are oriented to focus on the visible and the concrete. While that may work in the business world, it is a recipe for disaster in the personal world of relationships. Relationships are built on and dependent on their process (the "how"), not on the content (the "what"). "Perfect" content (for example, a beautiful woman with a great smile) fades, dissolves, and disappears as the relationship progresses, and its process actually begins to color the landscape while creating the actual emotions or feelings. *As process rises, content fades, and the most perfect partner theoretically can transform into a nightmare.*

First, men must recognize something that may be foreign to them, which is that finding the right partner is not a matter of searching and getting lucky. Subscribing to the content illusion that the right woman exists in the abstract, apart from the way they relate to each other, will only cause men to repeat their past failures. It is not a woman's content (what she is); it is her process (how she is to be with) and how that works for him.

Men have traditionally fallen into the content blind spot when looking for a partner, believing that the right woman is all about the way she looks, how she carries herself, and how she pleases him. Having typically approached relationships that way in the past, men have probably seen how a woman's "perfection" disappears under the weight of the way she is to be with and her ability to be a self-aware, nonblaming person who is comfortable with a full range of responses and emotions in herself and her partner.

INSIGHT 91: FORCING INTIMACY AND COMMITMENT

Intimacy and commitment are by-products of mutual liking, trust, and understanding. They are not needs to be filled, nor can they be demanded or artificially created by trying.

The Conversation

Armin, a bachelor in his early thirties, wondered whether he really had intimacy issues, which he'd heard from past girlfriends and family members who were pressuring him to get married.

> *Armin*: "I think I'm actually like a lot of guys in the way I tense up inside when I hear a woman talk about her need for intimacy or my supposed lack of ability to be close."

> *Dr. Goldberg*: "Men and women use the term so differently. For women, it seems to mean some intangible feeling of getting closer and closer. For guys, if they even use that term at all, it means having sex."

> *Armin*: "It seems like women believe men can push an on-off switch and become intimate or make a commitment. Women seem to think intimacy and commitment are just things men can decide to do if and when they really want to. But when I feel committed, it's because I

can't imagine being with any other woman. Likewise, I have feelings of intimacy when I don't have to hide anything about myself or when I feel loving toward a woman even when she acts as natural with me as she does when she's by herself and doesn't seem to have anything to hide. If she can look bad or get sick, or say silly or dumb things, or even go to the bathroom in front me, and I still feel the same, that's intimacy."

Dr. Goldberg: "To most women, it seems intimacy means you feel loving all the time. When I hear women talking about intimacy and commitment with a guy they've just started dating, it makes me realize how far off they are in their ideas from the way men see it. How can you be intimate with or committed to someone you're just getting to know? They don't seem to see it that way."

The Insight Explained

The feminine fantasy of intimacy and women's quest for commitment are forms of abstraction: ideals about relating that can somehow be brought about through an act of good will or by a man who is, in their eyes, "trying" to be a loving person. Women don't seem to see the self-defeating distortions behind their pressure. Instead of focusing on what they can do or be in order to make those things happen, women tend to see it as something that can be demanded of a man or something that some men are simply incapable of. As a result, they accomplish the opposite of what they want, much like when a man demands or pressures a woman for "hot sex" without an awareness of his part in generating that desire or lack of it in her.

What a Woman Can Do

I believe most men tense up and recoil when they feel pressure for commitment and are being confronted about their intimacy fears, similar to what many women experience when they are pressured for sex and told they are frigid and inhibited. Just as women know they are capable of intense sexual pleasure when they feel genuinely cared about and are attracted, men are as comfortable as women with commitment and closeness when they don't feel undue and premature pressure. Focusing on building a safe, relaxed, accepting relationship with a man without talking about intimacy and commitment is the best and easiest pathway toward achieving it.

Neither a man nor a woman can be pressured into intimacy or commitment. For intimacy and commitment to be genuine and of a lasting nature, they have to be the product of a balanced, nondefensive, transparent, and loving relationship. To the degree that either is artificially or prematurely created or coerced into being, they are destined to fail.

What a Man Must Do

A man must realize that pressure on him both to make a commitment to a relationship and to be more intimate is as misplaced and damaging as the pressure a man puts on a woman for sex.

If a woman accommodates a man's desire for sex, the resentment she'll feel by being used and not having her feelings respected will inevitably damage the relationship. Nondefensive, healthy sex requires two people who desire and support each other. Similarly, pressure for commitment and greater intimacy will have a downside of resentment and emotional withholding.

Men must be comfortably clear about their resistance to commitment, with the realization that commitment given to please the other at the expense of one's own feelings will have a lingering, negative effect on the relationship.

In a healthy relationship, both sex and commitment, a need for intimacy or space, will happen as a by-product of the feelings each partner has for the other. It cannot be prematurely given or demanded without risking damage to a relationship, which may not be physically visible immediately but will show itself increasingly in many forms as the relationship progresses.

Resisting commitment or intimacy does not automatically make a man the "bad guy" or commitment phobic any more than portraying a woman's resistance to sex as meaning she is frigid.

In a healthy relationship, neither partner will expect or demand from the other what the other is not fully ready to give, with the knowledge that forced accommodation by either partner means trading short-term gratification for a long-term authentically loving response.

INSIGHT 92: TRUE INTIMACY

When intimacy is authentic, love and closeness based on knowledge of the inner reality and experience of the other are present. When love is authentic, the relationship will not be put into crisis by a man honestly expressing his deeper feelings to a woman or when she exposes her true emotions to him.

The Conversation

"I don't get what women mean when they use the word *intimacy*," commented Chuck, an attorney, age forty-one. "How can you be intimate and still have to hide your true feelings and being?" In most relationships, when the man says things like "I'm feeling bored with us," or "You've gained weight," or "You're not making sense," the woman reacts as if she's been rejected, attacked, or criticized. Men learn early not to be honest in order to keep the peace and the relationship.

> *Chuck*: "When I'm really loved by a woman, I can tell because I just say what I think and express what I feel with no fear that she'll accuse me, break out in tears, or make judgments about whatever I'm showing to her. When I've been as real with her as I'm capable of being and she still says she loves me and acts that way, I can trust her. That to me is intimacy."

> *Dr. Goldberg*: "You're missing something in that idea, and it's a typical blind spot for men. You can't really tell if she's just accommodating and pleasing you unless she also fully reveals thoughts and feelings that don't show her in a 'nice' light and where she doesn't need to preserve a certain image of herself in front of you. So it's not just you being able to reveal yourself to her but also her doing the same with you that is authentic intimacy."

> *Chuck*: "Lots of couples appear to be very loving, but it's like a formal, careful, and respectful thing, and you get a sense they're always polite and cautious with each other. I've had times like that where I'm always mindful of being on my best behavior. In those situations, even when it feels good, there's a sense that it's fragile and could easily change."

Dr. Goldberg: "Relationships can look great from a distance when two people stay formal in their roles and respond according to what's expected of them. Maybe neither even knows it's going on until one of them crosses the line and does or says something 'out of character' and things explode."

Chuck: "I've heard it said that maintaining a good relationship takes a lot of work. But personally I think the hardest work is having to hide so much that's real and feeling drained by that."

The Insight Explained

Authentic intimacy doesn't exist as long as there is mutual guardedness and caution. At some point, hidden feelings, thoughts, and desires will leak through and create a crisis of trust. One or the other will feel the shock of betrayal and the sense that they never really knew their partners. In a sense, they didn't.

What a Woman Can Do

Perhaps men tune out or react with cynicism when they hear women talk about needing to feel closer or more intimate. Is this just one of those areas where men and women define a concept in completely different ways? For men, the definition of intimacy (if they think in those terms) would involve transparency and honesty without facing negative consequences and accusations. For women, intimacy seems to mean a more romanticized sense of a growing closeness between two people, almost to a point of becoming as one. For men, intimacy would also mean being able to maintain clear and separate identities and boundaries without their love being questioned.

Maintaining a relationship with rigid rules and boundaries as to what is or is not permissible to express is a game of postponing the inevitable. Avoiding conflicts and crises through careful, respectful interaction is a form of temporary escape from authenticity, with a price that has to be paid in some form later on. One way or another, the deeper feelings will manifest and create an overt crisis, or the crisis will take on the form of psychological or physical symptoms. Authentic intimacy, when it is present, is resilient even in the wake of brutal honesty.

What a Man Must Do

A man who hides his true feelings out of concern and fear of his partner's response or tarnishing his image is exchanging short-term peace and conflict avoidance for long-term frustration and assertions by his partner that he is closed, impossible to read, and fearful of intimacy. Love relationships are the centerpiece of a man's life, and they are sure to be damaged and eventually destroyed if men hide their true feelings from their partners.

A man must recognize that being in a relationship where he has to pretend to be someone he really is not is self-destructive and signals self-hate. Similarly, a woman accommodating a man falsely in order to please and hold him will be a major factor in her own development of low self-esteem and the anxious feeling that she is losing her identity.

Guarded, feigned, and denied feelings make intimacy and the sense of being truly loved impossible. Both men and women sense that and don't talk about it as they continually seek to reassure each other they feel loved. Continual and compulsive repetition in saying "I love you" suggests both partners sense that something is missing and wrong and are trying to hide it or run away from the deeper reality in the desire to convince themselves and their partners of feelings that neither truly have, as long as there is the fear of risking being fully oneself in the anticipation of being rejected.

INSIGHT 93: THE RELATIONSHIP THAT WORKS

The good relationship is not a "miracle" or luck of the draw but the result of each partner acknowledging and working through the distortions of their gender.

The Conversation

George, a man who had committed himself to therapeutic work for three years, articulates the perspective of a man who is becoming self-aware, open, and relatively free of the traditional relationship blind spots of men:

> *George*: "It's taken me years to let go of the fantasy that there is a magical soul mate out there just waiting for me. Sometimes I think

I finally can see the delusion in all that, but I still hear that occasional voice saying, 'Come on, you're being so cynical. It's okay to hold out for romance. *She* might actually exist. Keep looking!' To come back to earth I have to remind myself of that long trail of 'soul mates' I've already left behind."

Dr. Goldberg: "It's much like fighting an addiction, but because it's a popular notion, the craving for the soul mate is not really identified as such. After all, the media loves the idea, especially when movie stars play out that game in public. You know how addicts do the same self-defeating things over and over. It's like the person who has an eating addiction craving a quart of ice cream late at night. At that moment he or she can't remember how sick it made them each time before or how they promised themselves never to do it again. That's what the soul mate search is like. But a soul mate addiction is harder to kick because the latest one is a new person, so it's easy to delude yourself that it'll be different this time."

George: "I guess the idea of the soul mate is that your old patterns won't get repeated, 'this' woman won't be like all the rest, and you'll both avoid the usual issues and conflicts that bring relationships back down to earth. The need for that special 'miracle person' to love suggests there's something wrong to start with, that you need a ton of fantasy in order to let yourself open up and get close to someone."

Dr. Goldberg: "It also supposes that the guy won't have the usual masculine resistances men have in relationships to getting close, giving up control, relating to a woman as a person and not an object, expressing vulnerable emotions, needing space, and such, or that the woman won't have issues around maintaining boundaries, only reacting to the man's lead but then feeling controlled and diminished, and so on. In other words, it presupposes that the two people have miraculously escaped the traditional conditioning that gets in other couples' way when they relate."

George: "I used to rate relationships by the initial romantic high. It's hard to accept that a good relationship is about two people working on monitoring their own defensiveness to make it work."

Dr. Goldberg: "Letting go of that magical, romantic notion would cause many people to face the reality that relationships take mutual effort, and if they're not willing to do the work, the price of a relationship isn't worth the initial romantic high."

The Insight Explained

After the initial attraction, which is usually based more on the needs each person has rather than appreciation of the other person's uniqueness, any couple will have to confront each other's defensiveness, differences, and dysfunctional relationship patterns. This produces conflicts that will ground the relationship in some difficulties. If both people know why they want the relationship and are willing to take responsibility for looking carefully at those aspects of themselves that may alienate the other and undermine the connection, they are more likely to make it work. It's a matter of two people liking and enjoying each other enough that working through their mutual resistances feels as if it's all well worth the effort. The initial idea of and longing for a magical, preordained soul connection can only impede this process and produce the crisis that comes from having to let go of unrealistic expectations.

What a Woman Can Do

The notion of soul mate relationships is deeply embedded in most of us, perhaps less so in men who hide their neediness and hunger for love behind detachment or cynical humor. Authentic relationships that can continue to grow do not happen easily and may in fact require years of highs and lows before they are fully on track. For many people, it takes numerous failed relationship experiences before that difficult reality is accepted and the work required is acknowledged.

Why should relationships be easy when they involve developing a healthy connection between two complex and very different personalities with dramatically different socialization? Authentic and healthy relationships emerge from ragged journeys and can reverse the traditional relationship progression of *romance to boredom to rage*. They may not begin on an even course but steadily get better until they blossom into a naturally committed love. As men and women overcome their polarized conditioning and arrive on a level playing field, fulfillment and joy in the experience of intimacy becomes achievable.

Finally, successful relationships require that two people know themselves well enough that they can separate out the barriers they habitually create personally from the kind of issues that result when two people of different gender histories and personalities struggle to find common ground and strong footing. The greater each person's resistances and barriers, the more there will be a desire for the relationship to be a magical event. The hard work of a relationship begins by acknowledging and overcoming one's own dysfunctions and issues. In man-woman relationships, those dysfunctions exist in each person, if for no other reason than due to their opposing gender socialization. Not succumbing to powerful traditional romantic fantasy is the critical first step of the journey toward an authentic, enduring love.

What a Man Must Do

Negative stereotypes men and woman have about each other and that are used as rationalizations for giving up on changing or growing, while they may have a basis in reality, in fact are too often accepted as a given that each partner has to live with, like "you know how men are," rather than being seen as important information and guidance for growth and change in the service of the relationship.

Honest feedback should not be viewed or experienced as hurtful and insensitive or as criticism. Men and women are both in denial of aspects of themselves that are alienating and make communication difficult or impossible.

An authentically loving relationship is one that allows for identifying issues and the negative ways of seeing each other, which are usually perceived as part of being a man or a woman, that are bad for the relationship, bad for the individuals themselves, and act as a barrier between the partners, even if tolerated.

Men must know that the sign of a healthy relationship is one in which they and their partner feel trusting and loving enough that they can appreciate, welcome, and be grateful for honest feedback about the way they are as people, instead of needing to always be seen as positive and supportive.

An excellent way to identify a truly loving relationship that really works is the degree to which each partner can welcome as well as tolerate the harsher truths about their dysfunctions as men and women that usually neither are aware of.

Men have issues as a result of their externalization and their socialization to be a man. Women have issues for counterpart reasons due to their upbringing. Tests of a loving relationship that works and is healthy is the degree to which each partner can remain nondefensive when being given feedback about themselves while even inviting their partner's feedback as to what they observe and experience from the other and the feelings that generates. Authentic trust, when it exists in a relationship, can be recognized by the extent to which each partner can respond with appreciation to what they hear from the other—feedback that nobody else is likely to provide except perhaps out of anger or the desire to hurt the other.

The measure of a relationship that works is the degree to which each partner can educate the other about what they see and feel, and that feedback is met with a deep appreciation and seen as an impetus for growth and change. When a relationship works, it can handle even the most threatening of feedback, because who is more qualified to help us see ourselves and support our change than our partners?

BIBLIOGRAPHY

Bach, G. R., & Goldberg, H. *Creative Aggression*. New York: Doubleday, 1974.
Goldberg, H. *The Hazards of Being Male*. New York: Nash, 1976.
Goldberg, H., & Lewis, R. T. *Money Madness*. New York: William Morrow, 1978.
Goldberg, H. *The New Male*. New York: William Morrow, 1979.
Goldberg, H. *The New Male-Female Relationship*. New York: William Morrow, 1983.
Goldberg, H. *The Inner Male*. New York: New American Library, 1987.
Goldberg, H. *What Men Really Want*. New York: Penguin, 1991.
Goldberg, H. *What Men Still Don't Know About Women, Relationships, and Love*. Fort Lee, NJ: Barricade Books, 2007.

INDEX

achievement: costs of, 30–33, 151–153; gender socialization and, 43, men and, 28–30; and objectification, 77–79; versus spirit, 50–53; women and, 138, 148–151; at work versus love, 108–109

actor role, 1–2, 56–58; gender socialization and, 26; liberation and, 147; problems with, 2–3; relinquishing, 58–61; and women's power, 129–131

addictions, 186; alcohol, 48–50; food, 48–50, 184–186; work, 109

age: and neediness, 131–133; and withdrawal, 33–38

alcohol, men and, 48–49, 50

anger: children and, 170; victimhood and, 99–101, 105

anxiety, 15–17

appearances: and first impressions, 3–6; gender socialization and, 43; and irrational choices, 19–21; of perfect couple, 205–207, 270; versus reality, 269–284; and sex, 163–166

assertion, 26

autonomy, 26; versus closeness, 44, 45

being, men and, 28–30

blame, 124–126; flip-flop and, 98; as personality trait, 246–249; in poisoned relationships, 222; toxic men and, 231–235; toxic women and, 238–240

boundaries: problems with, and anger, 99–101, 105; women and, 15, 16, 65–66, 87

breaking up, 189–219; and blame, 124–126; and false love, 79; fatally poisoned relationships, 223–226; timing of, 225–226; and transformation, 34–35

chemistry, 6–8

children. *See* family; fatherhood

closeness, 44–46

cognitive dissonance, 12

commitment: fear of, 104; and flip-flops, 97–99, 110–111; and misunderstandings about sex, 14; and objectification, 77–79; recommendations for, 275–277; women and, 94–97

communication, recommendations for, 67–70

competitiveness, 133–136

conflict avoidance, 92–94

content, 2, 54, 179, 262; error regarding, 55, 275; and good relationships, 274

control: problems with, and anger, 99–101, 105; provider role and, 36; and touch, 119; traditional dynamic and, 77. *See also* actor role

counseling. *See* therapy

ABOUT THE AUTHOR

Herb Goldberg is a pioneering psychologist-author and practitioner whose books have broken new ground in the areas of male awareness, assertion and aggression, gender polarization and relationship behavior, and how people's personalities shape their financial attitudes and activities. He is passionately committed to the ways that psychology can become an effective tool for understanding and transforming the human experience, and he has dedicated his life to making that happen.

His well-known books include *Creative Aggression, The Hazards of Being Male, What Men Really Want, The New Male-Female Relationship, Money Madness, The New Male, The Inner Male,* and *What Men Still Don't Know About Women, Relationships and Love.* These volumes have inspired numerous other authors in the field of popular psychology.

Dr. Goldberg is currently working on projects that explore the ways social roles shape people's personal lives, the psychology of health and healing, and a recently completed book titled *Elvis in Therapy.*

He makes his home in the Mt. Washington area of Los Angeles, California; he is married and has one daughter.